THE CROSS
IN CHRISTIAN TRADITION

January 16, 2001

For Rose Anne, CSC

With appreciation for
all that you have done
for this endeavor and
so many others in the
Center.

Gratefully,
Keith

The Cross in Christian Tradition

From Paul to Bonaventure

Edited by
Elizabeth A. Dreyer

PAULIST PRESS
New York/Mahwah, N.J.

Acknowledgments
Shortened versions of portions of chapters 2 and 3 appeared in *Assembly* 24/1 (January 1998), a publication of the Notre Dame Center for Pastoral Liturgy, used with permission.

Cover design by Cheryl Finbow

Library of Congress Cataloging-in-Publication Data

The Cross in Christian tradition : from Paul to Bonaventure / edited by Elizabeth A. Dreyer.
    p.   cm.
    Includes bibliographical references and index.
    ISBN 0-8091-4000-4 (alk. paper)
    1. Holy Cross—History of doctrines—Early church, ca. 30–600. 2. Holy Cross—History of doctrines—Middle Ages, 600–1500. I. Dreyer, Elizabeth, 1945–

BT465 .C78 2000
246′.558′09—dc21

                 00-057485

Published by Paulist Press
997 Macarthur Boulevard
Mahwah, New Jersey 07430

www.paulistpress.com

Printed and bound in the United States of America

Contents

Contents

"...the passion of Christ Jesus is rather an amazement, an astonishment, an extasie, a consternation than an instruction."

The Sermons of John Donne

Ed. Evelyn Simpson and George R. Potter
(Berkeley, 1962), 2:132.

Contributors

John Cavadini has taught at Villanova University and Loyola University in Maryland and is presently serving on the faculty at Notre Dame University since 1990 where he is Associate Professor and Chair of the Department of Theology. He teaches courses in patristic and early medieval theology. Publications include *The Last Christology of the West* (University of Pennsylvania Press, 1993) and *Gregory the Great: A Symposium,* ed. (University of Notre Dame Press, 1996). He has also written journal and anthology articles on Augustine, Gregory the Great, Origen and Alcuin.

Elizabeth A. Dreyer is Associate Professor in the Religious Studies Department at Fairfield University. She has taught at The College of St. Catherine, The Catholic University of America, The Washington Theological Union and Hartford Seminary. She gives workshops, retreats and lectures on medieval women mystics, grace, pneumatology, lay spirituality and mysticism in the Christian tradition. Publications include *Passionate Women: Two Medieval Mystics* (Paulist, 1989); *Manifestations of Grace* (Liturgical Press, 1990); *Earth Crammed With Heaven: A Spirituality of Everyday Life* (Paulist, 1994); *A Retreat With Catherine of Siena* (St. Anthony Messenger Press, 1998).

Peter J. Gorday is an Episcopal priest on the staff of St. Anne's Church in Atlanta, GA, and a professional pastoral counselor on the staff of the Georgia Association for Pastoral Counseling in Atlanta. He has a Ph.D. in religion from Vanderbilt University, and a Th.M. in pastoral counseling from Columbia Presbyterian Seminary in Decatur, GA. He is a Fellow of the American Association of Pastoral Counselors. Published work includes *Principles of Patristic Exegesis: Romans 9–11 in Origen, John Chrysostom, and Augustine* (Edwin Mellen Press, 1983); journal and anthology articles on Origen, Gregory of Nyssa, and Eusebius of Caesarea; articles on the contemporary philosopher of comparative religion, Raimundo Panikkar, and the personality theorist David Bakan. He is currently working on a volume on the lesser Pauline epistles for the series, "Ancient Christian Commentary on Scripture," published by Inter-Varsity Press.

Nathan D. Mitchell received his M.A. in Religious Studies from Indiana University (1971) and his Ph.D. in theology, with concentration in liturgical studies, from the University of Notre Dame (1978). His books include *Cult and Controversy, Mission and Ministry, The Eucharist as*

Sacrament of Initiation, and *Real Presence: The Work of the Eucharist.* Since 1992, he has written "The Amen Corner" column for the journal *Worship.* He is presently associate director at Notre Dame's Center for Pastoral Liturgy.

Jerome Murphy-O'Connor, O.P. has been Professor of New Testament at the Ecole Biblique et Archeologique Française since 1967. He is a specialist in the letters of Paul and the topography of the Holy Land on which he has written extensively. His most recent books are *Paul: A Critical Life* (Oxford, 1996) and *The Holy Land: An Oxford Archaeological Guide* (4th edition; Oxford, 1998).

Foreword

I remember vividly how excited I was in the 1960s to read Father F. X.
Durrwell on the redemptive character of the resurrection of Jesus Christ.
It seemed to me, naive as I was, that the good news was being preached
for the first time. In the meantime, the cross and the death of Christ
have taken a back seat to the resurrection. But recently there have been
signs aplenty that a fuller appreciation of the paschal mystery of Christ is
on its way to a full restoration. No doubt Raymond Brown's *The Death
of the Messiah* was a landmark in this restoration. It was inconceivable
that the cross of Christ would be neglected indefinitely. The cross is too
central a Christian symbol to be hidden for long, even though in the
beginning of Christianity this instrument of humiliation seemed not to
have a glorious future.

From its earliest days in the beginning of the 1980s, the Center for
Spirituality at Saint Mary's College wanted to explore the meaning of the
cross of Jesus Christ. The founders and sponsors of Saint Mary's College
are the Congregation of the Sisters of the Holy Cross, whose principal
liturgical feasts are Holy Cross Day on September 14 and the feast of the
Seven Sorrows of Mary on September 15. Since soon after its inception,
this congregation has hailed the cross with the motto *Ave Crux, Spes
Unica*–Hail to the Cross, Our Only Hope. These words are from a
medieval addition to the hymn *Vexilla Regis Prodeunt* of Venantius Fortunatus, who died about 610 C.E. It was only natural for the Center of Spirituality to sponsor a summer seminar entitled "The Cross, a Biblical
Tradition" in 1996, and the following summer another seminar entitled
"The Cross: A Christian Tradition."

This book is a collection of papers presented at these two summer
seminars. We are grateful to the authors who so enriched our knowledge
of the cross during the seminars and who have generously prepared their
manuscripts for publication under the able and exacting editorship of.

Dr. Elizabeth Dreyer. Without Elizabeth's wholehearted commitment to the project, this book would never have come to fruition. To Elizabeth is owed appreciation beyond words by Saint Mary's College and its Center for Spirituality.

Many others had a hand in making these seminars and this book a reality. We thank them all, but I wish to make special mention of the gratitude owed to my collaborator in the Center for Spirituality, Sister Rose Anne Schultz, C.S.C., vice president for mission at Saint Mary's College, whose support is constant no matter what else she has on her plate. In addition, we wish to thank Sister Catherine O'Brien, C.S.C., president of the Congregation of the Sisters of the Holy Cross, and her council, who were avid and constant supporters of this project and who generously made a subvention toward the editorial costs entailed in the preparation of this book. As women of compassion, the Congregation of the Sisters of the Holy Cross live in our day the charism of the cross, imitating the women who courageously stood "near the cross of Jesus" (John 19:25).

This book had its origins at a center for spirituality in a women's college. A saint of recent vintage, Edith Stein, a woman from the modern domain of higher education, can inspire the young women who are and have been students at Saint Mary's College. In his homily for the canonization of Edith Stein, known in her Carmelite community as Teresa Benedicta of the Cross, John Paul II spoke of the school of the cross as a place for spiritual maturity. We at the Center for Spirituality hope that these essays will introduce the students at Saint Mary's College and the college's alumnae to the grace-filled curriculum of this school of the cross, wherein lies the blood that gives birth to the resurrection. But the wisdom of the cross, once the stuff of stimulating lectures in our summer seminars, and now rendered into lively prose, is destined for Christians everywhere. For the foolishness of the cross is surely the medicine needed for spiritual good health in a new millennium seeking wisdom about suffering and life. I think that these essays call us to stand with Mary and John at the foot of the cross. Then all who gather around the cross will discover the wisdom of Galatians 2:19–20: "I have been crucified with Christ. It is no longer I who live, but Christ who lives in me, and the life that I live in the flesh I live by faith, that of the Son of God, who loved me and gave himself for me" (translation by Jerome Murphy-O'Connor, O.P.).

2

FOREWORD

I bid the uncommonly gracious and gifted contributors to this book and its readers, wherever they may be, a lasting peace to be gained through participation in Christ's saving cross: "For in him all the fullness of God was pleased to dwell, and through him God was pleased to reconcile to himself all things, whether on earth or in heaven, by making peace through the blood of his cross" (Col 1:20).

Keith J. Egan
Director of the Center for Spirituality
J. M. Hank Aquinas Chair in Catholic Theology
Saint Mary's College, Notre Dame, Indiana
May 18, 1999

Introduction:
The Cross in the Tradition

Elizabeth A. Dreyer

The Cross and Tradition

Throughout Christianity's two-thousand-year history, the cross has been an anchor of its symbol system and, in its brutal violence, an inevitable stumbling block. In different eras, its primary meanings have shifted. It has been regarded as a divine necessity to overcome the sin of the world; as victory over the cosmic forces of evil; as a sign of identification for Christians; as God's infinitely loving gesture to humanity; as the source of a renewed covenant between the community and God; as a force for healing and even raising the dead; as a sacrificial action effecting forgiveness and reconciliation; as Jesus' act of obedience to the Father.

During the first millennium of Christianity, the cross served as a banner in battle, an assurance of victory over "pagans" and "barbarians." In the mid-fourth century, relics of the cross were gathered, venerated and fought over. In the seventh century, a vision of the holy cross gave birth to *The Dream of the Rood,* a poem that describes the crucifixion, in Peter Brown's words, "as if it were the bloodsoaked death of a warrior king."[1] In the Middle Ages, devotion to the cross took the form of repentance and ascetic practices, elicited by graphic, detailed descriptions of Jesus' suffering body on the cross in art and writing. Another group of Christians took up arms to recover the sacred places in the Holy Land and were said "to take the cross"—meaning to go off on crusade.[2] Throughout history, the cross has motivated believers to enter into spiritual and physical combat against what were perceived as forces of darkness. In another strain of piety, the passion has always provided a model for the saints—from fierce imitation of the Crucified to compassion for the suffering of others.

In the recent past, biblical, theological and historical discussions about cross and crucifixion in the Christian tradition have been infrequent. One can muse about this reticence. Did we need to correct what was now seen as an overemphasis on the cross? Does an affluent, comfortable culture lead us away from talk about the cross? Or has the cross simply become part of the woodwork—a symbol that is dull or virtually invisible in its familiarity? Many have argued that the very nature of the cross in all its scandalous, bloody violence causes the community to shy away from it—at root it is an offense to human sensibilities. Some have seen a tendency to neglect the cross when it is cut off from, or thought to be superseded by, the resurrection—a misguided approach that prevents a full and proper understanding of the paschal mystery in its fullness. Others see the root of neglect in the hegemony of the theory of atonement with which the cross has been linked for centuries—a view that is now challenged as the sole or primary way to understand the meaning of the salvific process. Or have theologies of the cross become a curious relic of history, perceived as dragging Christians, who are hanging on to the faith by their fingertips, through a slough of pessimism?[3]

On the other hand, interest in the cross has been renewed in certain contexts.[4] Perhaps a newly discovered need to think about the meaning of the cross emerges out of Canadian Douglas John Hall's suggestion that the "official optimism of North America is finally running off into the sand."[5] Indeed, when taken seriously, the cross confronts triumphalist attitudes in any form and can stand as a beacon against the kind of "export church" that sees only one brand of Christianity as the norm for everyone.

In addition, global communication makes first-world inhabitants more aware of the excruciating suffering experienced by a majority of peoples on the planet. And suffering inevitably draws the attention of thoughtful Christians to the cross. We are counseled to leave behind a "way of the cross" that leads Christians to destructive guilt or resignation in face of the world's ills. Rather, we struggle to allow the cross to issue a "call to minister to the wounded Christ as he is found broken and bruised on all the highways of the world."[6]

One may also take notice that as we advance into the third millennium, news reports are full of talk about forgiveness—nations across the globe seeking to make amends for past atrocities that include war, usurpation, colonialization and killing fields of various stripes. For example, in March 1998 John Paul II issued "We Remember: A Reflection on the Shoah," asking pardon for Christian passivity during the Holocaust. And in a pastoral letter, the Catholic Bishops' Conference in the Philippines apologized for clergy who sided with Spanish rulers and opposed the Philippine revolution 100 years ago. For Christians, the cross stands as a beacon demanding that we seek and grant forgiveness for the violence we visit on one another. Jesus' attitude to his executioners and to the thief at his side becomes the model for Christian existence.[7]

French philosopher René Girard analyzes the crucifixion as *the* event in history that put an end to the recurrent cycle of violent scapegoating.[8] He describes the mimetic violence woven into the very fabric of human culture and of each human being. We desire what we cannot have, and this acquisitive desire leads to violence. The death and resurrection of Jesus become for Girard the antidote to such violence. In the cross and resurrection, Christ refused to be drawn into these destructive cycles. Even though violence is the cause of Jesus' death, he refuses to retaliate. The resurrection is a judgment of grace not of condemnation.[9] In a joint interview with Girard, Ewert Cousins notes that if someone were to ask him to recommend a Christian classic on the spirituality of nonviolence, it would be hard for him to come up with a title.[10] This seems especially strange, given that Christianity claims as one of its cornerstones a brutal act of violence.

The Particularity of the Cross

This study of the cross in the tradition is part of a broader cultural development interested in the concrete, particular dimensions of human life. Native, aboriginal, ethnic and religious groups strive to recover and preserve the distinctive marks of their individual cultures. Historians have become more interested in demographic, legal and economic data than in dynasties and military engagements. There is impatience with grand, abstract schema that disregard information about specific situations.

Thus, curiosity about the "underside" of history is fueling much historical work these days.

This is also the case in biblical and theological disciplines. Over the centuries, major topics such as creation and redemption have suffered from a reductionism that eclipses the variety and detail of the biblical, theological and historical records. We forget that Christians in the past were not exempt from the intricate weave of life's complexities that we know to be true from our own experience. The comment that TV soap operas can never really compete with the vagaries of "real life" often rings true.

This "turn to the particular" applies in a distinctive way to study of the tradition, for the texts, art, music and customs of bygone eras are difficult to access and interpret. We know from experience that details fade with time, but we also know that the spice of life is found in those very details. It may be easier to settle for a streamlined history that has been boiled down over the years than to engage in the detailed, often painstaking work that is required to do justice to the nuances and complexity of the past in all its "messiness." On the other hand, we may tend toward oversimplification of the past as a way to cope with a level of complexity in contemporary life situations that threatens to overwhelm us.[11]

This penchant to shy away from the particular is even more understandable in the case of the doctrine of the cross. Christians spontaneously shrink from texts in the tradition that portray the painful, bloody, violent aspects of the cross in all their horror. The chapters that follow aim to redress this tendency by delving into some of the complex, symbolic resources of theologies and spiritualities of the cross from the first fifteen hundred years of Christianity. In an open yet critical fashion, authors have combed biblical texts and commentaries, lectionaries, liturgical poetry, sermons, theological treatises and spiritual works to bring to light the diverse ways in which some of our ancestors in the faith experienced, thought about and articulated the meaning and function of the cross. Our journey will take us to Paul's letters, early Christian liturgy, and the works of Origen, Augustine and Bonaventure.

The Cross in the Tradition

The following chapters lift up the language and imagery of the cross at select moments in the Christian tradition. Although the focus is the cross, there is no attempt to isolate this symbol in an overly narrow sense, for talk about the cross inevitably spills over into the wider context of the passion and death of Jesus. Each chapter provides a window onto texts from particular situations and asks what the cross meant and how it functioned. By shining a light on the tradition, we do not suggest that there is something absolute about the past that simply needs to be recouped. The most important thing to remember about "the good old days" is that they never existed. In any age, the cross resists exhaustive interpretation, and surely no generation can dictate the meaning of the cross for another. Each and every generation, in whatever situation it finds itself, must learn to return to the cross itself, there to encounter the crucified and hidden God.[12]

Knowledge of the past allows us not only to grow in appreciation of the work of some of the most illustrious ancestors in the faith, but also, by walking in their company, to enrich and enliven the ways in which we follow the Christian way of the cross today. History has an important role to play as modern questions are reframed in the light of the past. We are challenged to think of the cross not only through a private, but also a communal lens. We are not alone in grappling with its meaning. For Christians across the ages, the cross has been a symbol *out of which one lives*. And it continues to teach us something about how we are to be with one another. It is instructive to see how Christian communities and theologians down the ages have interpreted the role of the cross in their relationships with one another and with the world. The language and imagery of the past invite us to return to the cross with fresh expectation and new ideas and images about its meaning.

Paul

We begin our pilgrimage into the tradition with Jerome Murphy-O'Connor's essay on Paul, whose theology of the cross has been noted and celebrated throughout Christian history. Murphy-O'Connor notes that Paul's interest in the crucifixion is distinctive, since the theme of the cross is virtually absent in the primitive kerygma Paul inherited. Therefore, Murphy-O'Connor seeks to determine not only how Paul saw the crucifixion, but also why he gave it the emphasis he did. Murphy-O'Connor examines the abundant material on the cross in 1 Corinthians and Galatians; offers an explanation for the silence about the cross in 1 and 2 Thessalonians and Philemon; and suggests a hypothesis about why, in Romans, Paul frequently mentions the death of Christ but steers clear of any talk about the modality of that death.

Paul emphasizes that Jesus *chose* the cross in order to demonstrate in the most radical way the completeness of his love for humanity. For Christians, the way of love surpasses the way of the law as the model for the Christian life. Murphy-O'Connor suggests that for Paul "I have been crucified with Christ" is the only possible evidence for the truth of "it is no longer I who live, but it is Christ who lives in me" (Gal 2:19–20). The cross also redefines Paul's relationship to the world. He wants to convey to his hearers that the cross is important because it demonstrates what *life* is. The cross allows the community to see that this life was a real human possibility. Jesus' comportment on the cross set the standard of human love and revealed it to be attainable.

From the evidence in 1 Corinthians and Galatians, it seems clear to Murphy-O'Connor that Paul must have felt very deeply about the crucifixion of Jesus and that he wanted others to have a similar intense experience of it. Murphy-O'Connor goes on to explore the context of 1 Corinthians and Galatians. In both settings, Paul encountered alternative versions of the gospel that minimized the crucifixion. In response to Galatian Judaizers who insisted on circumcision, Paul explains how the modality of Jesus' death made the Law meaningless. The Galatians clung to circumcision out of concern about what others in the community would think of them. Because of their Jewish origins, they wanted to stay in the good graces of the Jewish community. But for Paul, not the Law but the cross was central to salvation.

In Corinth, Paul has to confront a community that opted for a gospel that gave it intellectual respectability, marked by fine rhetoric and sophisticated argument. But the image of a crucified Savior was neither intelligible nor palatable. Thus, Paul opposed the "wisdom of the world" to the "wisdom of God" that was the folly of the cross. He shows how divine goodness and the crucifixion could never be related by logic, but only by love.

INTRODUCTION: THE CROSS IN THE TRADITION

Murphy-O'Connor's essay brings to life the historical particulars of the communities to which Paul wrote and shows how each specific set of circumstances affected both *what* Paul chose to emphasize and *why* he presented the cross the way he did. This information brings to life aspects of the local situations in which Paul traveled; reminds us of the crucial way in which context shapes meaning; and challenges readers to reflect on how the presence, meaning or absence of the cross is affected by contemporary circumstances. Paul can serve as a resource for those Christians who judge that the cross is being eclipsed in contemporary culture, as Paul judged it to be in his.

Early Liturgies of the Cross

In chapters 2 and 3, Nathan Mitchell turns to the liturgy of the cross in the first millennium of Christianity, focusing in particular on its poetic and dramatic elements. He argues that the cross is the key that defines and interprets *all* aspects of the Christian tradition, and he invites the reader to ponder the statement, *history is hermeneutics with skin on.* Mitchell never allows us to forget that the church's liturgy must always be viewed in the context of the world liturgy. He notes ancient Rome's openness to diversity and cultural pluralism in liturgical practice, with the result that celebrations of the cross were influenced by global and multicultural factors. Ritual has never been shaped only by elite, "pure" forces, but is always also a product of the celebration of Christ's presence amid the poor of this earth.

Mitchell traces the development of the meaning of cross from Romans, Hebrews and John's gospel, where the cross is seen primarily as a soteriological *event;* to the ways the cross was linked to baptism and Eucharist in the early church; to an expanded understanding of the cross as a *cult object in its own right* by the tenth century. Evidence of Good Friday liturgies in fourth-century Jerusalem and in the tenth-century document *Regularis Concordia* suggests that, over time, the cross was imaginatively transformed in and by the liturgy and by the sensibilities of Christian poets into a central *character* with a speaking role that can also be hailed, held, clothed and greeted. The liturgy even portrays the cross as a symbol of the community itself. It becomes a *people.*

We are reminded in these chapters that the liturgical reenactment of the historical events of the passion is not an attempt to "imitate" history but is intended to transform the community engaged in this ritual action. In Mitchell's words, liturgies that call for the dramatic burying and raising of the cross are about "negotiating rapture," negotiating mystery for the participating community. Mitchell turns to folk rituals in Mexico and Chile to reinforce his point that ritual, art and culture are always "ordinary" before they are "fine." And like art, ritual makes things that keep on making—the lighting of the Easter fire has as its goal the re-creation of the world.

We are challenged by these essays to remember that when we engage in ritual, we are *making* ourselves, *inventing* ourselves as believers. When we wonder *why* Christians revisit the horrible events of Jesus' death in ritual, Mitchell wants us to ask not only "How do people make ritual?" but also "How does ritual make people?" In the rituals we celebrate from Palm Sunday to Easter, the violent way of the cross becomes the nonviolent way of rapture. Each year, we walk with Jesus on the way of the cross, not to recapture the past, but to empty ourselves so that God can once again take possession of us.

Origen (185–254)

Peter Gorday leads us on an extensive journey, mining the works of Origen for material on the cross. In spite of his "official" condemnation, Origen has been a substantial influence in the Christian tradition. In the past, he has been consulted primarily for his teaching on Christian dogma, but increasingly his insights into spirituality, ethics and the contours of faithful discipleship have come to dominate modern scholarship. Gorday reviews some of this literature as a backdrop to his interpretation of Origin's understanding of the cross and its place in Christian living.

Gorday suggests that Origen saw the cross in terms of the "drama" of human existence and the search for human transformation and wholeness. As a result, he suggests that Origen is much more in step with the concerns of later theologies of the cross—from Martin Luther to Jürgen Moltmann—than has usually been acknowledged. In Gorday's opinion, it is unfair to dismiss Origen as advocating only a "theology of glory," or to hold, as Andrew Louth does, that his is simply a "mysticism of light" and not one that includes darkness at its center as well.[13] Rather, Gorday sees aspects of Origen's theology/spirituality of the cross as a compelling option in terms of modern agendas for faithful praxis.

Gorday lays out the way Origen's valuation of spirit and body sets the parameters for Origen's exegetical method, in which he encourages Christians to move beyond the literal meaning of the scriptural word to the inner or spiritual meaning that is its true significance. Yet, for Origen, it is precisely through the weakness of his humanity that Jesus is able to speak effectively to ordinary human sinners, thereby making possible their conversion. Origen's view of the cross includes a conviction that salvation implies the transformation of the individual and the freely willed practice of virtue.

We revisit the great Catholic expositors of Origen, most notably Henri de Lubac, and the Anglican Henry Chadwick, who saw the vital center in Origen's construal of the Christian understanding of redemption. Like Origen, contemporary Christians are aware of "demonic powers" that the cross is meant to combat. It is only when individual believers are willing to go down into the trenches of human darkness (what Origen would call "mortality" and "corporeality") that the balance of power between truth and lies begins to shift. Origen's context may be radically different from ours, but the struggle for good remains the goal.

Thus, for Origen, it was necessary not only that Christ die so that the devil would be overcome, but also so that Christians would have a model for their own suffering and death. Origen's own desire for martyrdom plays a key role in his understanding of the cross. Origen writes, "Now let it be seen whether we have taken up our own crosses and followed Jesus." The virtue and integrity of Jesus' behavior throughout his entire life—including the cross—provide a paradigm for all Christian life. By following in the footsteps of Jesus, Christians make a moral contribution to society, rejecting idolatry and thereby bringing to light the true significance of the cross. For Origen, the cross becomes part of God's educative therapy for the illness of the world. The cross is about being human, about what it requires and means to be human. In Origen's theology, the incarnation/cross has a practical effect, for it allows Christians to form a clear image of their own path to a transforming and liberating view of their destiny and joy.

Augustine (354–430)

Like Origen, Augustine has left no discrete treatment of the theology of the cross. Augustine scholar John Cavadini consults sermons and treatises in search of Augustine's ideas on both the symbol of the cross and his broader treatment of the passion and death of Christ. Cavadini begins by exploring, in the sermons, a number of unusual but surely intriguing images Augustine associates with the cross—mousetrap, lampstand, classroom, boat and "silly fruit" (from Augustine's exegesis of the story of Zacchaeus). We are then led through a series of probing reflections that seek to penetrate the significance of the images. Among other things, the cross points to compassion, hospitality and humility. For Cavadini, Augustine invites the reader to climb the "tree of silly fruit," where even forgiveness of our enemies is not an occasion for pride in spiritual accomplishment, but a gesture of solidarity with the lowliness of God. Thus the cross is linked with becoming more human, more humane, more like God.

In chapter 7, Cavadini continues to probe the images of the cross as lampstand and as a "tree of silly fruit" by situating them in the larger context of Augustine's theology in his great apologetic work, the *City of God*. In this text, Augustine contrasts the character of the Roman citizen (which in many cases, he truly admired), which he judges led to the demise of the empire, with the way of Christ on the cross. Augustine suggests that Rome's fixation on its own virtue as behavior meriting praise—including compassion for those Rome conquered—had squelched its imagination by cutting off its ability to criticize itself. He concludes that domination, even by virtuous and glorious means, can never be a good.

This domination is overcome only by true worship—sacrifice—that Augustine describes as mercy or compassion. And only Christ on the cross accomplished the perfect sacrifice, the perfect work of mercy. In the cross, we are given a glimpse of genuine compassion that is *not* also a bid for praise or self-congratulation. Christ triumphs over empire. Augustine invites the reader to climb the "tree of silly fruit" where, like Zacchaeus, true vision is restored. Cavadini suggests that fidelity to the cross in the fourth or in the twentieth century involves dismantling the status quo in the form of received meanings that have been around for so long that they become like the air we breathe. For Christians in all ages, the cross has the potential to reinvest the imagination with new images based not on domination but on love.

Bonaventure (ca. 1217–1274)

With Bonaventure of Bagnoreggio, we advance to the high Middle Ages. And yet Bonaventure's texts on the cross are reminiscent of the lyrical poetry encountered in chapters 2 and 3 and—in Bonaventure's brand of provocative imagery—of the kind of imaginative mind encountered in the sermons of Augustine. Often called the "second founder" of the Franciscan order, after Francis of Assisi, Bonaventure also follows Francis in making the cross a centerpiece of his theology and spirituality.

Elizabeth Dreyer begins with an exposition of Bonaventure's christo-centric theology, in which Christ is seen as the exemplar for Christian life and for the entire creation. In a strain not unlike Origen's theology of the cross, Christ's suffering is seen by Bonaventure as a model of virtue that, when imitated, restores the harmonious functioning of the universe and of the Christian life. In what has come to be called "coincidence of opposites,"[14] Bonaventure sees the cross as a counterforce to sin: humility and obedience overcome pride; poverty overcomes greed; truth overcomes falsity. Each negative factor of the passion—the flagellation, trial, humiliation and abandonment of Jesus—accomplishes a good; that is, they free humans from suffering, condemnation and sin.

Dreyer suggests that, for Bonaventure, Christians are called to respond to the cross by embracing especially the virtues of poverty and humility in imitation of the Crucified. Bonaventure provides a rather detailed roadmap of the ways in which these virtues are to be practiced in the concrete circumstances of one's life. But above all, Bonaventure sees in the cross a particular image of God, a God who does not cling to status or power, but who "condescends" in love to be close to the world. Often in metaphoric language that soars to mystical heights, Bonaventure invokes the love affair of God with the universe, which finds its center and culmination in the cross and resurrection.

In chapter 9, Dreyer asks how images and metaphors function in Bonaventure's theology and suggests a framework in which language is understood as a never-ending flow that opens up conversations between past and present. She identifies six specific images of the cross: fire, tears, nakedness, the tree of life, the vine and "marked with the cross." The very nature of Bonaventure's language invites the reader to attend to his images of the cross with an inner contemplative eye and ear in order to experience a "felt sense" of the mystery of the cross of Christ.

Conclusion

This excursion into the past is not undertaken for its own sake. Rather, the historical quest has its starting point in the present—in questions about the meaning of the Christian life; in horror at the extent and violence of human sin and suffering; in fidelity to a story that continues to be told after two thousand years. A closer reading of the tradition holds out the possibility of greater connection and identification with our ancestors in the faith. We identify with them inasmuch as the patristic and medieval churches had good qualities and bad; fought ideological battles; made mistakes; went to war; turned to Jesus Christ in their agonies; and tried to serve the poor and love God.

The point of unearthing the past is not some antiquarian project that has no impact on present existence. Rather, it is to see history as a living, breathing resource and to enter into an ongoing dialectic in which past, present and future engage one another in informative and positive ways. In the chapters to follow, we are invited to open ourselves in a critical fashion, to be enriched, provoked and challenged by past thought on the cross. By thus expanding our awareness and horizons, we may discover—in agreement or disagreement—a new and genuinely authentic understanding of this foundational symbol of the Christian faith.

In North American culture, tradition is often perceived in a negative fashion. The transient nature of our existence often prevents the maintenance of customs that in earlier societies provided the "social glue" of communal life. To the extent that we live in a "presentist" culture, we rarely take time to inquire about or delve into the past. Some blithely discard the past as irrelevant baggage. Others read the past as a "golden age," clinging to it in literal and rigid ways, hoping to stave off the constant flux of contemporary life. Neither approach does justice to those Christians who have gone before, for the past is no more "perfect" or "bankrupt" than the present.

What is called for is an open, critical stance in which we approach the past with a receptive, respectful attitude, knowing that there will be parts of the tradition that can bring new life to the Christian faith today, and parts of it that are surely better left behind. Each generation has the privilege and responsibility to ask its own questions of the past, real questions that emerge out of the search for meaning and holiness. Too often, we settle for the dead faith of the living rather than discovering the living faith of the dead in ways that can contribute to the ongoing renewal and aliveness of faith today.[15] Whether we know it or not, the past is always with us, influencing and shaping present understandings and behaviors. We have the choice to be conscious participants, unconscious victims or passive bystanders.[16] The following exploration of the cross in the Christian tradition takes a confident step toward conscious, active participation and invites the reader to come along for the journey.

In all cases, the tradition will rise or fall by our ability to understand and articulate it "out of" and "to" the existential situation of this generation. Unless the tradition of the cross resonates with our deepest intuitions, our hunger for solidarity and our hopes for a suffering world, it will remain an empty symbol, and Christianity will remain a dream.[17] The material that follows is offered as a partial step in the recovery of the tradition of the cross, critically appropriated and aimed at contributing to a true and meaningful theology of the cross for our own time. Thus, these essays become part of the ongoing dialectic between past, present and future. In the end, the multivalent meanings of the cross in the past must open out to contemporary understandings of the cross that are both faithful to the integrity of the past and yet *truly* new and responsive to the needs of the present. The point is to examine the tradition of the cross, not simply to repeat it. A genuine doctrine of the cross will function to transform Christians into a people of compassion, courage, justice and love for the world.

NOTES

1. Peter Brown, *The Rise of Western Christendom: Triumph and Diversity,* A.D. *200–1000* (Oxford: Blackwell Publishers, 1996), 231.

2. Jaroslav Pelikan, *Jesus through the Centuries: His Place in the History of Culture* (New Haven and London: Yale University Press, 1985), 99.

3. Gerhard O. Forde, *On Being a Theologian of the Cross* (Grand Rapids, Mich.: Wm. B. Eerdmans, 1997), xiii.

4. A sampling of recent works: Jung Ha Kim, *Bridge-Makers and Cross-Bearers: Korean-American Women and the Church* (Atlanta: Scholars Press, 1997); George Martin, "The Scandal of the Cross," *New Covenant* 25 (April 1996): 34ff.; Terence McGuckin, "The Eschatology of the Cross," *New Blackfriars* 75 (July-August 1994): 364–77; Xavier McMonagle, "Solidarity through the Cross," *Priest & People* 8 (March 1994): 91–94; Larry Rasmussen, "Returning to Our Senses: The Theology of the Cross as a Theology for Eco-Justice," in *After Nature's Revolt: Eco-Justice and Theology,* ed. Dieter T. Hessel (Minneapolis: Fortress Press, 1992); Harold Wells, "The Holy Spirit and Theology of the Cross: Significance for Dialogue," *Theological Studies* 53 (September 1992): 476–92; Charles B. Cousar, *A Theology of the Cross: The Death of Jesus in the Pauline Letters* (Minneapolis: Fortress Press, 1990); William Hogan, "The Cross Reconsidered," *Review for Religious* 47 (March-April 1988): 197–201; Francis Martin, "The Power of the Cross," *New Covenant* 17 (March 1988): 12–15; Donna Korczyk, "Obedience, Absurdity of the Cross of Christ," *Review for Religious* 46 (May-June 1987): 371–76; Leo O'Donovan, "The Word of the Cross," *Chicago Studies* 25 (April 1986): 95–110.

5. Douglas John Hall, *Lighten Our Darkness: Toward an Indigenous Theology of the Cross* (Philadelphia: Westminster, 1981). See also his *God and Human Suffering: An Exercise in the Theology of the Cross* (Minneapolis: Augsburg Fortress, 1986).

6. Kenneth Leech, *We Preach Christ Crucified* (Cambridge, Mass.: Cowley Publications, 1994), 31.

7. See Maria Harris, *Proclaim Jubilee: A Spirituality for the Twenty-first Century* (Louisville: Westminster John Knox, 1996).

8. See René Girard, *The Scapegoat,* trans. Yvonne Freccero (Baltimore: The Johns Hopkins University Press, 1986); and idem, *Violence and the Sacred,* trans. Patrick Gregory (Baltimore: The Johns Hopkins University Press, 1979).

9. See L. Gregory Jones, "Roots of Violence," *The Christian Century* (July 15–22, 1998), 692.

10. Leo D. Lefebure, interview with René Girard and Ewert Cousins, *Christian Century* (April 8, 1998), 373.

11. See "'Why Are You So Interested in the Wandering People of God?': Michael Welker on Theology and Common Sense," *Soundings* 79/1-2 (Spring/Summer 1996): 128-31; and Michel René Barnes, "Augustine in Contemporary Trinitarian Theology," *Theological Studies* 56/2 (June 1995): 237-50.

12. Alister McGrath, *The Enigma of the Cross* (London/Sydney/Auckland: Hodder & Stoughton, 1987), 79-80.

13. Andrew Louth, *The Origins of the Christian Mystical Tradition: From Plato to Denys* (Oxford: Clarendon Press, 1981), 57.

14. See Ewert Cousins, *Bonaventure and the Coincidence of Opposites* (Chicago: Franciscan Herald Press, 1978).

15. See Jarosalv Pelikan, *The Vindication of the Tradition* (New Haven, Conn.: Yale University Press, 1984), 6, 65.

16. Ibid., 53-54.

17. Ibid., 60.

CHAPTER 1

"Even death on a cross": Crucifixion in the Pauline Letters

Jerome Murphy-O'Connor, O.P.

The cross is such a common Christian symbol that it has become decorative rather than meaningful. We notice it but do not attend to it. It nudges the periphery of our consciousness, but it does not demand our attention. It has become a generalized idea rather than a specific thing.

To rediscover the particularity of the cross we have to translate it into pictures of violent death that revolt us—the congested face and protruding tongue of a man hanging on the gallows, the convulsed body of a man dying in the electric chair. What would be our reaction if such pictures decorated children's classrooms? How would we respond if we met someone wearing a tasteful gallows or electric chair on a gold chain around her neck or in his buttonhole?

Death by crucifixion was infinitely more painful and degrading than is hanging or electrocution. During the first Christian centuries, the cross was a thing accursed. No one professed allegiance to Christ by wearing a cross. From personal witness, everyone was fully aware of what death on a cross meant in terms of atrocious, long, drawn-out suffering. The cross was not something to be contemplated with equanimity. It provoked shuddering horror.[1]

The attitude of Christians to the cross changed in the fourth century, due to a number of factors:

1. Before the decisive battle of the Milvian Bridge in 312, the emperor Constantine (c. 280–337) had a vision of a luminous cross with the words, "In this conquer." His victory opened the way to the legalization of Christianity.[2]

2. Out of respect for the way Christ died, Constantine forbade crucifixion as a means of execution.[3] Consequently, people began to forget precisely what was involved in this horrible form of murderous torture. It was no longer part of their experience.

3. A new, more pleasant meaning for the cross was facilitated by the discovery of the True Cross during the construction of the Church of the Holy Sepulchre in Jerusalem. The emphasis that it was made of wood transformed it into a positive symbol of the tree of life.[4] Thus, for example, in the fifth-century monastery at Saqqara in Egypt, none of the twenty-two painted crosses bears a figure and virtually all show new branches sprouting from the intersection of the two arms.[5]

Even after the cross had been widely accepted as a symbol, there was a consistent refusal to accept its reality. Only two crucifixion scenes survive from the fifth century. On an ivory casket in the British Museum, London, a beardless Christ with arms at right angles seems to hover on the cross. On one of the doors of the Church of Santa Sabina in Rome, the arms of Christ are bent at the elbow (the posture of prayer) and nailed to the architectural background; no crosses are visible.[6] There is no hint that the crucified figures are dying in agony. The situation remains unchanged until the twelfth century.

Such ambivalence throughout history highlights the contribution of Paul. He alone among the missionaries of the early church insisted that it was important to recall, not merely the death of Christ, but the way he died. Given the tendency of the primitive kerygma, the gospels would probably have passed over in silence the modality of the death of Christ. There would have been a reference to his execution, and then all attention would have focused on the resurrection. Without Paul, it is unlikely that the gospels would have contained such detailed accounts of the crucifixion. In the last analysis, therefore, it is due to Paul that the cross, an instrument of torture, became a Christian symbol.

My aim in this chapter is to attempt to explain why Paul felt so strongly about the crucifixion, and how he integrated the cross into his understanding of the mystery of salvation. His reflections are the revealed foundation of all cross-related theology and spirituality.

The Uniqueness of Paul

If we leave aside the gospels, "cross" and "crucify" are Pauline terms. Elsewhere in the New Testament *stauros*, "cross," appears only in Hebrews 12:2, and *stauroô*, "to crucify," only in Revelations 11:8. *Anastauroô*, "to crucify" (Heb 6:6), is unique in the New Testament. Other New Testament writers use the neutral "tree"; "by hanging him on a tree" (Acts 5:30; 10:39), "took him down from the tree" (Acts 13:29), and "bore our sins in his body on the tree" (1 Pet 2:24), all of which reflect Deuteronomy 21:22-23, which is cited in Galatians 3:13.

If we rearrange the Pauline references according to the chronology of the letters,[7] a curious pattern emerges:

	Cross	Tree	To Crucify	Blood
1 Thessalonians				
2 Thessalonians				
Galatians	3	1	4	
Philippians	2			
Colossians	2			1
Philemon				
1 Corinthians	2		4	3
2 Corinthians 1–9				
2 Corinthians 10–13			1	
Romans			1	2
2 Timothy				

No mention of "cross" or "crucifixion" appears in Paul's earliest and latest letters. Nonetheless, 1 Thessalonians mentions the death of Christ three times (1:10; 4:14; 5:10),[8] and in 2 Timothy it is evoked once (2:8). Even though the redemptive value of the blood of Christ is twice mentioned in Romans, how that blood was spilled is not made explicit.

Crucifixion language appears for the first time in Galatians, and then eight times. This number is challenged only by the six references in

1 Corinthians, whose three references to "blood" are also relevant, even though all occur in the context of the discussion on the Eucharist. These two letters exhibit the greatest concentration of crucifixion language and chronologically bracket the other letters that use such language, namely Philippians and Colossians, which were written during Paul's stay in Ephesus from the late summer of A.D. 52 to the early fall of A.D. 54. There are two allusions to crucifixion in Philippians and three in Colossians. Nothing similar appears in Philemon.

The singularity of Paul's emphasis becomes apparent when it is contrasted with the primitive kerygma, the common doctrinal base that Paul shared with the rest of the early church. There is a wide consensus that fragments of traditional teaching appear in a series of passages in the letters, namely 1 Thessalonians 1:9-10; Galatians 1:3-4; 1 Corinthians 15:3-5; Romans 1:3-4; 4:24-25; 10:9.[9] Paul also quotes the eucharistic words (1 Cor 11:23-25) and two liturgical hymns (Phil 2:6-11; Col 1:15-20). Not a single one of these formulae that he inherited from his Christian environment mentions the crucifixion. Not only that, but one can detect a reticence regarding the fact of the death of Jesus. Only two texts formally state that he died (1 Cor 15:3; Phil 2:8). In all the others, the death of Jesus has to be inferred from the fact that he was raised from the dead!

Paul's stress on the modality of Christ's death is therefore startling and certainly set him apart from his contemporaries. It forces us to begin with the question of why Paul gave such prominence to the crucifixion and what it meant to him.

I have not been able to find any recent exegetical study that deals explicitly and at length with this question. Many titles are promising, such as Charles B. Cousar, *A Theology of the Cross: The Death of Jesus in the Pauline Letters* (1990), but like many others,[10] this book focuses almost exclusively on the fact of the death of Christ and devotes only marginal attention to its modality. Modern scholars, it would appear, have found a new way to deny the scandal of the cross. It is subsumed under the death of Jesus and becomes merely convenient shorthand for what is distinctive in Paul's understanding of the death of Jesus. This is explicit in the arrangement of title and subtitle in Cousar's book. The subtitle spells out what the title really means. It is appropriate, therefore, to attempt to determine how Paul saw the crucifixion and why he gave it the emphasis

24

it has in his letters. In thus narrowing the focus, I deliberately abstract from a whole range of other perspectives on the death of Jesus.

Paul Preaches a Crucified Christ

In his first letter to the Corinthians Paul recalls his experience when he began to preach among them, "When I came to you, I did not come proclaiming to you the testimony of God in excellence of speech or wisdom. I did not think it appropriate to know anything among you except Jesus Christ and him crucified" (1 Cor 2:1-2). Here he expands slightly what he has said in the previous chapter, "we preach Christ cruci-fied" (1 Cor 1:23). The structure of the phrase is designed to make the modality of Christ's death inescapable. If to speak of the death of the Messiah[11] can be described as "an unprecedented novelty,"[12] which flew in the face of all popular expectation, what can be said of Paul's emphasis on the horrible way in which the Messiah met his death? The question highlights the issue of Paul's missionary strategy.

The emphatic negative *(ou)* at the beginning of 1 Corinthians 2:2 is designed to emphasize the contrast introduced by "except" *(ei mê).*[13] Every-thing that is not the crucified Christ is excluded from Paul's proclamation of the gospel. Paul relates this decision to his arrival in Corinth. Was it merely a reaffirmation of his normal practice or a new initiative? A prima facie case for the latter has been made on the grounds that Paul's failure in Athens (Acts 17:22-23) necessitated a change in his missionary approach when he moved on to Corinth. However, this seductive correlation is rejected by commentators, principally on methodological grounds. There is no guarantee that Luke gives an accurate picture of Paul's method of preaching at Athens.[14] Correct as this is in principle, it is less satisfying than Galatians 3:1, which furnishes a decisive argument in favor of the hypothesis that Paul is merely confirming his usual practice.

None of the current translations of Galatians 3:1[15] brings out the full force of the Greek verb *baskainô*, whose literal meaning is "to injure with the Evil Eye."[16] That this dimension should be made explicit in any translation is confirmed by what Paul says of his arrival in Galatia. He was a very sick man, one who might be thought to envy the good health of others and so wish to injure them. He was not, however, rejected as a threat. On the contrary, "You did not despise me, or spit, but you received me as an angel of God, as Christ Jesus" (Gal 4:14). Spitting was considered one of the most effective defenses against the evil eye.[17]

The economy of effort in Galatians 3:1 is extraordinary. By his use of this one verb, *baskainô*, Paul simultaneously tapped into the deepest fears of the Galatians and emphasized the value of what they had received from him. If the intruders tried to detach them from Paul's gospel, it must be because they envied the Galatians. The Judaizing mission, therefore, was a specific form of the Evil Eye, and highly injurious.[18] Thus warned, the Galatians should fight back and not permit themselves to be overwhelmed. As far as Paul was concerned, however, they should have been immune, because "before their eyes Jesus was portrayed crucified" *(hois kat' aphthalmous Iêsous Christos prographê estaurômenos)*. This half verse is packed with an extraordinary amount of concentrated meaning.

The verb here is *prographô*, which is literally "to write before." But "before" is ambiguous. It can be understood in both a temporal sense (e.g., "whatever was previously written" [Rom 15:4]) and in a locative sense "to set forth as a public notice."[19] This meaning fits the context because of the reference to "eyes," and it is in fact adopted by some commentaries.[20] Jesus, however, is not a document (despite Col 2:14!). Paul is evidently thinking in terms of a word picture. Hence recent translations and commentaries all rightly opt for the reading "to portray" (RSV)—or a synonym, "to exhibit" (NRSV), "to display" (NAB)—even though this meaning for *prographô* is attested nowhere else.[21] This unusual departure from the only attested meaning is made all the more exceptional by the fact that translations and commentaries feel constrained by the context to introduce a reinforcing adverb that has no correspondent in the Greek text—"publicly" (RSV, NRSV), "openly,"[22] "so vividly,"[23] "clearly."[24] The paraphrase of J. B. Phillips perfectly articulates Paul's activity in terms of its impact on the Galatians, "O you dear idiots of Galatia, who saw Jesus the crucified so plainly."[25]

Crucifixion was not alien to the culture of the Galatians; they knew perfectly well what was involved.[26] On the one hand, this facilitated Paul's graphic description of the modality of Christ's death. In common with the best theory of oratory, he was able to make the members of his audience believe that they were spectators.[27] On the other hand, he was disadvantaged by the fact that their acceptance of the image was not weakened by any tinge of disbelief in such cruelty.

The essence of Paul's argument in Galatians 3:1 now becomes apparent. In popular imagination a crucified person must have been the ultimate source of the Evil Eye. He envied and hated everyone. Anyone else's lot was better than his, no matter how much pain and misery were involved. He could not possibly wish anyone well. The Galatians had been confronted with such a person. They had caught the eye of someone nailed to a cross, yet they had been blessed, not injured.

Before continuing with the line of thought that Galatians 3:1 opens up, we must underline its relevance to the question raised by 1 Corinthians 2:2. A crucified Christ was the kernel of Paul's preaching from the beginning of his independent missionary effort.[28] Further confirmation is provided in 2 Corinthians 11:4, "If someone comes and preaches another Jesus than the one we preached, or if you receive a different spirit from the one you received or a different gospel from the one you accepted, you readily put up with him." Since the spirit (Gal 3:2) and the gospel (1 Cor 15:1; cf. 1 Thes 2:13) are given through the preaching, their authenticity is conditioned by the accuracy of the way "Jesus" is presented. A survey of Paul's usage of this name unambiguously indicates that it carries "the connotation, not only of an earthly, historical existence, but of one marked by weakness, humiliation, and suffering."[29] What more effective way to preach such a "Jesus" than by highlighting the modality of his death? Crucifixion was the most extreme demonstration of weakness (2 Cor 13:4). We must assume, in consequence, that Paul also preached a crucified Christ in the areas evangelized en route from Galatia to Corinth, namely Philippi and Thessalonica (Acts 16–18), and that he did so in the same graphic way as at Galatia.

According to Quintilian, only those who had the imagination to re-create the event for themselves to the point where they experienced the appropriate emotions could achieve the verbal vividness that Paul claims in Galatians 3:1.[30] Paul, therefore, must have felt very deeply about the crucifixion of Jesus. It was somehow an intense experience that he had to make possible for others. He presumably told his audiences why the crucifixion of Jesus was so central to his vision of salvation, but we have to work it out from the hints scattered throughout his letters. The natural place to begin is with those texts which suggest that, for Paul, Jesus chose to die in this particularly horrible way.

Jerome Murphy-O'Connor, O.P.

The Self-Sacrifice of Christ

The meaning of the Philippian hymn (Phil 2:6-11) is still vigorously debated. I am convinced, however, that the thrust of the first two strophes (in Jeremias's classical analysis) is that Jesus did not merely accept death. He chose to die.[31] As the Sinless One (2 Cor 5:21), he was not subject to the penalty of death inflicted on those who had ratified the sin of Adam.[32] If Christ died, therefore, it was because he freely chose to submit himself to this fate. Thus the principal verbs of the hymn and their associated reflexive pronouns—"he emptied himself," "he humbled himself"—have to be taken literally. Jesus was not sacrificed. He sacrificed himself. This perspective is in perfect harmony with one of the texts commonly considered to reflect the primitive kerygma, namely, "the Lord Jesus Christ, who gave himself for our sins to deliver us from the present evil age" (Gal 1:3-4).

To the common statement of the faith in the kerygma and the hymn, Paul adds the crucial words *thanaton de staurou*, "even death on a cross" (Phil 2:8d).[33] The Greek *de* has been understood in intensive and explanatory senses. Both are probably intended.[34] Given the subject matter, it is impossible that the latter should not imply the former. No first-century hearer/reader acquainted with the reality of crucifixion could have understood the phrase as neutral information. The words would have provoked a shudder of horror. The point is so obvious that Paul's intention is unmistakable. The English word *even* cannot be bettered as a translation.[35]

In context, the addition "even death on a cross" can only mean that Christ chose this form of death.[36] He opted to die in this particular way. Why? The hymn speaks of "obedience." To whom is not specified, but it is impossible to think of anyone other than God. Obedience in itself, however, is not the answer. It must be understood in such a way as to do full justice to the formal statements of Jesus' self-determination in the hymn, for example, "he emptied/humbled himself." Jesus, in other words, was free to have done otherwise. His decision to be obedient, therefore, needs to be explained. What motivated him?

The letter to the Galatians suggests that he was motivated by love. "I have been crucified with Christ. It is no longer I who live, but Christ who lives in me, and the life I live in the flesh I live by faith/fidelity, that

28

of the Son of God who loved me and gave himself for me *(en pistei zô tê tou hyiou tou theou tou agapêsantos me kai paradontos heauton hyper emou)"* (Gal 2:20). The use of the reflexive pronoun with the verb, "he gave himself," is immediately reminiscent of the Philippian hymn.[37] It reflects the same pattern of thought, which is here carried a step further because "he gave himself for me" explains "he loved me."[38] Christ chose death by crucifixion in order to demonstrate in the most radical way possible the completeness of his love for humanity. Nothing is held back. Such totality in the gift of self is the only adequate response to divine election and grace. It can never be spelled out by precepts ("the works of the Law"), no matter to what extent they are multiplied. Discrete demands, which are fulfilled successively, can never coalesce into the completeness exemplified by the behavior of Christ. Henceforth the law *is* Christ (Gal 6:2).[39] As the immediate context indicates—"Bear one another's burdens" (Gal 6:2; cf. Rom 15:1-9)—love is the sole binding imperative of the new law (Rom 13:8-10), and the standard required is revealed by the love displayed in Christ's choice of crucifixion.

Paul Crucified

Only now does it become possible to see that "I am crucified with Christ" is the only possible evidence of the truth "I live now, not I, but Christ lives in me" (Gal 2:20). The tense of the verb *synestaurômai* is perfect and evokes a completed act whose results continue to the time of writing, "I have been nailed to the Cross with Christ, and am still hanging there with him."[40] In context, the immediate reference is to Paul's death to the Law, but he dies to the Law by adopting a lifestyle governed, no longer by rules and regulations, but by the sacrificial love of Christ.[41] The making of that commitment is an intellectual act, but it is not a once-for-all that sustains itself. Its continuing reality depends on its decisive influence on all subsequent choices. Selflessness ("not I"), being totally given over to the other ("Christ lives in me"), must impregnate his entire comportment.

The theme of Paul's crucifixion recurs later in Galatians in a context that gives it new depth. It appears in the handwritten postscript (Gal 6:11) in which Paul summarizes the salient point of the letter, "May it not be in me to boast—except in the cross of our Lord Jesus Christ, through whom/which the world has been crucified to me and I to the world"

29

(Gal 6:14). This text exhibits a number of extraordinary features. The unique combination of "cross" and "Lord" accentuates the paradox insinuated by the combination of "boasting" and "cross," particularly since boasting is by definition *self*-praise.[42] Crucifixion should produce revulsion, and the penalty was never inflicted on a "lord."[43] Moreover, three crucifixions are mentioned, those of Christ, the world, and Paul. Finally, it is the only passage to combine the noun "cross" and the verb "to crucify."

What is new in this text is the insight that the cross of Christ is the instrument that redefines Paul's relationship to the world, and the meaning of the latter. There is a theoretical ambiguity in *di' hou*, because the pronoun can be either masculine referring to "Christ" (a minority view) or neuter referring to "cross" (the majority view), but there is in fact no difference, because for Paul, "cross" always evokes the way Christ died, and Christ is always the crucified savior.[44]

"World" renders *kosmos*. The translation is easy—to determine the meaning less so. In usage, the basic distinction is between animate and inanimate reality. The inanimate sense is rare in Paul.[45] The animate sense is the predominant one, and two subdivisions are discernible. Parallel to Paul's use of "flesh," we can distinguish neutral (e.g., "God will judge the world" [Rom 3:6]),[46] and pejorative senses, the latter implying a negative value judgment (e.g., "we have not received the spirit of the world but the spirit which is from God" [1 Cor 2:12]).[47]

Which sense does Paul have in mind in Galatians 6:14? All commentators opt for the pejorative meaning but content themselves with generalizations, for example, "the mode of life characterized by earthly advantages";[48] "the totality of creation (human as well as nonhuman) in its distance from God, in its as yet unredeemed state,"[49] "the entire range of moral and spiritual possibilities of enfleshed humanity."[50] It is possible to be considerably more specific if one pays close attention to the context in which Galatians 6:14 is embedded.[51] The verse is bracketed by references to circumcision; 6:12–13 speaks of the circumcised and of those whom they wish to circumcise. Manifestly, for such people, circumcision retains all its value as the symbol of belonging to the Chosen People, the channel of salvation. It is the defining feature of their "world." Galatians 6:15–16 asserts the complete irrelevance of such symbolism, "Neither circumcision or uncircumcision counts for anything."

We have to do with a different world, another Israel, a new creation. The "world" of Galatians 6:14, therefore, can only be that of Jews and Judaizers. It is an ironic reversal, for Jews used it pejoratively of all non-Jewish humanity; it had become a synonym for Gentiles (cf. Rom 11:12).[52]

All the English translations that I have been able to consult render the datives *emoi* and *kosmô* by "to me" and "to the world." They are understood to indicate the place of crucifixion. This makes Paul the cross to which the world is crucified, and then the world becomes the cross on which he is crucified. The crucified becomes the cross of another. The paradox is so extreme that commentators make no attempt to explain it.

If one remains within this framework, the only possibility that I can see is to take the phrases as a rhetorical inversion implying completeness.[53] From this perspective the meaning would be, "Both I and the world have been completely crucified." But this is far from satisfying. Just as one cannot be half-pregnant, there is no half-crucifixion. It is always total. Moreover, this interpretation makes the datives irrelevant and assumes that the verse is structured like Galatians 5:24.

Grammar and usage are two further objections to the standard translation of Galatians 6:14. The dative of place is not found in the New Testament.[54] In all contemporary sources when the verb "to crucify" is employed, the place is never evoked directly or indirectly. It would be tautological, since "to crucify" necessarily implies a cross. When "cross" is in fact used, the verb is "to nail" (Col 2:14).

Hence, we must explore other meanings of the dative attested in the Pauline letters. Lagrange opted for the dative of advantage,[55] "the cross of our Savior, Jesus Christ, by which the world was crucified to me and I to the world."[56] It is difficult, however, to see what advantage accrued to the Judaizing world from the crucifixion of Paul. A preferable alternative is the dative of respect, "with reference to, as regards."[57] In this perspective Galatians 6:14b should be translated "the cross of Christ through which, as regards myself, the world has been crucified, and I, as regards the world." The function of the datives is to highlight Paul's experience, which to his profound regret was not shared by others. Their "world" had not been shattered by the crucifixion of Jesus.

The use of the verb "to crucify" in this context (as in Gal 2:20) is obviously metaphorical. "World" has to be personified, and Paul was not actually crucified (cf. 1 Cor 1:13). The choice of the metaphor goes to the heart of Paul's theology. If the cross of Christ is central, then the fundamental action is crucifixion. The content of words like "Messiah" and "Lord" were radically transformed by the crucifixion of the one who bore such names. Thus, no word was more appropriate than "crucifixion" to bring out the fundamental devaluation of all that the pre-Christian Paul had inherited from his Jewish "world." "For his sake I have suffered the loss of all things, and count them as refuse" (Phil 3:8). He was once as committed to Jewish values and symbols as the Judaizers, but all that has been changed, and permanently (*estaurôtai* is the perfect passive). A new creation means a new "world" whose most basic value is the self-sacrificing love displayed by Christ in the way he died.

One final dimension of Paul's crucifixion must be mentioned. In his discussion of ministry in 2 Corinthians, Paul uses the image of the wrestler thrown down so often that he is covered in sand to the point where he resembles a clay statue (4:7–9).[58] It is a metaphor for Paul's own struggle. He is being ground down physically and mentally (2 Cor 4:16) and sees clearly that the future holds only death. In this sense, his life is a "dying," "always carrying in the body the dying *(nekrôsis)*[59] of Jesus, so that the life of Jesus may be manifested in our bodies. For while we live we are being handed over to death for Jesus' sake so that the life of Jesus may be manifested in our mortal flesh" (2 Cor 4:10–11). Paul existentially identifies his "dying" with that of Jesus (Rom 6:5–6). We know, however, that the "dying" of Jesus was the long, drawn-out agony of crucifixion. Here, as in Galatians 2:20 and 6:14, Paul has in mind his being "crucified with Christ." But the Apostle introduces a new dimension that brings to light what was latent in Galatians 2:20. Paul's "dying" manifests "the life of Jesus."

In his agonized dying Jesus manifested the love for others that is literally the redeeming feature of authentic humanity. It is what restores the quality of being "the image of God" to human beings (Gen 1:27). Jesus thereby *demonstrated* what true "life" is. This had two effects. It showed those under the power of sin that they were "dead" and at the same time offered them the hope of "life" by revealing that sin was not omnipotent. By his act of love on the cross, Jesus enabled others to *see* that "life" was a real possibility. Talk can create utopias, but only achievement makes dreams a reality. It is easy to talk about loving to the limit, but where is the limit? Is it not necessary to hold back something in order to continue to love? Jesus' comportment on the cross set the standard of human love and revealed its attainability. He was human as we are, and what he did we can do.

It should now be clear why Paul was at such pains to make the crucifixion of Jesus as real as possible for the Galatians (Gal 3:1) and others.[60] It was the key to their salvation. Jesus in his suffering revealed to them what they could become. His generosity shattered the stifling bonds of their egocentricity. "He died for all that those who live might live no longer for themselves" (2 Cor 5:15). Words about love, however, could never be an adequate substitute for actual loving. For this reason, Paul was forced to assume the burden of being another Christ (1 Cor 11:1) in order to demonstrate that love without limit remained a real possibility for humans. He gave meaning to the slow death of his sufferings by finding in them the opportunity to manifest in his own way the quality of love that Jesus had shown in his horrible "dying." Thus, the "life of Jesus" once again became *visible* "in our bodies...in our mortal flesh" (2 Cor 4:10-11). Could there be any other explanation for his willingness to carry on to the end, despite all the anxiety and pain (2 Cor 11:23-29), except the same sacrificial love that inspired the choice of Jesus? Paul's wounds, therefore, are "the marks of Jesus" (Gal 6:17).

Enemies of the Cross of Christ

The predominance of crucifixion language in 1 Corinthians and Galatians must be explained by the circumstances of those two letters. Both in Galatia and in Corinth, Paul was confronted by alternative versions of the gospel. Although radically different in content, each had the effect of reducing the crucifixion of Christ to insignificance. In the light of what I have said above, Paul's reaction comes as no surprise; it remains a salutary corrective to tendencies that continue to distort Christianity. Only the cross exposes the extent to which the "world" has corrupted the body of Christ.[61]

The Judaizers

Paul was profoundly shocked when missionaries from Antioch appeared in the churches he had founded in Galatia. From his point of view, they were intruders. These churches, however, had been founded when he was commissioned by Antioch. Its emissaries believed that they were simply communicating to its daughter churches the new orientation of Antioch. Under pressure from James, the church there had opted for a heightened level of Jewish observance, which meant that Gentile believers effectively had to become Jews in order to stay in the community. Paul had lived through this change (Gal 2:11-14), and it brought home to him that if law in any form was given the slightest toehold in a Christian community it would inevitably become a rival to Christ. Law inexorably bred legalism. To follow a pattern of external observances was infinitely easier than living the sacrificial love of the Crucified. It became imperative for Paul to demolish the arguments his adversaries used to justify their position.

The sophistication of Paul's intelligence is evident in the elegant economy of his refutation. "Christ redeemed us from the curse of the law, having become a curse for us, for it is written, 'Cursed be everyone who hangs on a tree'" [Dt 21:23] (Gal 3:13). This unambiguous, but enigmatic, allusion to the crucifixion of Jesus becomes intelligible only in the light of the argument that Paul develops in Galatians 3:10-14, where, as C. K. Barrett has well said, "If the Judaizer appeals to Scripture to Scripture he must go; and Paul will beat him at his own game."[62]

The missionaries from Antioch could, and presumably did, argue that since Paul and his followers in Galatia refused circumcision, ignored the dietary regulations and disregarded the festivals, they were condemned by Deuteronomy 27:26, "Cursed be everyone who does not continue in all the things written in the book of the Law to do them" (Gal 3:10). Paul turns this accusation on its head by insisting that those who thought that their behavior merited a blessing were in fact under the curse of the disobedient (cf. Dt 11:26-27). How does Paul reach this conclusion, which to the intruders was the height of paradox?

He does so by invoking (Gal 3:11) an aspect of the covenant that the Judaizers had failed to take into account, namely, "The righteous person from faith will live" (Hab 2:4). The existential meaning of "life" here is identical with that in 2 Corinthians 4:10-11 (see above). It is the authentic humanity revealed by the faith/fidelity of Christ. The key element in the covenant relationship is no longer "the works of the Law" but faith. In order to drive home the fact that the Law is not "from faith"

(Gal 3:12), Paul quotes Leviticus 18:5, "The one who does them [the commands of the Law] will live by them."

Paul at this point seems to have worked himself onto the horns of a dilemma. Equally authoritative parts of scripture specify two different sources of "life." For Habakkuk it is "faith." For Leviticus it is "obedience." Paul would seem to have played into the hand of the intruders, because the most natural hypothesis is that both texts are saying the same thing. In other words, "faith" is articulated in "obedience," or "obedience" is the authentic expression of "faith."

This, however, is precisely the conclusion that Paul does not want to reach. In his view the two texts are mutually exclusive. If "the works of the Law" produce "life," then it cannot also come from "faith," and vice versa. It is illogical to postulate two causes to explain the same effect, if each is by definition adequate. Hence, a choice has to be made, and Paul justifies his option for "faith" by excluding the Law.

In terms of the Law, Jesus must be considered "accursed" because he had been hung on a tree (Gal 3:13). But for any Christian this is absurd. Even the intruders recognize that Jesus is the Messiah, whose inauguration of the eschaton is the justification for their mission to Gentiles. "The Messiah of Israel could never ever at the same time be the one who according to the words of the Torah was accursed by God."[63] If the Law is wrong on such a fundamental issue, it must be set aside. The intruders were hoisted with their own petard.

Here Paul transforms the crucifixion, which should be a major difficulty in acceptance of the gospel, into a powerful argument for liberty. In the process, he emphasizes that the crucifixion is the decisive objection to any attempt to reconcile Christ and the Law. Were it not for the modality of Jesus' death, it would have been feasible for the Judaizers to present him as a faithful observer of the Law. He had been circumcised (Luke 2:21). He obeyed the Law, for example, by going to Jerusalem on pilgrimage. He affirmed the enduring validity of the Law (Matt 5:17–19) and recommended obedience to it (Mark 1:40–45). According to that same Law,[64] however, Jesus must have been a criminal because he was hung on a tree. The way he died showed that he did not respect the Law.

The radical incompatibility of the Law (here concentrated into the symbol of circumcision) and Christ (associated with persecution) is evoked by Paul on two further occasions in Galatians. "But if I, believers, still preach circumcision, why am I still persecuted? Then the scandal of the cross has been annulled" (Gal 5:11). The first part of this text has given rise to a wide variety of interpretations as commentators speculate on when and where and in what sense Paul preached circumcision,[65] but it is the second that concerns us. Paul insists that he is still being persecuted; therefore, he cannot be preaching circumcision. In fact, he must be opposed to it. The whole Jewish Diaspora would have been up in arms against anyone who advocated the abolition of circumcision.[66] Synagogues did indeed inflict punishment on Paul—"Five times I have received at the hands of the Jews the forty lashes less one" (2 Cor 11:24)—presumably for such deeply offensive teaching. He could not have proclaimed Christ as savior without asserting the pointlessness of circumcision.

Unless "of the cross" in Galatians 5:11 is treated as a genitive of content or of apposition,[67] the verse is made to say the opposite of what is intended. To give importance to circumcision is not to nullify the scandalous nature of the crucifixion of Jesus but to negate the scandal that is the cross. The Judaizers believed that they could have both Christ and circumcision, but Paul's use of *katargeô*, "to annul," reveals that for him they were mutually exclusive. Just as the crucifixion of Jesus made the Law meaningless (Gal 3:13), so acceptance of circumcision makes his sacrifice irrelevant. Once again, it was the modality of Christ's death that revealed the inherent powerlessness of any other channel of salvation.

Paul articulates his assessment of why the Judaizers acted as they did in the words, "As many as wish to look well in the flesh, these compel you to be circumcised only in order that they may not be persecuted for the cross of Christ" (Gal 6:12). They were cowards motivated only by what people thought of them. Because of their Jewish origins, they wanted to retain the favor of the Jewish community. Their good standing, however, would be put at risk if they associated with uncircumcised Gentiles. Not only would such behavior lower the barriers essential to Jewish identity, but it would seriously weaken the argument for the indispensable salvific character of circumcision. Thus, in order to avoid persecution, they refused to proclaim a crucified Messiah, for the modality of his death revealed the radical inadequacy of circumcision.

This made those whose Jewishness remained the fundamental salvific factor "enemies of the cross of Christ" (Phil 3:18). That the reference here is to Judaizers is made unambiguous by the following phrase,

"Their god is (a) the stomach and (b) the glory in the shame of them" (Phil 3:19). This awkwardly literal translation is necessary in order to bring out the fact that in Paul's mind the two elements belong together.[68] Even though each phrase taken separately can be interpreted differently, the force of the combination is inescapable. The dietary laws were in fact more sacred than God,[69] and Jews gloried in circumcision, which for their pagan contemporaries was shameful mutilation.[70] Paul certainly has in view those whom he has qualified earlier as "dogs" who "mutilate themselves" (Phil 3:2). For the Judaizers kashrut and circumcision were the only matters of ultimate concern. They scaled the role of Christ down to irrelevance. Paul's blood boiled at such callous dismissal of what Christ suffered for us. The Judaizers, in consequence, were not merely misguided. They were "enemies," who by definition are destructive of Christianity.

The Spirit-people

The Judaizers also tried to make inroads at Corinth, but they were not successful. The real danger there came from a different source, a group within the church whose needs were not met by Paul's insistence that all they needed to know was a crucified Christ and how to live like him. For convenience, I call them the Spirit-people.[71] They desired a speculative theology and turned to Apollos (1 Cor 3:6). He gave them a rational framework derived from Philo of Alexandria, which they developed in a way that radically distorted Paul's teaching.

They believed that their possession of "wisdom" made them "perfect." Religion was essentially a matter of the mind. Theistic discussion was the most appropriate response to divine election. The body and physical actions were fundamentally irrelevant. The "wise," in consequence, could do whatever they liked; "all things are lawful to me" (1 Cor 6:12; 10:23). Sin was a mental stance, not a corporeal act void of love (1 Cor 6:18).[72] These attitudes spawned divisions in the community (1 Cor 1:11–12).

Paul's immediate reaction was to repudiate his own supporters, "Was Paul crucified for you? Or were you baptized in the name of Paul?" (1 Cor 1:13). The rhetorical questions were designed to force the Corinthians to see the absurdity of their behavior. The formulation of the first admirably illustrates how intimately salvation and crucifixion were linked in Paul's mind, and what the meaning of crucifixion was.

Paul, Cephas and Apollos may have done a lot for different churches, but none of them had suffered in the atrocious way Christ had. None of them had given everything with the totality of Christ. The love he exhibited gave him alone an absolute claim on all the members of the church. They "belonged to Christ" (1 Cor 3:23) exclusively. There was no basis for saying that they "belonged to Paul" or to anyone else.

Paul then moved to the root of the problem. He refuses "wisdom of word" (1 Cor 1:17), which is most naturally understood as a reference to the preferences of the Spirit-people.[73] The problems latent in these three words are borne out by the variety in major translations, for example, "eloquent wisdom" (NRSV) and "wisdom of language" (JB). The first puts the emphasis on content, whereas the second highlights the modality, "studied rhetoric,"[74] "rhetorical skill."[75] If one limits oneself to the phrase alone, the need to make a choice appears imperative, but as so often with Paul, matters are not that simple. His reason for repudiating "wisdom of word" is "lest the cross of Christ be emptied of its power" (1 Cor 1:17). The paradoxical association of "cross" and "power" is repeated in the next verse, "The word of the cross is folly to those who are perishing, but to those who are being saved it is the power of God" (1 Cor 1:18). These words immediately direct our attention to a parallel saying, "The gospel is the power of God for salvation" (Rom 1:16), and oblige us to conclude that "the gospel" *is* "(the word of) the cross." This inference is confirmed by Paul's insistence that "we preach Christ crucified" (1 Cor 1:23); "I did not think it appropriate to know anything among you except Jesus Christ and him crucified" (1 Cor 2:1–2).

This concatenation of references to the crucifixion of Jesus in the first two chapters of 1 Corinthians betrays Paul's awareness of the seriousness of the threat to its centrality in his gospel.[76] In opposition to the Judaizers, who wished to retain the traditional salvific role of their observances, the Spirit-people sought a faith that would give them intellectual respectability, a religious option that would satisfy the canons of accepted rhetoric, a rounded whole that could be set against the other religious systems of the day. The Spirit-people were a more subtle danger than the Judaizers. The appeal of the latter was diminished by the pain of circumcision and its widespread condemnation in the Greco-Roman world. The Spirit-people, on the contrary, could capitalize on the human desire to be on the cutting edge of religious thought.

No orator, even the most skillful, could devise arguments to make a crucified Savior either intelligible or palatable. Such arguments have to be rooted in commonly accepted values. Both Jews and Gentiles, however, agreed that the idea was "scandal" and "folly" (1 Cor 1:23). This consensus condemned any attempt to present a crucified Christ in a favorable light. Thus, there was an inherent contradiction between rhetoric and the Pauline gospel. The former manifested "the wisdom of the world," whereas the latter was the product of "the wisdom of God." The gospel could be made rational only by suppressing its most distinctive feature, the crucifixion of Jesus. The insidious danger at Corinth was that those who wished to give the gospel an attractive rhetorical presentation did not have to deny the crucifixion formally. All they had to do was to pass over it in silence. It sufficed to stress "the Lord of Glory" (1 Cor 2:8) and to make no mention of crucifixion.

There is also an inherent contradiction between a gospel centered on the crucifixion and a speculative theology. Such a theology rationalizes the data of revelation by organizing it logically. The only logic capable of accommodating death by crucifixion is the political logic of deterrent punishment. But it is ridiculous to think of God sacrificing an innocent human being in order to deter humanity from further sin. The crucifixion simply cannot be brought into any rational pattern that respects the creative goodness of God.

For Paul, however, the goodness of God was a given (Rom 8:28), and the crucifixion of the Savior a fact. He had no choice but to relate them, but he recognized that logic could never work. Incapable of dynamic tension, it would have to deny one of the elements in one subtle way or another. As we have seen, divine goodness and crucifixion could be related only in terms of love (Gal 2:20). The love that Jesus showed in the choice of that particular mode of death for us became the revelation of God's efficacious love for humanity (Rom 8:39) and manifested that such creative love was constitutive of authentic humanity. However irrational it might be, true "life" was the surrender of "dying" for others. It is only in giving, in enabling, that we become human and Christian.[77] Paul had to insist that the Lord of Glory had been crucified (1 Cor 2:8) in order to prevent the Spirit-people from reducing Christianity to a vacuous verbalism in which conceptualization took the place of charity. It is precisely as crucified that Jesus is "the power of God and the wisdom of God" (1 Cor 1:24).

Blood

In 1 Corinthians Paul three times speaks of the "blood" of Christ (10:16; 11:25; 11:27), and in Romans there are two references (3:25; 5:9–10). "Blood," however, has no necessary connection with crucifixion. Thus, there may be some hesitation as to the appropriateness of dealing here with these texts. The basis of a prima facie case, however, as far as Paul is concerned, is provided by his explicit association of the two in his addition to the Colossian hymn, "making peace by the blood of his cross" (Col 1:20).[78]

The three references in 1 Corinthians all allude to the Eucharist.[79] The first appears in the context of Paul's discussion of the propriety of eating meat offered to idols (1 Cor 8–10), "the cup of blessing, which we bless, is it not a communion of the blood of Christ?" (1 Cor 10:16). Paul's point in bringing in the Eucharist is not at first sight apparent, but it is in fact intimately related to the issue under consideration. The initial link is the similarity between the eucharistic assembly and meals in pagan temples, and the bonds that are forged in such rituals. Although there was nothing intrinsically wrong in the participation of Christians in temple meals, Paul wished those who felt so inclined to desist because of the damage it did to the weaker members of the community (1 Cor 8:10-12; 10:20-21). Out of love for others, they should make the sort of sacrifice that Paul did (1 Cor 8:13–9:18). Understandably, therefore, Paul thinks in terms of the ultimate self-sacrifice of Christ in which his blood was spilled. Union with Christ necessarily means acceptance of self-sacrifice as a way of life.

The second reference occurs in Paul's argument that lack of genuine love among the participants in the liturgical assembly at Corinth (1 Cor 11:21-22) made the valid celebration of the Eucharist impossible (1 Cor 11:20). He quotes the words of Jesus, "This is the cup of the new covenant in my blood" (1 Cor 11:25), on which he then comments in 1 Corinthians 11:26. Paul shows that the sharing of the eucharistic meal was designed to be a proclamation of the death of the Lord, which, we have seen, was an act of self-sacrificing love. Words and gestures, however, accomplished nothing. Only when the table fellowship accurately reflected the Christlike love of the believers for each other did such a proclamation really take place. Then alone did the Eucharist fulfill its promise. Once again, "blood" unequivocally evokes what Jesus revealed in his choice of crucifixion.

A slightly different aspect appears in the third reference, "Whoever eats the bread or drinks the cup of the Lord in an unworthy manner will be guilty of the body and blood of the Lord" (1 Cor 11:27). "To be guilty of the blood of someone" is to be responsible for that person's death (cf. Deut 19:10). Those who attempt to celebrate the Eucharist without love put themselves in the position of the executioners who crucified Christ (cf. Heb 6:6).

If the thought of the crucifixion of Jesus lies just beneath the surface of the allusions to his "blood" in 1 Corinthians, the same does not appear to be true of the two references in Romans. Since there is but one passing and indirect mention of the crucifixion of Christ in this letter (6:5–6), Paul's readers would have understood the references to "blood" in both 3:25 and 5:9 in purely sacrificial terms, without any awareness of the modality of Christ's death.[80] He was the divinely designated victim, whose blood produced expiation and justification.

Silence

The silence of Romans with regard to the crucifixion is paralleled by three other letters, 1 and 2 Thessalonians, and Philemon. Given the importance that Paul attached to the precise way in which Christ died, both in his oral preaching and in his letters to Galatia and to Corinth, this reticence calls for an explanation.

If Paul preached a crucified Christ in Galatia (Gal 3:1) and in Corinth (1 Cor 2:2), then he certainly did in Thessalonica. One could say that neither of the problems that called forth Paul's emphasis on the crucifixion in Galatians and 1 Corinthians arose in the church at Thessalonica. That is certainly correct, but there may have been another factor.

R. Jewett has argued that the success of Christianity among the working class at Thessalonica was due to the fact that it offered a satisfactory substitute for the Cabirus cult, which had been co-opted as part of the official religion. Like Cabirus, Jesus was a young man, unjustly killed, who had risen from the dead and would help the poor. It is not difficult to surmise, as Jewett has emphasized,[81] that the hint of a new "god," who would radically transform the situation of the underprivileged, would have been perceived by the municipal authorities as subversive. In consequence, they were the source of the persecution that worried Paul so much (1 Thess 3:3–8).

This meant that the members of the Jesus movement would have been labeled, not merely as adherents of a religion of doubtful legality, but as politically dangerous. According to Roman law—and Thessalonica was a Roman colony—rebellious subjects were treated as common bandits, who were punished by being crucified or thrown to wild beasts.[82] If Paul had some doubt about the ability of the Thessalonians to withstand harassment, perhaps economic deprivation, even some physical brutality, he was probably insightful enough to recognize that it was not the moment to remind them that they might be crucified like Jesus, even though he had warned them to expect suffering. The cross was a frightful deterrent. Under these precise circumstances, to emphasize crucifixion might have led to the Thessalonians abandoning their faith.

A similar hypothesis can explain the silence of the letter to Philemon. Onesimus was a slave (Phlm 16) who had inflicted severe damage on his master (Phlm 18). Were Philemon to assert his rights, Onesimus could be crucified.[83]

The case of the letter to the Romans is completely different. The death of Christ is a recurrent theme in Romans. Paul evokes it no less than seventeen times.[84] Seven are variations of the phrase "raised from the dead,"[85] whereas of the rest, eight focus on the purpose of his death,[86] one highlights the effect of his death (5:10), and the last relates his death to sin (6:10). If Paul did not take so many opportunities to mention the modality of Christ's death, it looks as if he had made a deliberate decision not to do so. Why?

The external circumstances that provided a reasonable explanation for the silence of 1–2 Thessalonians and Philemon were not replicated in Rome. The inhabitants of the Eternal City were fully aware of the horrors of crucifixion, and the two groups of Christian slaves—the Aristobuliani (Rom 16:10) and the Narcissiani (Rom 16:11)[87]—were liable to crucifixion, but there is no hint that they or any other member of the Christian community were directly threatened by this punishment.

I have argued elsewhere that Paul's purpose in going to Rome was to be commissioned by that church for the mission in Spain (Rom 15:24).[88] If this is correct, it provides an alternative explanation for the silence of Romans. The convergence between the formulations of Romans and those of the traditional kerygma suggests that Paul abandoned his characteristic stress on the crucifixion of Jesus in order to make clear to the Roman church that he stood in the mainstream of the Jesus movement. It was a concession that he felt he had to make in order not to compromise his return to a representative role. The divine origin of his commission (Gal 1:1) could be demonstrated by hindsight (1 Cor 9:2; 2 Cor 3:2), but it provided no defense against accusations that he was a maverick preaching his own religion. His sense of the unity of all Christian churches was so great that his isolation became ever more irksome. He needed to be the envoy of a church. I am sure that in Paul's mind, the *suppression* of the truth was only temporary. A crucified Christ was too deeply interwoven with so many other aspects of his soteriology to be abandoned definitively.

A Concluding Reflection

The attitude that Paul had to counter in Galatia and at Corinth remains a perennial problem in the church. The temptation to adopt a vision of salvation that will not make us look ridiculous, and that can be defended by logical arguments, is ever present. The temptation to take refuge in the discussion of the niceties of legal demands and to lose oneself in legalism is always with us. The cross is still a scandal that must be suppressed or buried in busyness.

Contemporary sermons and retreats emphasize discernment of the will of God. It is a mystery, we are told, that must be probed with patience. A director is essential if we are serious in our quest for enlightenment. We put such emphasis on the will of God, however, because it can be made anything we want it to be. It can be made to excuse the tortures of the Inquisition and the massacres of the Crusades. It can be made to justify mass suicides as the tragic ends of so many cultists illustrate.

For Paul, the will of God is very simple, and this lack of ambiguity terrifies us. It mandates the following of Christ who is defined by the cross. This is the revealed will of God. We must exhibit the self-sacrificing, empowering love that Christ showed in his crucifixion. We must bear in our bodies the dying of Jesus in order that the life of Jesus may be manifested to the world. Crucifixion is what makes a Christian.

NOTES

1. There are two major studies of crucifixion: Martin Hengel, *Crucifix-ion in the Ancient World and the Folly of the Message of the Cross* (London: SCM, 1977), and Heinz-Wolfgang Juhn, "Die Kreuzesstrafe wahrend der fruhen Kaiserzeit: Ihre Wirklichkeit und Wertung in der Umwelt des Urchristentums," ANRW 25/1 (1982): 648-793.

2. *Life of Constantine*, 1.28. On the historicity of this event, see John Julius Norwich, *The Early Centuries* (London: Penguin, 1990), 38-43.

3. Sozomen, *Ecclesiastical History*, 1.8.

4. The glorification of the cross is well documented by Nathan Mitchel in chapter 3 of this book.

5. Paul van Moorsel, "The Worship of the Holy Cross in Saqqara: Archaeological Evidence," in *Theologia Crucis–Signum Crucis*, festschr. for Erich Dinkler, ed. C. Andresen and G. Klein (Tübingen: Mohr, 1979), 409-20.

6. *New Catholic Encyclopedia*, s.v. "Crucifixion (in Art)," 486, with illus-trations on 488.

7. For justification of the proposed order and of the authenticity of Colossians and 2 Timothy, see J. Murphy-O'Connor, *Paul: A Critical Life* (Oxford: Clarendon Press, 1996).

8. There is another reference in 1 Thessalonians 2:15, but I consider this verse and the following a post-Pauline interpolation.

9. J. A. Fitzmyer, *Paul and His Theology: A Brief Sketch*, 2d ed. (Engle-wood Cliffs, N.J.: Prentice-Hall, 1989), 32.

10. E.g., most recently, John T. Carroll and Joel B. Green, "'Nothing... but Christ and Him Crucified': Paul's Theology of the Cross," in John T. Car-roll and Joel B. Green, *The Death of Jesus in Early Christianity* (Peabody, Mass.: Hendrickson, 1995), 113-32.

11. 1 Corinthians 15:3 is the only kerygmatic formula to use "Christ."

12. M. Hengel, *The Atonement: The Origins of the Doctrine in the New Tes-tament* (Philadelphia: Fortress Press, 1981), 40.

13. The assumption that *ouk ekrina* is the same as *ekrina ou* is rightly refused by A. Robertson and A. Plummer, *A Critical and Exegetical Commentary on the First Epistle of St Paul to the Corinthians*, ICC (Edinburgh: T. & T. Clark, 1911), 30.

14. So, most recently, G. D. Fee, *The First Epistle to the Corinthians*, NICNT (Grand Rapids, Mich.: Eerdmans, 1987), 61; H. Merklein, *Der erste Brief an die Korinther. Kapietl 1–4*, Okumenischer Taschenbuch-Kommentar zum Neuen Testament 7/1 (Gütersloh: Mohn/Würzburg, 1992), 209.

15. "You foolish Galatians! Who has bewitched you? It was before your eyes that Jesus Christ was publicly exhibited as crucified!" (NRSV). "You stupid people in Galatia! After you have had a clear picture of Jesus Christ crucified, right in front of your eyes, who has put a spell on you?" (JB). "You senseless Galatians! Who has cast a spell over you—you before whose eyes Jesus Christ was displayed to view upon his cross?" (NAB).

16. See in particular J. H. Elliott, "Paul, Galatians, and the Evil Eye," *Currents in Theology and Mission* 17/4 (1990), 262–73. In more detail, idem, "The Fear of the Leer: The Evil Eye from the Bible to Li'l Abner," *Forum* 4/4 (1988), 42–71.

17. Pliny, *Natural History* 28.36, 39; Theocritus, 6. 39; 20.11.

18. It is not impossible, as Elliott has argued ("Paul, Galatians, and the Evil Eye," 269), that Paul's adversaries in Galatia claimed that the circumstances of Paul's arrival were such that he must have put the Evil Eye on them, but this is to make the argument more convoluted than is necessary.

19. LSJ, 1473b.

20. E. de Witt Burton, *A Critical and Exegetical Commentary on the Epistle to the Galatians*, ICC (Edinburgh: T. & T. Clark, 1921), 144–45; H. Schlier, *Der Brief an die Galater*, MeyerK (Göttingen: Vandenhoeck & Ruprecht, 1962), 119; P. Bonnard, *L'épitre de saint Paul aux Galates*, CNT 9, 2d ed. (Neuchatel: Delachaux & Niestlé, 1972), 60.

21. *Graphô* is used in the sense "to paint" only in centuries remote from the beginnings of Christianity (Burton, *Galatians*, 144).

22. J. D. G. Dunn, *The Epistle to the Galatians*, BNTC (Peabody, Mass.: Hendrickson, 1993), 152.

23. H. D. Betz, *Galatians: A Commentary on Paul's Letter to the Churches in Galatia*, Hermeneia (Philadelphia: Fortress Press, 1979).

24. R. N. Longenecker, *Galatians*, WBC 41 (Dallas, Tex.: Word Books, 1990).

25. J. B. Phillips, *Letters to Young Churches* (London: Fontana, 1955), 114.

26. "In pursuance of their savage ways the Celts manifest an outlandish impiety also with respect to their sacrifices. They keep their criminals for five years and then impale them in honour of the gods" (Didorus Siculus, *Library of History*, 5.32.6). The incursions of the Galatians into Asia brought a vigorous Roman response (Livy, *History*, 38.16–29), but I have not found any references to the crucifixion of captives. From 25 B.C., however, Galatia was a Roman province, in which criminals and slaves would have been crucified on a fairly regular basis in accordance with Roman practice elsewhere.

27. "From such impressions arises that *enargeia* which Cicero calls 'illumination' and 'actuality,' which makes us seem not so much to narrate as to

exhibit the actual scene" (Quintilian, *Institutio Oratoria* 6.2.32). Paul's disclaimer of any rhetorical ability in 2 Corinthians 11:6 is a mere rhetorical convention. In fact, he was so well trained that his skill had become instinctive (see H. D. Betz, *Der Apostle Paulus und die sokratische Tradition: Eine exegetische Untersuchung zu seiner Apologie 2 Korinther 10–13*, BHT 45 (Tübingen: Mohr, 1972), 47–69; C. Forbes, "Comparison, Self-Praise and Irony: Paul's Boasting and the Conventions of Hellenistic Rhetoric," *NTS* 32 (1986), 1–30. The negative position on the quality of Paul's secular education taken by older authors (e.g., J. Knox, *Chapters in a Life of Paul* [New York/Nashville: Abingdon-Cokesbury, 1950], 75–76) is due to inadequate analysis.

28. Was this departure from the common kerygma the real reason for the decision of Barnabas to let Paul go his own way (Acts 15:36–41)? Luke could hardly say that Barnabas wished to ignore the fact of the crucifixion.

29. J. Murphy-O'Connor, "Another Jesus (2 Cor 11:4)," *RB* 97 (1990), 248.

30. "We must identify ourselves with the persons of whom we complain that they have suffered grievous, unmerited and bitter misfortune, and must plead their case, and, for a brief space, feel their suffering as though it were our own" (Quintilian, *Institutio Oratoria* 6.2.34).

31. See J. Murphy-O'Connor, "Christological Anthropology in Phil 2:6–11," *RB* 83 (1976), 25–50.

32. There was a widespread Jewish tradition that to die was not intrinsic to human nature but was an extrinsically imposed punishment (see Gen 3:2–3; Wis 1:12–14; 2:23–24; Philo, *Quaest. in Gen.*, 1.55; *1 Enoch* 69:9–11; *4 Ezra* 3:7; *2 Baruch* 23:4; 54:15; *Gen. Rab.* 8.11 on Gen 1:27). Other references are given in M. E. Stone, *Fourth Ezra: A Commentary on the Book of Fourth Ezra*, Hermeneia (Minneapolis: Fortress Press, 1990), 65 n.26.

33. G. D. Fee objects to the hypothesis of a Pauline addition on the grounds that it is a rhetorical climax (*Paul's Letter to the Philippians*, NICNT [Grand Rapids, Mich.: Eerdmans, 1995], 217), but the argument is circular and ignores both the tightly woven structure of the hymn and the thrust of the common kerygma. My argument, however, does not depend on my source analysis.

34. J. Gnilka, *Der Philipperbrief*, HTKNT (Freiburg: Herder, 1968), 124.

35. Fee's attempt to respect the word order of the Greek, "death, that is, of a cross" (*Philippians*, 217) is not successful. G. Hawthorne's paraphrase. "and that of all things, death on a cross" brings out the sense admirably (*Philippians*, WBC 43 [Waco Tex.: Word Books, 1983], 75).

36. Fee, *Philippians*, 216.

37. The shift from "Christ" to "son of God" in Galatians 2:20 may hint at the theme of obedience that is found in the hymn, because for a Semite a true child is one who obeys (Matt 21:28-31).

38. As frequently in the Pauline letters (BDF §442[9]), the *kai* "and" linking the two phrases is explanatory.

39. The genitive is appositive (BDF §167), and so *nomos Christou* should be translated as "the law which is Christ." The underlying idea is clearly articulated by Philo, "The lives of those who have earnestly followed virtue may be called unwritten laws" (*De Virt.* 194; cf. *Vita Moysis* 1.162). While arguing that Galatians 6:2 presents Christ as the paradigm of Christian existence R. B. Hays ignores the grammatical point and is completely silent on the fact that the Christ of Galatians is above all the Crucified ("Christology and Ethics in Galatians: The Law of Christ," *CBQ* 49 [1987], 268-90).

40. Dunn, *Galatians*, 144.

41. Despite the parallel with Romans 6:6, there is no allusion here to baptism; against Schlier, *Der Brief an die Galater*, 101.

42. Betz, *Galatians*, 318.

43. See in particular Cicero: "To bind a Roman citizen is a crime...to crucify him is—what? There is no fitting word that can possibly describe so horrible a deed" (*In Verrem* 5.66); "The very word 'cross' should be far removed not only from the person of a Roman citizen, but from his thoughts, his eyes, and his ears" (*Pro Rabirio Postumo* 5.16).

44. So rightly Betz, *Galatians*, 318.

45. Out of thirty-seven instances only five can be classified in this way, e.g., "the creation of the world" (Rom 1:8; cf. 4:13; 1 Cor 3:22; 5:10; 8:4).

46. Other examples: Rom 1:8; 5:12; 11:12; 16:19; 1 Cor 1:21; 4:9; 5:10; 14:10; Phil 2:15; Col 1:6.

47. Other examples: Rom 11:15; 1 Cor 1:20; 3:19; 11:32; 2 Cor 5:19; 7:10; Col 2:20.

48. Burton, *Galatians*, 354.

49. Dunn, *Galatians*, 340.

50. Bonnard, *Galates*, 130.

51. See in particular P. Minear, "The Crucified World: The Enigma of Galatians 6,14," in Andresen and Klein, *Theologia Crucis–Signum Crucis*, 397-98.

52. Minear notes the disparaging use of "world" by Christians of Jews (John 18:20) and by Jews of Christians (John 12:19); the pot calling the kettle black ("Crucified World," 400 n.14).

53. In virtually all cultures it is common to express totality by the combination of opposites. God's order to Laban in Genesis 31:24, when translated

literally is, "Do not say to Jacob from the bad to the good," but the meaning is obviously, "Say absolutely nothing to Jacob." In moving from one extreme to another the mind traverses the totality of what could be said. We still use expressions such as "I will support you through thick and thin" to mean "I am completely on your side." See G. Lambert, "'Lire-délire': L'expression de la totalité par l'opposition de deux contraires," *Vivre et Penser* 3 (1943-44) [= *RB* 52 (1944)], 91-103.

54. BDF §199.

55. BDF §188.

56. St. Paul, *Epître aux Galates* (EBib; Paris: Gabalda, 1925), 165. He is followed by S. Lyonnet in the *Bible de Jérusalem*, "...qui a fait du monde un crucifié pour moi et de moi un crucifié pour le monde." A curious halfway position is taken by Bonnard, "...par laquelle le monde est crucifié pour moi et moi au monde" (*Galates*, 128).

57. BDF §197. Phillips paraphrases, "the cross of our Lord Jesus Christ which means that the world is a dead thing to me and I am a dead man to the world" (*Letters to Young Churches*, 121).

58. C. Spicq, "L'image sportive de 2 Cor 4:7-9," *ETL* 13 (1937), 209-29.

59. The predominant translation "death" on the basis of the use of the same term in Romans 4:19 is inappropriate here because the context indicates that it is question of a process. So rightly C. Wolff, *Der zweite Brief des Paulus an die Korinther*, THNT 8 (Berlin: Evangelische Verlagsanstalt, 1989), 92 n.217, against V. P. Furnish, *II Corinthians*, AB (Garden City: Doubleday, 1984), 256.

60. Cousar (*A Theology of the Cross*, 23) rightly criticizes E. Käsemann's insistence that Paul evokes the cross exclusively in polemical situations ("The Saving Significance of the Death of Jesus in Paul," in his *Perspectives on Paul* [Philadelphia: Fortress Press, 1971], 35-36), but fails to explain how crucifixion functions in missionary discourse.

61. No one has argued this point more passionately or more cogently than Käsemann in his "The Saving Significance of the Death of Jesus" (see note 60). An alternative translation is given in "The Pauline Theology of the Cross," *Int* 24 (1970), 151-77.

62. C. K. Barrett, *Freedom and Obligation: A Study of the Epistle to the Galatians* (London: SPCK, 1985), 26.

63. Hengel, *Atonement*, 43.

64. Deuteronomy 21:22-23, whose actuality for the period with which we are concerned is confirmed by 11QTemple 64:6-13. According to 4QpNah iii-iv 1:7-8, individuals were crucified alive.

65. A list of six different views is given by Dunn, *Galatians*, 278-79. I do not think that Paul ever preached circumcision. As a Pharisee, he took it for

granted. Early in his career Paul tolerated circumcision among his Jewish converts (cf. 1 Cor 9:20). After the incident at Antioch (Gal 2:11-14), however, he realized that circumcision was only the thin end of the wedge of legalism. Thereafter he forbade his Jewish converts to circumcise their children. The accusation of Acts 21:21 is entirely accurate. Paul's enemies inflated this well-motivated change of attitude into a charge of unprincipled inconsistency by claiming that he had once "preached" circumcision.

66. The prohibition of circumcision by Antiochus Epiphanes (1 Macc 1:48, 60-61) unleashed a holy war. P. Borgen interprets Philo's *De Migratione Abrahami* 86-93 as criticism of Jews who opted for ethical circumcision against physical circumcision ("Paul Preaches Circumcision and Pleases Men," in *Paul and Paulinism: Essays in Honour of C. K. Barrett* [London: SPCK, 1982], 39-40).

67. BDF §167.

68. Although he fails both to let the observation influence his translation and to recognize its significance, Fee rightly points out that "grammatically, the two clauses are held together by a single relative pronoun indicating that in Paul's intention they go together" (*Philippians*, 372 n.37).

69. See Murphy-O'Connor, *Paul: A Critical Life*, 337-38.

70. Martial, *Epigrams* 7.35 and 82; see ABD 1.1027.

71. Elsewhere I have argued that they were at the root of virtually all the problems dealt with in 1 Corinthians (see J. Murphy-O'Connor, "Pneumatikoi in 2 Corinthians," *Proceedings of the Irish Biblical Association* 11 ([1988], 59-61).

72. See J. Murphy-O'Connor, "Corinthian Slogans in 1 Corinthians 6:12-20," *CBQ* 40 (1978), 391-96.

73. So rightly Robertson and Plummer, *First Corinthians*, 16.

74. Robertson and Plummer, *First Corinthians*, 9.

75. Barrett, *First Corinthians*, 49.

76. Unfortunately, the one study devoted to this specific issue makes little or no contribution, R. S. Barbour, "Wisdom and the Cross in 1 Corinthians 1 and 2," in Andresen and Klein, *Theologia Crucis–Signum Crucis*, 57-74.

77. J. Macquarrie, *Principles of Christian Theology* (London: SCM, 1966), 212, 288.

78. See J. Murphy-O'Connor, "Tradition and Redaction in Colossians 1:15-20," *RB* 102 (1995), 231-41.

79. For more detail, see J. Murphy-O'Connor, "Eucharist and Community in First Corinthians," *Worship* 50 (1976), 370-85; 51 (1977), 56-69.

80. J. D. G. Dunn, *Romans*, WBC 38 (Dallas, Tex.: Word Books, 1988), 171.

81. R. Jewett, *The Thessalonian Correspondence: Pauline Rhetoric and Millenarian Piety*, Foundations and Facets: New Testament (Philadelphia: Fortress Press, 1986), 132.

82. Hengel, *Crucifixion*, 47–48.

83. Juvenal, *Satires*, 6.219–22.

84. Rom 4:24, 25; 5:6, 8, 10; 6:3, 4, 5, 8, 9, 10; 7:4; 8:11, 32; 10:7, 9; 14:9.

85. Rom 4:24; 6:4, 9; 7:4; 8:11; 10:7, 9.

86. Rom 4:25; 5:6, 8; 6:3, 5, 8; 8:32; 14:9

87. BDF §162(5).

88. Murphy-O'Connor, *Paul: A Critical Life*, 329–30.

CHAPTER 2

"Washed Away by the Blood of God"

Nathan D. Mitchell

Introduction

Both this chapter and the one that follows focus on the relation between the cross and the liturgy. In the previous chapter, Jerome Murphy-O'Connor showed that this relationship developed very early in Christian history, as seen, for example, in the Philippian hymn (Phil 2:6-11). This liturgical hymn celebrates the self-emptying of Christ, who "did not count equality with God a thing to be grasped" (Phil 2:6). Christ, the hymn explains, chose to accept death, even death on a cross. As a result, "God raised him high and gave him the name which is above all other names" (Phil 2:9). Throughout subsequent centuries, Christian poets and hymn writers—especially those whose work made its way into the liturgy—celebrated the cross as an icon of Christ's self-surrender and of our salvation in him. This present chapter offers selections from this poetry, and focuses on the way its images influenced the evolution of Christian festivals that celebrate the cross. In chapter 3 I will look more closely at the ways both liturgical practice and devotional custom transformed the cross itself, as image, icon, object of veneration.

To begin, permit me to cite three examples of how the cross has awakened poetry over the centuries. The first example is early, Byzantine and liturgical.

> All creation was gripped by terror when it beheld you,
> > suspended on the Cross, O Christ!
> The sun was darkened, and the foundations of the earth were shaken:
> > All things suffered in sympathy with the One who had created all
> > things...

51

Today the Virgin undefiled, beholding you, the Word, uplifted on the
Cross,
wept with the tender love of a mother...
Woe is me, O my Son!
Woe is me, O Light of the world!
Why have you departed from my eyes, O Lamb of God?[1]

The Cross...commands every created being to sing the most pure Passion
of him who was lifted up...
Come...Let us adore the blessed Tree,...
For the [Evil One] who beguiled our forbear Adam with the tree
is himself beguiled by the Cross...
The poison of the serpent is washed away by the blood of God,
and the curse of condemnation is abolished...

For it was fitting that the tree should be healed by the Tree
and that, by the Passion of the Passionless One upon the Tree,
the passions of the condemned...should be destroyed.
Glory, O Christ our King, unto your wise providence,
whereby you saved us all:
for you are good and love humankind![2]

The second example is early, Irish, and devotional.

At the cry of the first bird
They began to crucify Thee, O cheek like a swan
It were not right ever to cease lamenting —
It was like the parting of day from night.

Ah! Though sore the suffering
Put upon the body of Mary's Son—
Sorer to Him was the grief
That was upon her for His sake.[3]

The third example is by a twentieth-century poet who might not
even claim to be a Christian.

The prairie melts into the throats of larks
And green like water green begins to flow
Into the pinto patches of the snow.

I'm here, I move my foot, I count the mountains:
I can make calculations of my being
Here in the spring again, feeling it, seeing...
[...]
A mountain range ago the sea was here,
Now I am here, the falcons floating over,
Bluebirds swimming foredeeps of the blue,
Spindrift magpies black and splashing white,
The winged fins, the birds, the water green...

Not ocean ever now but lilies here,
Sand lilies, yucca lilies water-petaled,
Lilies too delicate, only a little while,
Lilies like going away, like a far sound,
Lilies like wanting to be loved
And tapping with a stick,
An old man tapping
The world in springtime with a stick.
[...]
I know the myth for spring I used to know:
The Son of God was pinned to a wooden truss
But lived again, His blood contiguous

To mine, His blood still ticking like a clock
Against the collar of my overcoat
That I have buttoned tight to warm my throat.
Who was His lover? That might keep Him nearer.
Whom did He love in springtime fingering
All fruit to come in any blossom white?
Cupping His hand for tips of nakedness
And whispering:

   "You are the flowers, Beloved,
You are the footstep in the darkness always,
You are the first beginning of forever,
The first fire, the wash of it, the light,
The sweetest plume of wind for a walled town"? [...]⁴

What extraordinary images confront us in these poems, ancient
and modern. They help us understand why poets like W. H. Auden
spoke of their art as "memorable speech." Slow down and let these

images seep into your mind and heart for a few moments: The serpent's poison is "washed away by the blood of God." The tree of creation is "healed by the passion of the Passionless One upon the Tree." "At the cry of the first bird, they began to crucify Thee, O Cheek like a swan!...It was like the parting of day from night." The son of God was pinned to a wooden truss, "his blood contiguous to mine, his blood ticking like a clock...."

Language, especially the memorable speech of poetry, is the way human experience is constituted, embodied and retrieved—the way its power is continually released into life. For Christians, "the cross that spoke" goes beyond all frontiers; it *reinvents* language.

> You are the mystical Paradise, O Birth-giver of God! Though you were untilled, you budded forth Christ, by whom the life-bearing Tree of the Cross was planted on earth!
>
> Today, the Ruler of creation, the Lord of glory, is nailed upon the cross, pierced in the side! Today, the Sweetness of the church drinks gall and vinegar! Today, the One who clothes the heavens with clouds is wrapped in a robe of scorn, beaten and wounded....
> (From the Orthodox Liturgy for Great and Holy Friday)

In a word, from the beginning Christians have found that they cannot speak about what is, what was, or what will be, without speaking about the cross. "The cross stands," ran an old Arthurian motto, "while the world goes spinning on" *(Crux stat dum volvitur orbs)*.

The cross is not, therefore, simply one theme among many in cultic data. The hermeneutic defines and interprets everything else. The cross is the climax of what Karl Rahner called "the liturgy of the world," that sublime and terrible liturgy smelling of death and sacrifice, lilies and urine, that God celebrates and causes to be celebrated throughout the length and breadth of human history. It is *within* this vast "liturgy of the world" that the church's liturgy takes place, and not vice versa. Christian worship—word and sacrament—is but a small sign, a humble landmark that points to that liturgy of the world where God lives, present and powerful, in human sweat and soot, in vigils, wrinkles and dreams, in the confused impurity of the human condition. Karl Rahner once wrote in an Easter homily:

Christ is already in the midst of all the poor things of this earth, which we cannot leave because it is our mother....He is in all tears and in all death as hidden rejoicing and as the life which triumphs by appearing to die. He is in the beggar to whom we give, as the secret wealth which accrues to the donor. He is in the pitiful defeats of his servants, as the victory which is God's alone. He is in our powerlessness as the power which can allow itself to seem weak, because it is unconquerable. He is even in the midst of sin as the mercy of eternal love patient and willing to the end.[5]

The cross is thus that place of ultimate transformation where God is revealed precisely as One who becomes Something—and Someone—*other*, dangerously other, dangerously different. On the cross, God's powerlessness meets our own, to the undying benefit of both.

The Cross in the Liturgy

Let us look, then, at the cross in the liturgy. It hardly needs to be said that references to the cross abound in the literature of the Second (or "New") Testament. The presence of the cross in gospel and letter, in memoir and diatribe, is simultaneously literal and figurative, polemic and theological. In a word, the cross is both script and symbol. It not only *testifies* to the brute historical facts of Jesus' suffering and death "under Pontius Pilate," it also interprets the life of discipleship ("Take up your cross and follow me...") and *defines* the power of sacraments like baptism and Eucharist (Rom 6; 1 Cor 11). As John Dominic Crossan has said, Christian faith itself was understood as "the experience of Jesus' continued empowering presence...the continued presence of absolutely the same Jesus in an absolutely different mode of existence."[6]

The event of Easter did not diminish the importance of the cross; on the contrary, it loomed larger than the empty tomb, greater than stories of fish for breakfast at the seashore. Although we often think of the earliest Christian literature as "arising from the Easter experience," it may be far more accurate to think of it as an imaginative and often polemical response to the *scandal* of the cross. After all, the horror of Jesus' execution did not lead instantly to the conclusion that "this is the divine plan for God's prophet" or "this sacrifice purchased salvation for all the world." Eventually, of course, such conclusions *were* reached—but only after much trial and error, and only after decades of heated and divisive debate.

Nor was it immediately evident to all Christians that the cross is, or should be, the focus of liturgical veneration or remembrance. Some Christians, like Paul, saw the cross as a generative source of "sacramental" power in baptism and Eucharist. In a similar vein, the noncanonical *Letter of Barnabas* (written sometime between 70 and 150 C.E.) links the waters of baptism to Jesus' cross. In a commentary on verses from Psalm 1, with its allusions to water, trees, leaves and fruit, Barnabas writes,

> Observe how [the psalmist] describes the water and cross [the "tree"] together. He obviously means to say, "Blessed are they who go down into the waters with their hope firmly fixed on the cross."[7]

The author of Barnabas clearly believed that baptismal washing and the cross together constitute a theological unit. He defended his position by alluding to both the Torah (Exod 17, "water from the rock") and extracanonical sources (*IV Esdras* 4:33; 5:5; the tree that "drips blood, droops and rises").

However, other early Christian documents describe communities whose ways of worship do not seem to have been cross-centered at all. For example, in chapter 1, Jerome Murphy-O'Connor discussed those Christians whom Paul calls "enemies of the cross of Christ." These were believers who, in Paul's judgment, were so intent on "the wisdom of the world" and the "Lord of glory" that they ignored the scandal of Jesus' crucifixion. Or consider the *Didache*, a church manual probably from the important interracial community of Antioch that dates from the late first century. In the *Didache*, none of the Pauline ideology about baptism as access to the power of Jesus' death or Eucharist as its proclamation is to be found. When baptism is described (*Didache* 7), we are told about the water and the trinitarian formula that accompanies the washing, but our source is utterly silent about Jesus' passion, death, cross or resurrection.[8]

Similarly, in the eucharistic table prayers of *Didache* 9 and 10,[9] neither the cross of Jesus nor Easter is mentioned. The texts speak instead of Jesus as "God's child," as the "Holy Vine of David," as the "Holy Name" who has "pitched a tent in our hearts." Jesus is acclaimed not as the One who "died and rose," but as God's servant, who brought us knowledge, faith and immortality. Sunday worship is described, and Christians are admonished to confess their transgressions and to put aside quarrels when gathering to "break bread and hold Eucharist," but these actions are not interpreted as a proclamation of the "death of the Lord."[10] Instead, the *Didache* alludes to the prophet Malachi: "In every place and time offer me a pure sacrifice, for I am a great king," says the Lord, "and my name is great among the gentiles."

As startling as it may seem, one can read the entire *Didache* (including its opening catechesis on the "two ways"—the way of life/light versus the way of death/darkness) without once encountering the cross or Easter. The *Didache's* concluding chapter (16), an eschatological peroration, does refer to the final "resurrection of the dead" and to Jesus "coming on the clouds of heaven," as well as to "the sign of extension" (possibly the cross), but that is all. We are clearly in the presence of a community whose theological beliefs and liturgical practices differed markedly (and, I would argue, *deliberately*) from those advanced by writers like Paul.[11]

Aside from the New Testament literature, the first signs that the cross had begun to assume liturgical importance appear in church orders like *The Apostolic Tradition* attributed to Hippolytus.[12] This document, originating in the early second century, was composed in Greek but translated into many other languages—Latin, Coptic, Arabic, Ethiopic. Many scholars used to believe that the detailed descriptions of Christian rites and practices found in *The Apostolic Tradition* reflected Roman usage of the early third century (ca. 214 C.E.). Today this view is regarded as rather implausible. Still, the existence of numerous translations—and the fact that portions of ApTrad (its shorthand designation) appear in other important church orders (e.g., the *Apostolic Constitutions*, the *Testamentum Domini* and the so-called *Canons of Hippolytus*)—testifies to its longevity and influence.

The content of ApTrad resembles that of later liturgical books like the *ordines Romani*, the sacramentary, the *rituale* and the *pontificale*. In it we find descriptions of baptism and the catechumenate, of Eucharist, of the ordination of bishops, presbyters and deacons. Prayer times, fasting, lucenarium ("lamplighting," the time for evening prayer), church suppers, the ministry of widows, crafts and professions, as well as blessings for food and oil are also described. I want to draw attention to three passages that help us trace the evolution of the cross in the liturgy. As we will see, the cross is first of all a *gesture,* used in both personal and public prayer (see passage 1, below). But there is more; the cross is also a devotional *motif*–an inspirational source that guides the Christian in the daily round of prayer (see passage 2, below). Finally, the cross is perceived as the theological *fulcrum* or *pivot* enshrined at the heart of the Eucharistic Prayer (see passage 3, below).

The first passage deals with the "sign of the cross" as both a liturgical act and a devotional custom. ApTrad 42A reads:

> If you are tempted, sign your forehead. For this sign of the passion is displayed against the Devil, if it is made in faith, not to please men, but through knowledge, presenting it like a breastplate. For when the Adversary sees the power of the Spirit (which comes) from the heart, outwardly displayed in the likeness of baptism, he will tremble and flee, when you do not strike him but breathe on him. Moses did this symbolically with the sheep which was sacrificed at the Passover. By sprinkling the blood on the threshold and by anointing the two doorposts, he signified that faith which is now in us, in the perfect sheep. Let us sign forehead and eyes with the hand, and escape from him who is trying to destroy us.[13]

This text is extremely revealing because it shows us that the cross is understood not only as a protective sign that repels Satan during times of temptation, but is also intimately linked to the rites of baptism and to the power of the Spirit. The cross is a protecting breastplate (recall the "breastplate" prayer of St. Patrick, "Christ beneath me, Christ above me"); its effects parallel those of the Passover sacrifice in Exodus. Here we meet a rich set of images and ritual allusions (e.g., the *signing* and *breathing* found in the liturgy of baptism; Exodus and Passover; the power of blood) that will dominate Christian understandings of baptism for two millennia.

The second passage, found in ApTrad 41, deals with times of daily prayer, personal and public.[14] Seven such times are discussed—upon waking; at the third, sixth and ninth hours of the day; before going to bed; at midnight; and at cockcrow. ApTrad interprets these times (some of them private and individual, some of them public and corporate) in light of Jesus' passion, cross, death and resurrection. Thus, at the third hour of the day, the Christian is told to pray in your heart. For at that hour Christ was nailed to the tree. For this reason also...the Law prescribed that the shewbread should be offered continually as a type of the body and blood of Christ; ...the slaughter of the lamb...is [the] type of the perfect lamb. For Christ is the shepherd, and also the bread which came down from heaven.[15]

This is obviously a daily horarium derived from the twin themes of cross and Eucharist. Similar instructions govern prayer at the sixth and ninth hours; they connect the Christian to Christ who was "nailed to the wood of the cross," and whose side, pierced by a spear, poured out water and blood.[16]

For our purposes, the most important text in ApTrad is its Eucharistic Prayer, a text that served as the model for Eucharistic Prayer II in the postconciliar Roman rite. It reads,

We render thanks to you, O God, through your beloved child Jesus Christ, whom in the last times you sent to us as saviour and redeemer and angel of your will; who is your inseparable Word, through whom you made all things, and in whom you were well pleased....Fulfilling your will and gaining for you a holy people, he stretched out his hands when he should suffer, that he might release from suffering those who have believed in you.

And when he was betrayed to voluntary suffering that he might destroy death, and break the bonds of the devil, and tread down hell, and shine upon the righteous...and manifest the resurrection, he took bread and gave thanks to you....

Remembering therefore his death and resurrection, we offer to you the bread and the cup, giving thanks because you have held us worthy to stand before you and minister....[17]

This prayer leaves no doubt that Jesus' passion and cross are at the heart of what Christians do at the eucharistic table.

The ritual of the sacred meal is a memorial of Jesus' own paschal transitus, his journey through death and "hell" to new life in God's presence. Indeed, the Eucharistic Prayer itself becomes the ritual means by which Christians join Jesus in that same Easter journey. His *transitus* becomes their own, as they offer themselves in faith and self-surrender through the power of the Holy Spirit. "We ask that you would send your holy Spirit upon the offering of your holy Church," the prayer says, so "that gathering [it] into one, you would grant to all who partake of the holy things to partake for the fullness of the holy Spirit, for the strengthening of faith in truth."[18] Through the power of the cross, the body of Christ is both *on* the table, as hallowed food and drink, and *at* the table, as holy church.

As I will show in chapter 3, the cross eventually became an object of veneration in its own right—a kind of Christian "totem," a prop in a dramatic liturgical action, a "person" or "character" with scripts and festivals of its own. But in my view, the deepest and most ancient connection between cross and liturgy emerges from the Eucharistic Prayer tradition and from the rituals of baptism. In one of our earliest Latin Christian treatises on baptism, the North African author Tertullian, who died about the year 225 (thus a contemporary of the material in ApTrad), wrote:

> How mighty is the grace of water, in the sight of God and Christ....Never is Christ without water....He is baptized in water. When invited to a wedding feast, he begins, in water, the first displays of his power. He invites the thirsty, while speaking of that water of his which springs up to eternal life. When he teaches about love, he approves, among the works of mercy, the cup of water offered to the poor. He regathers his strength at [the water of] a well, walks over the water, willingly crosses the sea, ministers water to his disciples. Onward he presses, to the passion—and it too witnesses to [the water of] baptism. For as he surrenders to the cross, water again intervenes—witness the washing of Pilate's hands; witness the wound in his side, where water gushes out; witness the soldier's lance! (*De Baptismo*, 9)

The cross is thus inseparable from the Easter sacraments, from the rituals of font and table. Within the liturgies of baptism and Eucharist, the cross is transformed from an object of horror, torture, violence and degradation into a sign of the self-bestowal that begets life. Shame becomes surrender; the gibbet becomes a garden; the passion becomes a paradise; the tomb becomes a womb. We can feel and hear this transfiguration of images in the "invitations to the baptismal font" composed by Zeno, bishop of Verona (+ ca. 375).

Why are you so slow?...Rush to the fountain, to the sweet womb of your virgin mother!...She incorporates us in one body after gathering us from every race and nation....

Run, children, hasten to the bath that will purify you! The living water, tempered by the Holy Spirit and by fire, invites you with its tender murmur....children, you burn with a thirst deep and fierce. The sweet murmur of the flowing nectar invites you. Fly quickly to the milk of this life-bearing font. Drink with confidence while you may. Be bathed in the waves of the river flowing over you. Fill your vessels with urgency and devotion, so that you will always have enough water. (*Invitations* 4, 6, 7)

Feasts of the Cross

Perhaps the kind of "baptismal piety" represented by Tertullian and Zeno of Verona did not have a very long life. What we sometimes think of as the Golden Age of Christian initiation—in the fourth century especially—was perhaps neither "golden" nor an "age." The cross is, after all, an enormously powerful symbol in its own right, and while it became the hermeneutic that defines and interprets everything else, it also became the object of a cult. The anonymous eighth-century Anglo Saxon poem "The Dream of the Rood" portrays the cross as a bejewelled apparition, a character with its own costume and lines:

> It seemed to me that I beheld bright in the air
> a wondrous cross of wood speeding its way
> brightest of beams: and all that blessed sign,
> glorious with gold, glittered with jewels,
> one on each earth-o'erstretching arm, and yet a fifth,
> glowing upon its heart...
> Blessed was this triumphal sign....To me the glorious tree appeared
> sumptuously shining
> decked in solemn vestments, and royal jewels
> radiant with rich gold.[19]

And as the poet gazes on this shimmering sight, the tree changes, becomes "red with blood, running in torrents." The cross then tells the story of its youth in the forest, its selection for a dread and shameful deed, its cutting and transport to the high hill where it is "stabbed with nails of iron black."

Inevitably perhaps, the "cross that spoke" came to be considered a *character*–a person with its own costumes, cosmetics and ceremonies. The cult of the cross was also connected with the "discovery" (whether real or imagined, factual or legendary) of the True Cross and the traffic in relics that resulted. In the West, the first clear mention of a feast of the Exaltation of the Holy Cross occurs in the *Liber Pontificalis* (a collection of early papal biographies) in connection with the pontificate of Sergius, a native of Syria, who sponsored several liturgical innovations (most notably, the singing of the *Agnus Dei*) while bishop of Rome from 687 to 701.[20] It is probable that this feast developed in the West as a way to commemorate a specific historical occasion, namely, the recovery and exposition of a relic of the True Cross at Jerusalem by the Emperor Heraclius in 629. This dramatic event seems to have taken place in the springtime, so the question naturally arises, Why is the Western feast of the Exaltation of the Holy Cross celebrated toward the beginning of autumn (on September 14)? The reason may be rooted in confusion about just *what* was being celebrated *when*.

In the Greek church, a feast of the Finding of the Holy Cross was indeed celebrated on September 14 and was linked to legends about the discovery of the true cross by St. Helena and to the building of a basilica on the site of the holy sepulcher by her son, Emperor Constantine, in 335. Perhaps the West confused these two historical events (one from the fourth century, the other from the seventh), so that September 14 was attached to the "recovery" of relics by Heraclius, while the commemoration of the building of the Constantinian basilica was assigned to the spring season, and so was celebrated on May 3 as the feast of the Invention of the Holy Cross. Whatever the precise historical process may have been, the Western feast of the Invention of the Cross on May 3 was almost certainly linked to an apocryphal Latin document entitled *De inventione crucis dominicae*. Thus this feast (suppressed in 1961) probably originated in northern Europe (Gaul?) sometime in the seventh century. It later made its way to Rome, perhaps during the Carolingian era (ca. 800).

Scholars have noted that over time, a kind of "naturalism" developed, a liturgical *verismo* similar to what emerged much later in Italian opera (at the end of the nineteenth century), in the work of Puccini, for example. (The term *verismo* is derived from the arts and refers simply to realism or naturalism.) If you examine a Roman Missal published at the turn of the century, for instance, you will discover a series of "votive Masses" connected with the events of Jesus' passion and crucifixion.[21] The list includes complete Mass formulas (proper prayers and readings)

- for Jesus' prayer in the garden (assigned to Tuesday after Septuagesima Sunday);
- for the holy pillar where Jesus was scourged (assigned to Tuesday after Quinquagesima Sunday);
- for the holy crown of thorns (assigned to Friday after Ash Wednesday);
- for the spear and nails (assigned to Friday after the First Sunday of Lent);
- for the holy shroud in which Jesus' body was wrapped (assigned to Friday after the Second Sunday of Lent);
- for the five wounds of Jesus (assigned to Friday after the Third Sunday of Lent);
- for the precious blood (assigned to Friday after the Fourth Sunday of Lent).

A second "feast" of the crown of thorns was assigned to Friday after "Low Sunday," and later in the spring (on April 24) the Roman Missal provided texts for a "feast" in honor of "the good thief, confessor."[22]

All this constitutes a somewhat bizarre but interesting development in the history of Christian worship. It indicates that in the centuries following the Council of Trent (when the earlier church's respect for local diversity and liturgical pluralism was replaced by the imposition, in 1570, of a single, standard Missal for the entire Latin West), a kind of "parallel universe" or "shadow government" developed in the liturgy. Alongside the official church year (with its cycle of Sundays and feasts, its structured seasons of Advent, Christmas, Lent and Easter), there developed a second, shadow or parallel church year rooted in liturgical "naturalism" or *verismo*. Because the primacy of Sunday and Easter were no longer very evident, it was often possible within the rubrics of the so-called Tridentine rite to replace the Sunday liturgy with "special-interest" feasts and to strew the weekdays either with votive Masses of the kind I just reviewed, or, at the priest's choice, with a votive Requiem. Ironically, the very charge that is often leveled against the postconciliar liturgy—namely, a smorgasbord or "ad lib" mentality on the part of presiders and planners—could be made with equal justice against the practices of the Tridentine period.

Poetry, Passion and Prayer:
The Cross in the Evolving Roman Liturgy

I do not mean to suggest that the votive formularies connected with the cross and passion of Jesus were simply liturgical kitsch, works of inferior quality or defective imagination (like pictures of Elvis painted on black velvet!). On the contrary, many of them were quite beautiful and appealing. For example, the rather improbable feast of the Pillar of Flagellation includes as its first reading a generous portion of the fourth "servant song" from Isaiah 53: "All we like sheep had gone astray....He was like a sheep led to slaughter"—a text worthy, surely, of "choral listening" and communal contemplation. Or consider this prayer from a votive Mass of the Passion, assigned to the Tuesday after Sexagesima Sunday:

> Almighty, eternal God,
> for the sake of humankind,
> our Savior took flesh and suffered the cross
> as an example of lowliness for us to imitate.
> Graciously grant that just as we remember and celebrate his passion,
> so we may deserve to hold the tokens of his patience
> and to have fellowship in his resurrection.[23]

This is by no means a poor prayer—nor can it be dismissed as an example of medieval neurosis—erotic hysteria masking as naturalism or *verismo*. The prayer is in fact reminiscent of the sort we encounter in Carolingian sources on the continent and in insular (British) sources of the tenth century. Two brief examples will illustrate my point. In the *Manual of Dhuoda*, a booklet written by a Carolingian noblewoman whose son William was pursuing a career at court, we find these instructions for prayer at bedtime:

Sign yourself and your bed with the image of the cross that redeemed you—like this (+)—and say: "I adore your cross, O Lord, and I believe in your holy resurrection. Your holy cross is with me. It is the cross that, as long as I've known it, I have always loved, and always adore. The cross is my salvation, the cross is my defense, the cross is my protection, and always my refuge. The cross is my life— but it is death to you, Devil, enemy of the truth and lover of vanity. The cross is life for me and death for you. Your cross, Lord, I adore; your glorious passion I remember. For you willed to be born, to suffer, die and rise from the dead.[24]

These bedtime devotions are rooted in both liturgical texts and personal piety. For despite fantasies to the contrary, the liturgical rites of the Latin West were not always "Roman," nor were they always "sober, succinct, hieratic and juridical" in tone.

Take, for instance, this prayer from the *Regularis Concordia*, a Latin document produced in England about 970, which I will discuss at greater length in the next chapter:

Lord Jesus Christ, I adore you ascending the cross;
I beg you to free me, by your cross, from the attacks of the devil.
Lord Jesus Christ, I adore you wounded on the cross;
I beg you, by your wounds, to heal my soul.
Lord Jesus Christ, I adore you, laid in the tomb;
I beg you, let your death be my life.
Lord Jesus Christ, I adore your descent into hell to free those in prison;
I beg you not to let me enter there.
Lord Jesus Christ, I adore your rising from the dead and ascending into heaven;
I beg you, have mercy on me.
Lord Jesus Christ, I adore your coming as judge;
I beg you not to judge me as a sinner, but to forgive rather than condemn.[25]

As Lilli Gjerlow notes, this prayer was most certainly "extraliturgical" in its origins. Its sources "are the medieval books of private devotions, such as the Book of Cerne and the [Carolingian] 'Precum libelli' edited by Dom Wilmart."[26]

But one must also point out that in the period that produced this Good Friday prayer, sharp distinctions between "liturgical" and "devotional (or extraliturgical)"—like distinctions between "sacred" and "secular" music—were not all that easy to make. Indeed, even our earliest "Roman" liturgical evidence shows a mixture of "ritual sobriety" and popular "devotionalism." This is the case, in part, because our earliest "Roman" data in the sacramentaries and *Ordines Romani*, for example, are rarely "purely Roman." Most of it is hybrid material that shows a mixture of Roman and Frankish elements.[27] And the Latin liturgical tradition outside Rome, especially in nations north of the Alps, seems to have been more willing to incorporate ritual elements that purists of a later period denounced as "popular" and "devotional" (i.e., "extraliturgical" or "paraliturgical") in character.

Still, we do have reliable evidence for the ways the Roman rite celebrated Good Friday at an early stage of its evolution. I say ways (in the plural) because what was done at the *papal* liturgy (outlined, for example in *Ordo Romanus XXIII*) and what was done in Rome's presbyteral *tituli* (parish churches staffed principally by presbyters) was not identical.[28] *Ordo Romanus XXIII* (abbreviated OR) dates from the first half of the eighth century and describes a liturgy at which the pope in person presided. Antoine Chavasse believes that this papal ordo, along with data found in the eighth-century Gelasian sacramentary, reflects liturgical practice from the late seventh century.[29]

According to OR XXIII, the pope left his residence at the Lateran about two o'clock in the afternoon. He and his entourage proceeded to the stational church where the liturgy would be celebrated that day—"Holy Cross in Jerusalem." During that procession, which was accompanied by the singing of Psalm 119 ("Beati immaculati in via," "Blessed are they whose way is blameless"), a deacon carried a relic of the True Cross. When the party arrived at "Jerusalem," the deacon placed the precious reliquary ("capsa") containing the fragment of the cross on the altar. Then the pope prostrated before the cross in prayer. After a time, he rose, kissed the relic, and took his seat. Thereupon, the bishops, presbyters, deacons and subdeacons who were present came forward to kiss the cross. When they were finished, a similar act of veneration by the people followed. Once the ceremony of adoration ended, the Good Friday liturgy continued with readings and psalmody (texts from Hosea, Deuteronomy and the passion according to John were read), and the whole celebration concluded with the solemn intercessory prayers. There was no distribution of communion. Instead, the party returned to the Lateran, once more singing "Beati immaculati."[30]

The information contained in the eighth-century Gelasian sacramentary shows how this papal liturgy for Good Friday was adapted for use in Rome's parish churches. The celebration took place about three o'clock in the afternoon. The cross had already been placed on the altar, so the presbyter, accompanied by other ministers, simply proceeded from the sacristy to the altar "in silence, singing nothing" ("cum silentio, nihil canentes"). After an opening prayer, the readings followed. The passion according to John was read, then the presbyter intoned the solemn prayers ("orationes sollemnes"). These completed, the liturgy of the presanctified followed; it included adoration of the cross and reception of communion from the reserved sacrament.[31] Note that the parish celebration relocated the adoration of the cross and included a rite of communion *not* found in the papal rite. Such changes were possibly a pastoral response to popular desire among the people to unite more closely with their Lord in holy communion on the day devoted to remembering his passion and death.

Evidence from later in the eighth century also shows how parish liturgy had come to influence the ritual organization of Good Friday in Rome's suburban dioceses, where a bishop—but obviously not the pope—presided. OR XXIV describes a double system of celebration for Good Friday—one episcopal, the other presbyteral (or parochial). The episcopal rite, led by a suburban bishop and attended by all the presbyters as well as by lower clergy and lay people, began in the morning with a relatively brief Liturgy of the Word that concluded with the solemn intercessory prayers ("orationes sollemnes"). It contained no liturgy of the presanctified, that is, no adoration of the cross and no reception of communion. After it ended, the presbyters returned to their parish churches to celebrate a Good Friday service with their people toward evening. At this parish liturgy, the Word service and prayers from the earlier "episcopal" rite were repeated—this time for the local community—but then the parish celebration continued with adoration of the cross and distribution of holy communion. Meanwhile, in the evening, back at the "chief church," the bishop proceeded with a liturgy of the presanctified like the one the presbyters celebrated in their parishes.[32]

It seems obvious that the basic shape of this double system of celebration has been influenced by what we find in the eighth-century

Gelasian sacramentary, a book intended for presbyters serving in parishes.[33] The motive behind this double system may have been to encourage the presence and participation of the presbyters in at least that part of the liturgy celebrated by the bishop in the chief church on Good Friday morning. However, it was the ritual format practiced *in the parishes*, with cross and communion rites coming after the Liturgy of the Word, that became the truly influential one. It seems to have shaped the episcopal, and later the papal practice, rather than vice versa. Indeed, this basic parish format—liturgy of the Word, solemn prayers of intercession, adoration of the cross, and communion—reflects the order of the Good Friday liturgy as we know it today in the Roman rite.

To summarize, we may say that at an early period, the Roman liturgy celebrated the mystery of the cross by combining the parochial with the papal, the solemn and hieratic with the popular and trendy, poetry with drama, transcendent vision with real-life *verismo*. The old Gelasian sacramentary already contained texts for the two major feasts of the cross outside Holy Week (September 14 and May 3).[34] It probably imported these, as I noted earlier, from the East, perhaps by way of northern Europe.[35] Tracing the path of the cross in Latin Christendom shows quite well how the ancient Roman temper tended to tolerate, indeed, to welcome, local diversity and cultural pluralism in liturgical practice. The influences that shaped celebrations of the cross in the Latin West were thus truly global and multicultural. Indeed, this process continues today. In large cities such as Chicago and Los Angeles, one hears a variety of languages—English, Spanish, Vietnamese—at a single celebration. And modern celebrations such as the popular Taizé community's "Prayer at the Cross," employ Byzantine icons and elements of the old Latin liturgy that mingle comfortably with modern chants. In all these expressions, one can hear strife and solemnity, passion and pathos, triumph and anguish, the wild night of suffering and the numb pain that knows only "an element of blank."[36]

I conclude as I began, with the poetry of the cross:

O king of the Friday
    Whose limbs were stretched on the cross,
    O Lord, who did suffer
    The bruises, the wounds, the loss,

We stretch ourselves beneath the shield of thy might,
Some fruit from the tree of thy passion
Fall on us this night!

And from the Brussels Missal (MS 451), a prayer for Good Friday:

Lord Jesus, son of the living God, I beg you
that through your cross I may become worthy
to receive pardon and forgiveness of all my sins.
Through the joyful cross, keep my body and my soul.
Through the glorious cross, guard my head.
Through the blessed cross, guard my eyes.
Through the venerable cross, guard my mouth.
Through the holy cross, guard my hands.
Through the glorious cross, guard my knees.
Through the honorable cross, keep my feet and all the members of
    my body
        free from the devil's tricks
        and free from all my enemies, visible and invisible.
Through the cross hallowed in the body of Christ, keep my
        soul and free me, Lord my God, from all adversaries on the last day.
Through the holy nails hallowed in the body of Christ, grant me
        undying life.
And may your mercy and your holy presence, Lord Jesus Christ,
        keep my spirit always. Amen.[37]

NOTES

1. These passages are taken from the office of Vespers for Great Friday in the Russian church. See Isabel Hapgood, trans., *Service Book of the Holy Orthodox-Catholic Apostolic (Greco-Russian) Church* (Boston: Houghton, Mifflin and Company, 1906), 218.

2. Ibid., 167 (texts from the all-night vigil for the feast of the Elevation of the Cross).

3. See Kuno Meyer, trans., *Ancient Irish Poetry* (London: Constable, 1913; ppb., 1994), 99.

4. "The Prairie Melts," in Thomas Hornsby Ferril, *New and Selected Poems* (New York: Harper & Brothers, 1952), 14-15.

5. Karl Rahner, "Easter: A Faith That Loves the Earth," in *The Great Church Year*, ed. A. Raffelt, trans., Harvey D. Egan (New York: Crossroad, 1994), 196.

6. John Dominic Crossan, *Who Killed Jesus? Exposing the Roots of Anti-Semitism in the Gospel Story of the Death of Jesus* (San Francisco: Harper, 1995), 210.

7. See the Greek text in Kirsopp Lake, ed., *The Apostolic Fathers*, 2 vols., Loeb Classical Library (Cambridge, Mass.: Harvard University Press, 1912), 1:380.

8. A convenient (though not a critical edition) Greek text and translation of the *Didache* may be found in Kirsopp Lake, ed., *The Apostolic Fathers*, 1:308–33. For the section on baptism, see 1:318–21.

9. Ibid., 1:322–25.

10. Ibid., 1:330–31.

11. See Nathan D. Mitchell, "Baptism in the *Didache*," in *The Didache in Context: Essays on Its Text, History and Transmission*, ed. Clayton Jefford (New York: Brill, 1995), 226–55.

12. A convenient translation, with notes and commentary, may be found in Geoffrey J. Cuming, *Hippolytus: A Text for Students* (Bramcote, Notts.: Grove Books, 1976).

13. Ibid., 28.

14. Ibid., 29–31.

15. Ibid., 29.

16. Ibid., 30.

17. Ibid., 10–11.

18. Ibid., 11.

19. From "The Dream of the Rood," trans. Edmund Colledge, cited in *A Christian's Prayer Book*, ed. Peter Coughlan, Ronald C.D. Jasper and Teresa Rodrigues (Chicago: Franciscan Herald Press, n.d.), 231.

20. See *Liber Pontificalis*, ed. Louis Duchesne, 2 vols., Bibliotheque des Ecoles Francaises d'Athenes et de Rome (Paris: E. De Boccard, 1955 [originally, 1886–92]), 1:371–82. A third, supplemental volume was edited by C. Vogel and published in 1957. The entry for Pope Sergius indicates that during his pontificate (687–709) a festival of the cross was known in Rome. This festival, celebrated on September 14, is now referred to in Western liturgical sources as "The Triumph of the Cross."

21. See *Missale Romanum* (New York: Benziger Brothers, 1903), 126–35.

22. Ibid., 135; 137–38.

23. Ibid., 128; my translation.

24. Latin text in Pierre Riche, ed., *Dhuoda: Manuel pour mon Fils*, Sources chretiennes 225 (Paris: Les Editions du Cerf, 1975), 128-30; my translation.

25. Latin text in Thomas Symons, ed. *Regularis Concordia* (New York: Thomas Nelson and Sons, 1953), 43; my translation.

26. Lilli Gjerlow, *Adoratio Crucis: The Regularis Concordia and the Decreta Lanfranci*, Manuscript Studies in the Early Medieval Church of Norway (Norwegian Universities Press, 1961), 15.

27. See Cyrille Vogel, *Medieval Liturgy: An Introduction to the Sources*, trans. and rev. Niels Rasmussen and William G. Storey (Washington, D.C.: The Pastoral Press, 1986), 66-67.

28. See Antoine Chavasse, *Le sacramentaire gelasien*, Bibliothèque de théologie Série IV: Histoire de la Théologie (Tournai: Desclée, 1958), 1:87-96.

29. Ibid., 1:96.

30. Ibid., 1:88.

31. Ibid., 1:89-93.

32. For these rites, see ibid., 1:94.

33. Ibid., 1:95.

34. Ibid., 1:350-64.

35. Ibid., 1:357-64.

36. A line from Emily Dickinson's poem that begins, "Pain has an element of blank." In *Selected Poems and Letters of Emily Dickinson* (Garden City, N.Y.: Doubleday Anchor Book, 1959), 89.

37. Latin text in Gjerlow, *Adoratio Crucis*, 128; my translation.

CHAPTER 3

"The Cross That Spoke"

Nathan D. Mitchell

Introduction

This essay will explore some of the ways that both liturgical practice and devotional custom transformed the cross of Christ. For the earliest Christians, the cross was above all an event, something that happened in history, a horrific, bloody deed carried out under the auspices of Roman imperial authority. "He was crucified under Pontius Pilate, suffered, died, and was buried." Nevertheless, during the first millennium, a multitude of new and expanded meanings accumulated around the cross. It became not only an event in salvation history, but also the pious object of veneration in its own right. The purported discovery of the True Cross during the reign of Constantine contributed to this development, as did an increasingly dramatic approach to the liturgy itself.

Understanding this evolution in the meaning of the cross is a bit like following clues in a detective story. Many readers may be fans, as I am, of the fictional medieval monk Brother Cadfael, an apothecary, herbalist and former Crusader, whose career at the Benedictine abbey of Sts. Peter and Paul in Shrewsbury (in Shropshire, near the border with Wales) the late Ellis Peters chronicled in some twenty novels. Cadfael is now widely known to American audiences from six PBS features starring British actor Derek Jacobi as the cunning, devout—and slightly roguish—sleuth. If you have read any of the Cadfael novels, you know how important the city of Winchester was in the political and religious life of medieval England. At times, the royal court itself made its home there. One of its late medieval bishops was the notorious Thomas Cardinal Wolsey, who served many years (until 1529) as Lord Chancellor of England under King

72

Henry VIII. A century later, the distinguished Anglican divine Lancelot Andrewes served as Winchester's bishop (from 1619 to 1626).

It was in this same royal city of Winchester, more than a thousand years ago (ca. 970), that an important ecclesiastical synod met during the peaceful and prosperous reign of King Edgar (+975). A pressing pastoral item on the synod's agenda was the need for a code of uniform monastic observance that would determine the details of daily life and liturgy in communities of nuns and monks who followed the Rule of St. Benedict. Continental models for such a code were already available in the work of the Carolingian reformer Benedict of Aniane, and in the *consuetudines* (the books called "customaries") formulated by the great French monastery of Cluny.[1] The monastic code drawn up for "the English nation" has come down to us in a document known as the *Regularis Concordia*.[2] The *Regularis Concordia* was written anonymously, but we can be fairly certain that its principal authors were Ethelwold (bishop of Winchester from 963 to 984) and Dunstan (archbishop of Canterbury from 960 to 988).[3] These two had been leaders in what Dom Thomas Symons, the modern editor of the *Regularis Concordia*, called "the English monastic revival of the tenth century," a period that saw the restoration of Benedictine monks (in place of secular canons) at several influential English cathedrals.[4]

Ethelwold appears to have been responsible for just such a reform at Winchester, shortly after the middle of the tenth century. But Dunstan was the figure destined for greater renown—in part because of his spiritual stature as monk and later abbot of Glastonbury; in part because of his upward ecclesiastical mobility (he became archbishop of Canterbury and hence the primate of England); and in part because of his brains and good looks. Dunstan was so smart and good-looking, in fact, that people wrote poetry about him! A celebrated acrostic composed by Abbo, a monk of Fleury, addressed him with the words, "angelicam qui fers faciem" ("you have the face of an angel"). Another of Dunstan's friends wrote—in classical Latin meter, no less—

Carne es sic pulcher, sic pulcher acumine sensus
Alter te nullus pulchrior esse queat.

(Your body, so handsome! Your mind so sharp and subtle
No one else can be counted as comely as you.)[5]

73

It isn't every day that someone with the brains of Stephen Hawking and the looks of Mel Gibson produces a memorable document on the reformation of monastic life, but apparently this is exactly what happened in tenth-century England!

Indeed, we should be grateful, because among its rules for celebrating Holy Week, the *Regularis Concordia* gives us a vivid and detailed description of how the cross was venerated in the liturgy of Good Friday. Readers today will find this description quite familiar. For in the tenth century, as now, the Western liturgy for Good Friday consisted of three principal parts: (1) the Liturgy of the Word, climaxing in a solemn reading of the passion from John's Gospel and prayers of intercession; (2) the veneration of the cross; and (3) holy communion. This basic structure remains in place even after the liturgical changes promulgated by the Second Vatican Council. The principal difference is that the *Regularis Concordia* exploits the dramatic potential inherent in the rite. In the *Regularis Concordia*, we can observe how the liturgy has begun to change from "a ritual action done by priest and people" to a kind of dramatic tableau in which past historical events are reenacted. Some modern liturgical scholars argue that the *Regularis Concordia* shows us how history and drama (with focus on the past) are beginning to replace mystery and symbol (with focus on God's action in the present). This is a point I will discuss further in the second section. To begin, however, I will sketch the shape and content of this ancient Good Friday liturgy. Then I will suggest an interpretation of its structure and its significance.

Good Friday in Early Medieval England (ca. 970 C.E.)

The liturgy of Good Friday occurred in the late tenth century, as it does now, in midafternoon.[6] It began, as now, with a period of prayerful silence, followed by two readings from the First Testament (Hos 6:1–6; Exod 12:1–11),[7] psalm responses, and prayer. Then the passion account from John's Gospel was read, as now, with an intriguing note that instructs two deacons to act "like thieves" ("in modum furantis") and to strip the altar of the cloth that lies under the gospel book when the words "partiti sunt vestimenta mea" are read (John 19:24: "they divided my garments among them"). After bringing this word-and-deed drama of

John's Gospel to a close, the monks (or nuns) continued the liturgy with the solemn prayers of intercession, as we still do today.

Once the *orationes sollemnes* were completed, a covered cross was set up in front of the altar, and the veneration began. The lyrics or libretto that accompanied this dramatic action are familiar to us. Included are the reproaches *(improperia)*: "My people, what have I done to you?"; the ancient acclamations in Greek and Latin ("Hagios ho Theos, Hagios Ischyros, Hagios athanatos, eleison hymas—Sanctus Deus, Sanctus fortis, Sanctus immortalis, miserere nobis"—"Holy God, Holy and Strong, Holy Immortal One, have mercy on us!"); the hymn "Pange lingua gloriosi" (with the verse "Crux fidelis")[8] by Venantius Fortunatus (bishop of Poitiers + ca. 610); and the antiphons, "Ecce lignum crucis" and "Crucem tuam adoramus."[9]

While these lyrics are being sung, the cross is laid on a cushion before the altar, unveiled by the deacons and presented for veneration. "As soon as it has been unveiled," the *Regularis Concordia* directs, "the abbot shall come before the holy Cross and shall prostrate himself thrice with all the brethren of the right hand side of the choir, that is, seniors and juniors; and with deep and heartfelt sighs shall say the seven penitential psalms and the prayers in honor of the holy Cross."[10]

What is important about this Good Friday afternoon ritual?

First, it is evident that tenth-century monastic communities in England had already begun to capitalize on the dramatic elements inherent in the Good Friday ritual, using liturgical objects (altar cloths, the gospel book, the covered cross) as props, and as I will show below, even as *characters*. We heard, for instance, how two deacons are instructed to "stalk" the altar like a couple of thieves. They denude it, despoil it, by stripping away the cloth under the gospel book. Both altar and book are, of course, common symbols of Christ's presence. In effect, these ministers *perform* or *reenact* the violent assault on Jesus' body that preceded his passion and death—just as, later in the ceremony, the abbot and community function as a Greek chorus, commenting upon the action with deep, "heartfelt sighs" and words of lamentation drawn from the seven penitential psalms. It is now well known that many scholars discern in such dramatic, liturgical details, the origins of modern, Western theater.[11]

However, something else also seems to be happening in the liturgy described by the *Regularis Concordia*. In earlier Christian tradition, the cross was not only (or even primarily) an object. It was an outcome, a soteriological event that demonstrates who Jesus is (the savior, the redeemer, the high priest whose sacrifice supersedes all the propitiatory rites of the Israelite priesthood)—and at the same time, shows how salvation flows from this "lifted" Christ into the hearts and bodies of believers. Such is the ideology represented, for instance, by the Letter to the Hebrews and by the Pauline interpretations of baptism and Eucharist found in Romans 6 and 1 Corinthians 11. Paul argues in Romans 6 that baptism plunges us into Jesus' death, while Eucharist (1 Cor 11) "proclaims" that same "death of the Lord until he comes." Similarly, Hebrews 5 speaks about Jesus as the compassionate high priest whose "loud cries and tears" are heard by God and whose all-sufficient sacrifice makes him "the source of eternal salvation for those who obey him."

Some decades later, in John's Gospel, the crucifixion of Jesus has become a ritual consecration, a royal enthronement, a solemn coronation liturgy. Though each has its own perspective, these three sources—Paul, Hebrews and John—all agree that the cross is both the event that demonstrates Jesus' true identity and the radical source of sacramental power. This ideology will contribute mightily, over time, to the twin traditions of high Christology and high sacramentalism that came to dominate a Christianity that was increasingly Gentile rather than Jewish and Hellenic rather than Semitic in character. In sum, the cross, as understood by Paul or John or the author of Hebrews, is the symbolic nexus of a whole set of relationships that define and connect Christ and the Christian, Jew and Greek, past and present, source and sacrament, cult and culture.

In the *Regularis Concordia,* however, a rather different ideology seems to be at work. For by the tenth century (and indeed, much before), the cross had become a cult object in its own right, worthy of acclamation, address and adoration—worthy, in short, of *liturgy.* The cross is no longer just a soteriological event, a theological outcome or even a prop in a monastic drama. Rather, it has become a central *character,* with a speaking role of its own. It can be hailed, held, clothed and greeted like any other character. And like any person, it can talk. The cross thus becomes both *One who speaks* and *One who is spoken to.* We hear, for example, the visionary Anglo-Saxon poet of the *Dream of the Rood* quoting words the cross has spoken.

Much did I suffer, standing on the mount,
at many hostile hands, as I watched the Lord of hosts
dolorously labor. Clouds of darkness
covered in blackness the body of the Lord,
his shining radiance, as his shade departed,
wan beneath the heavens and all creation wept,
proclaiming the King's death. Christ was upon the Cross.[12]

Moreover, when the cross is not speaking for itself, it can be *spoken to*. Examples of this appear rather early in the history of Christian poetry and hymnody. Thus, the famous verses in Venantius Fortunatus's hymn "Pange lingua gloriosi":

Flecte ramos, arbor alta, tensa laxa viscera,
et rigor lentescat ille, quem dedit nativitas,
ut superni membra Regis mite tendas stipite.

Sola digna tu fuisti ferre pretium saeculi,
atque portum praeparare nauta mundo naufrago,
quem sacer cruor perunxit fusus Agni corpore.[13]

(Bend your branches, towering tree, and your rigid sinews bend;
for a moment, all the rigor that your birth bestowed, suspend;
members of the great King's body gently on your crossbeam tend.

You alone were counted worthy this world's ransom to uphold;
for a ruined, shipwrecked people you prepared a safe stronghold,
smeared with sacred blood that from the Lamb's own broken body
     rolled.)

By the early Middle Ages, this custom of addressing the cross as a person reaches a passionate, almost erotic intensity.

Salve crux, signum Dei vivi, vexillum dexterae excelsi;
Salve, signum triumphale, signum salutare,
     signum potens et admirabile;
Salve, signum honorabile coelestibus, amabile terrestribus,
     inferis horribile.
Salve, crux, signum benedictum, lignum pretiosum et electum,
     lignum fructiferum super omnia ligna silvarum,
     et super omnia aromata quae ab origine mundi
     super terram germinaverunt...

O lignum praeclarum et nobile, cuius cedunt dignitati
   cedrus et cypressus, laurus et platanus, palma et oliva,
   vitis et ficus et malus, cinnamomum et balsamum,
   et myrrha et libanus, storax et galganus,
   gutta, casia et terebinthus, ligna Setim,
   ligna thyina pretiosa de ophir.[14]

(Hail O Cross, sign of the living God, Banner in God's right hand!
Hail, sign of triumph, sign of salvation, sign potent and amazing!
Hail, sign honored by the hosts of heaven, loved by earthlings,
   feared by the denizens of hell!
Hail, O Cross, sign of blessing, Wood precious and chosen,
   Wood more fruitful than all the trees of the forest,
   more fragrant than anything grown on earth
   since the beginning of the world!
Wood shining and noble, to whose dignity all others yield—
the cedar and the cypress, the laurel and the plane tree, palms and olive
   trees
   grapevines, figs and apple trees, cinnamon and balsam,
myrrh and frankincense, aromatic gums and resins,
aloe, cassia and terebinth, the trees of Setim,
the precious citron tree of Ophir.)

One is reminded here of both the sumptuous imagery found in Sirach's description of the high priest Simon, son of Jochanan (Sir 50) and the exotic, erotic "aromaticism" of the Song of Songs. The "cross that speaks" as a "character" in a drama—whether liturgical and actual or poetic and imagined—is now the flower-strewn marriage-bed *(lectus sponsae)*—and by implication, the marriage *partner*—of the bridegroom Christ. An example of this "eroticizing" or "nuptializing" of the cross appears in an anonymous work *(Vitis Mystica)* attributed to Bernard of Clairvaux (1090–1153):

> The cross was a wedding chamber *[sedes sponsalis]*, in which the True Spouse joined the church, his bride, to his own body *[sponsam suam ecclesiam sibi copulavit]*. He bought her with the outpouring of his very own sacred blood. Therefore, Christ listens intently not, any longer, to the soul of the [repentant] thief, but to the soul of his bride. He comforts her, as she prays, with a suitable response: "Amen I say to you,"—truly to *you* I say it—"today *you* will be with me in paradise." Why "to *you?*" "Because you acknowledged me even when I was being

tortured on the cross. You will be with me in a paradise of pleasures."
With me, he says. What an exquisite tenderness! He doesn't say simply
"You will be in paradise," or "You will be with the angels." No. He
says "You will be *with me!*" You will be filled and satisfied by the One
you desire. You will see in majesty the One whom you now acknowledge as crushed by infirmity.[15]

In this passage, the author is commenting on the "seven last words
of Christ on the cross"; earlier, the author had compared Jesus' words to
leaves on a vine. A little later in the treatise, the images shift again, and
the reader's attention is drawn to the flowers that grow on the mystical
vine *(vitis mystica).*

Who can overlook the fact that bees build their honeycomb from
the nectar gathered from flowers?...If, then, we are truly "spiritual
bees," let us, from the flowers of our Nazarene paradise (i.e., from
the blooming garden that is the beautiful Christ) hold fast in our
memory things that can never wither....Let our memory be
equipped to receive the mark of the "seal," that is, of the crucified
Jesus, so that we may remember him always. For he said "Place me
as a seal [upon your heart]." That royal seal is the cross. If we
remember and bear it constantly in our heart, we shall be able to
pass over securely into the kingdom that knows no end.[16]

The author goes on to explain, rather fancifully, that the very word
Nazarene means "flowering," and that it points to the pleasure and
delight we experience in Jesus. Of course, this image of the cross as a garden of delights, a paradise, a fruitful, flowering tree, is quite ancient. It
appears very prominently in a verse of Venantius Fortunatus's hymn
"Pange lingua gloriosi."

Crux fidelis, inter omnes arbor una nobilis—
nulla talem silva profert, flore, fronde, germine—
dulce lignum, dulce clavo, dulce pondus sustinens![17]

(Faithful cross, above all others, noblest tree in all the wood,
none can ever equal you in foliage, flower, fruit or frond;
Sweet the wood and sweet the nails, sweet the weight that hangs on you!)

By the end of the first millennium, therefore, the cross had been
imaginatively transformed in and by the liturgy—as well as in and by

the devotional sensibilities of Christian poets. This transformation occurred nearly four centuries before the rise of the *devotio moderna,* that late-medieval revival of spirituality that focused on the life and passion of Christ. The christological and soteriological themes of earlier Christianity were expanded and transfigured. For Paul, as I noted above, baptism and Eucharist embody and proclaim the cross as event, as outcome, as the launching of an irreversible process that will culminate in Jesus' triumphant return, the resurrection of Christians, and the transfiguration of the cosmos. By the time one reaches the *Regularis Concordia,* however, the cross, as both event and symbol, has been reimagined, redefined. It has absorbed a host of new meanings— becoming part cult-object, part totem, part prop in liturgical drama, part person and character, part role, part one who speaks and is spoken to, part marriage-bed and marriage partner.

A second, and briefer, point should also be noted here. The Good Friday liturgy in the *Regularis Concordia* did not end with the veneration of the cross by abbot, monks and people. It continued (then as now) with what used to be called the Mass of the Presanctified, a communion service that commences with the Lord's Prayer and its embolism, and then continues with the distribution of the consecrated bread that had been reserved the evening before, after the liturgy of Holy Thursday.[18] What is of interest for us here is not the obvious parallelism between the liturgy of the tenth century and that of today, but rather the provision made in section 46 of the *Regularis Concordia* which reads,

> Since on that day [i.e., Good Friday] we solemnize the burial of the Body of our Saviour, if anyone should care or think fit to follow...certain religious men in a practice worthy to be imitated for the strengthening of the faith of unlearned common persons..., we have decreed this only: on that part of the altar where there is space for it there shall be a representation...of a sepulchre, hung about with a curtain, in which the holy Cross, when it has been venerated, shall be placed in the following manner: the deacons who carried the Cross before shall come forward and, having wrapped the Cross in a napkin there where it was venerated, they shall bear it...to the place of the sepulchre. When they have laid the cross therein, in imitation as it were of the burial of the Body of our Lord Jesus Christ, they shall sing the antiphon *Sepulto*

*Domino....*In that same place the holy Cross shall be guarded with all reverence until the night of the Lord's Resurrection. And during the night let brethren be chosen by twos and threes, if the community be large enough, who shall keep faithful watch, chanting psalms.[19]

These directions clearly set up a drama, complete with Greek chorus—the faithful watchers, "twos and threes" chanting psalms at the tomb. Note also that the cross is not simply a prop or a totem that represents the body of Christ dead and buried. It has also become a *condensed symbol for the community itself* as it enters the tomb with Jesus to await resurrection. The cross is not just a person; it's a *people.* And just as this people is joined to Jesus' death and lies with him in the tomb, so too it shares the events of Easter morning.

This is exactly what we find, dramatically rehearsed, in the *Regularis Concordia.* At the office of Vigils (Nocturns, Matins) for Easter Sunday, the drama that began with the adoration of the cross and its "burial" on Good Friday reaches its ritual dénouement. Three monks vested in copes assume the roles of the spice-bearing women (they carry smoking thuribles with them), while a fourth monk, clad only in an alb, represents the angelic messenger at Jesus' tomb. At the third responsory to the third reading of the Night Office, these four monks ritually reenact the question and answer scene.

"Quem quaeritis?" asks the messenger, "softly and sweetly."

"Jesum Nazarenum," the "women" reply.

"Non est hic. Surrexit," the messenger answers, as he pulls aside the veil of the "supulchre" to reveal an empty tomb. Then the monks playing the spice-bearing women lift up the linen that lay within the sepulchre, show it to the community, and carry it to the altar. The church bells peal, the *Te Deum* is sung, and the office of Lauds begins.[20] Those acquainted with the history of medieval liturgy will recognize at once that this short drama (the "Quem quaeritis" play, as it is sometimes called) continued to develop throughout the Middle Ages. Eventually, the object "hidden" in the tomb on Good Friday and "raised" on Easter morning was not the totemic *cross,* but *the consecrated eucharistic species.*[21]

Sources of the Good Friday Liturgy

Many of the features of the Good Friday liturgy outlined in the *Regularis Concordia* still survive today, more than a millennium later. Nor were they at all new in late tenth-century England. As any student of the liturgy can tell you, our present Latin Holy Week rites had already begun to take shape in the late fourth century—not in Rome but in Jerusalem, where a European pilgrim, a woman named Egeria, kept a travel diary of her experiences in the Holy Land (ca. 384 C.E.). Egeria's descriptions tell us that the Jerusalem church was already celebrating a "paschal triduum" with a "developed system of stational services" that followed "the sequence of events of Jesus' Passion."[22]

Rome itself did not have such a system at this time, nor did Constantinople, but eventually the influence of Jerusalem's shrine-centered, "stational" liturgies (ever popular among pilgrims) was widely felt. Over several centuries, Western churches that already had indigenous Holy Week traditions of their own adopted and adapted elements from the stational liturgies that were rooted in the chronology of Jesus' last days and hours. Eventually the Roman church also made these adaptations, although what we call the *modern* Roman rite is a hybrid structure that took final shape largely in the liturgical practices of the papal court during the twelfth and thirteenth centuries.

It is sometimes argued that by importing the stational liturgies derived from Holy Week in Jerusalem, Latin Christians replaced mystery (a unified, comprehensive celebration of Jesus' passion, death and resurrection) with history (a chronological drama or tableau that imitates what happened to Jesus in the final week of his life).[23] I want to suggest, however, that this familiar dichotomy between mystery and history is misleading and, finally, false. When the pilgrim Egeria described how Christians in Jerusalem gathered for worship at the places where Jesus suffered agony, arrest, trial, sentencing, flogging, torture and crucifixion, she understood quite well that their ritual actions did not simply imitate, retrieve or repeat the past by recalling it to language and gesture. She understood that ritual is really an inventive and resourceful "folk technology" that provides access to a world of mystery. Not a world of the past, but a world alive in the present and awaiting a future. Not a world that lies *behind* deeds and texts, but a world that *lies in front of them*. As philosopher Paul Ricoeur has argued, meaning is not a calcified object, an opaque system of references that lurks behind words, deeds and narratives. Rather, meaning is an outcome that lies *in front of* speech, *up ahead* in our unfolding, evolving world.

The so-called imitative rites of Holy Week were thus never intended to be an exercise in liturgical archaeology. The "history" that such rites "remember" or appear to "reenact" is actually *hermeneutics*–an act of interpretation, a rereading, a retelling of experience. *History is hermeneutics with skin on.* That is why, as I have suggested, the dichotomy between history and mystery—between history and eschatology—is not particularly useful for understanding what happens in Christian liturgy. After all, history is the essential, palpable milieu, anchored in space and time, within which we encounter the eschatological. More simply, we meet mystery by meeting history. We meet God by meeting the least and littlest among us. We find heaven in the thick, encrusted textures of earth. We experience resurrection by embracing the cross.

If, therefore, we seek to discover the meaning of the dramatic, imitative, cross-centered Holy Week liturgies found in documents like the *Regularis Concordia*, we must focus not upon ritual props or totem objects, but upon *the people who make use of them*. It is my argument that what the *Regularis Concordia* reveals is a community "caught in the act" of negotiating its relation to rapture, to mystery. *Negotiating rapture*–that is what the liturgies of "burying" the cross on Good Friday and "raising" it on Easter Sunday are all about. The nuns or monks of the *Regularis Concordia* conduct this negotiation through a series of ritual acts that appear to imitate history, to mimic Jesus' final days and hours. But the goal is not repetition or imitation; the goal is the transformation of the community engaged in the ritual action.

To say this is to argue that ritual is not rubric. Ritual is not only doing, it is a *making*. Like art, ritual does not merely perform, it *produces*; it does not merely mime, it *makes*. The arts negotiate rapture by making objects and outcomes—a painting, a poem, a play, a sculpture, a skyscraper, a string quartet. *Art makes things that keep on making.* And so does ritual. Ritual is embodied, kinetic technology that combines the discipline of learned skill and acquired craft with the panache, the singularity, of creative invention. Art is a passionate human outcry against extinction; it rebels against the ending of the waltz, the fading of the rose, the dying of the light. So too, ritual is not merely remembrance or imitation: It is resistance—even rage and rebellion. The fire we light at the beginning of the Easter Vigil is more than a source of warmth or illumination. It is a ritual shout, an exclamation, a bold defiant outcry. Blazing light lifted against the encroaching night. Fire flung out in all directions. A conflagration! The world as we know it torched, reduced to rubble, burned down to a hot, flocculent ash. The fire of the Easter Vigil is not a *natural disaster*. It is a human conspiracy; it is something we make, *ritually*. It is a ritual re-creation of the world.

In short, rituals are ways to *negotiate* communal access to the Sacred, to mystery. They are not a symbol system, designed to produce meanings, but a folk technology whose purpose is to *redefine*, to *reconfigure* the people who make and use the rituals. The importance of the rites in the *Regularis Concordia* lies not in what they tell us about the cross as a prop or an object of veneration or an ocular focus, but in what they reveal about *people making ritual* and *ritual making people*. This dual process of ritual-making and people-making is never pure or precise. It is a homely, improvised art. It is not a process that originates in the hallowed precincts of official theology; it arises, instead, from the far messier instincts of popular piety and folk religion, from what the Chilean poet Pablo Neruda called "the confused impurity of the human condition."

A perfect example of this process appeared in the cover story of the *National Catholic Reporter* for February 7, 1997. The story opens with a photo of dancers in Espinazo, a small Mexican village two hours from Monterey. Twice a year, in March and October, these dancers—clad in colorful native costumes topped with elaborately plumed ceremonial headdresses—perform in the village plaza near the tomb of a folk saint who is known as El Nino Fidencio. They are joined by throngs of pilgrims carrying "flowers and copal incense like ancient Aztec celebrants." The pilgrims come from all over Mexico and from the United States as well—from Wisconsin, California, New Mexico and the Rio Grande Valley in Texas.[24]

The object of their veneration—El Nino Fidencio—was a local *curandero*, born in 1898, who possessed remarkable gifts of healing and a detailed knowledge of medicinal plants and their uses. During his lifetime, El Nino (who is also called El Guadalupano, son of the Virgin of Guadalupe) was famous throughout Mexico for his power to cure the desperately ill—victims of leprosy and cancer, for example. He was also a source of bitter controversy. El Nino loved music and parties and "often wore a dress as he carried a cross through Espinazo['s] streets." As a result, some of his detractors concluded that El Nino was a fraud, or a transvestite, or an alcoholic who drank himself to death.[25] None of these objections, however, has stopped the Fidencistas, whose numbers have grown steadily since the *curandero*'s death in 1938. Their rituals of prayer and healing continue to attract even the most skeptical. Indeed, Fidencista *materias* (spiritual mediums) have established missions, and some "have sought to have the Fidencista church receive official recognition by the Mexican government."[26]

To Roman Catholic officials, like Monterey's archbishop, and to liturgical purists, the cult of El Nino Fidencio sounds utterly outré—scabrous, syncretistic, sensationalistic. Ever since the Second Vatican Council, ecclesiastical "insiders" and liturgy professionals have warned that ritual reform must be planned; that it must unfold slowly and carefully; that the process of change must be ordered, reasonable and decorous. Jowls atremble, scholars have insisted that they alone have the skill and authority to determine what is historically appropriate and traditional in Roman Catholic worship.

All this is very commendable, perhaps, but it is *not* the way ritual—or art—customarily negotiates human access to the sacred. Neither ritual nor art is immaculately conceived. Their origins are untidy, their pedigree suspect. Our longstanding membership in the "cultural religion of the privileged" often leads us, of course, to equate "high religion" with intellectual superiority and refinement—Catholicism with Mozart, for example—and so to conclude that God loves the poor but *hates* their art.[27] We fall easily into the elitist habit of seeing "culture" as the implacable and superior enemy of "kitsch." We ridicule pictures of Elvis painted on black velvet, and forget—to our peril—that the men who conceived the ovens of Auschwitz as a "final solution" to the "Jewish problem" were the very ones who attended Mozart operas and listened to Haydn's quartets.

My point here is that ritual, art and culture are always "ordinary" before they are "fine."[28] As the fourth-century pilgrim Egeria realized, we cannot understand how or why Holy Week developed unless we pay close attention to folk religion, to the followers of El Nino Fidencio, to the thousands who throng the grounds of Graceland every year for the ritual celebration of the King's birthday in Memphis. In short, we can't understand how rituals develop without paying attention to people who have neither property nor privilege; people without social advantages; people for whom *culture* means *making a living,* not a trip to the museum or the concert hall; people who are pushed down and shut out; people who show us bodies of hurt and hope; people who are so marginalized they live only at the edge of the raft.

To understand where rituals come from, we have to watch and listen to those Chilean women who create *arpilleras,* patchwork narratives, little cloth murals that tell the story of sons and daughters who "disappeared" courtesy of General Pinochet's military regime. "These miniature street murals in cloth became [the language of these poor women]. They provided a way of not only seeing but feeling and thinking: a language."[29] Indeed, to make *arpilleras* is to make culture, art and ritual. Like pilgrims in fourth-century Jerusalem shuffling from one shrine to another, like the *Regularis Concordia's* tenth-century monastics "sneaking" to the altar like thieves ready to strip the body and bury the cross, the Chilean women of Santiago "make well what needs making." They create a ritual theater of the disappeared, the dispossessed, the disadvantaged—the marginalized "whom our society makes least, makes lost and makes last."[30] As Bob Haveluck has written in reference to the religious situation at the time of Jesus,

> In those days, even as now, the holy and high things had come to be seen as part of the furniture of those who live secure. The holy and high things—God, the practices and places of worship, neighbors, values, the dominant artistic forms—had become a part of [a] familiar, comfortable world. It was as if the Holy Temple had been reduced to a royal chapel with its comforting likenesses to kinship itself. Almost everything had been fashioned to confirm the ruling orders and their definitions of disorder...the dirty, the sick, the ugly, the lay-abouts, the malcontents, those who do not know their place, in short, the dangerous and disorderly.[31]

Jesus, of course, democratized religion and its rituals—gave equal access to the dirty, the sick, the ugly, the malcontents, the dangerous and the disorderly. This created a scandal we Christians have never quite gotten over.

In all the examples I have used, people are *making ritual*—equipping themselves with a technology that crafts words, fabrics and movements, a technology that gives access to the Sacred. By making rituals they are making *themselves*, inventing themselves as believers. As Simon Schama demonstrates in his book *Landscape and Memory*, a landscape is more than nature; it's *culture*. It's the human work of human minds.[32] So too the landscapes (some imitative, some purely imaginary) that we create through ritual. Keith Thomas has written, "Our perception of the...natural world is shaped by our inherited attitudes, myths, and traditions. It is therefore wrong to think that in the modern world, the attitude to nature has been wholly exploitative, and it would be equally wrong to see nature as having a purely benign objective existence apart from human perceptions of it. On the contrary, our present-day perceptions of trees, mountains, or rivers are shaped by cultural traditions of great antiquity."[33]

Such is also the case with religious ritual. Ritual is a way of painting *places* with culture. Ritual action not only "marks" the spot, for example, where Jesus walked, fell, trudged, was tortured and crucified. It also *redefines* that spot, rewrites it, paints it over with the layers of experience embodied in the celebrating assembly's *culture* (where *culture* is defined as a complex of values and meanings ever in need of review and renewal). As I noted above, *history is hermeneutics with skin on*. Our question must be not only "how do people make ritual?" but "how does ritual make people?" In a document like the *Regularis Concordia*, we meet a community "caught in the act" of rewriting its sacred history, of reinterpreting its hallowed spaces—in short, of renegotiating *rapture* through the strategies of *ritual*. The story of Jesus' cross and triumph, the scenes of his passion and suffering, become the ritual optic within which we view our own.

This helps explain why the Christian community has chosen for nearly two millennia to revisit ritually those horrible scenes of torture, violence, degradation and death that make up the "way of the cross," that form the heart of our Holy Week liturgies. Ritual is a strategy that works in much the way that negative capability works in poetry and negative space in art. "Negative capability" was poet John Keats's term for the ability to accept the terrifying *absence*, the *lack* of certainty that encircles human affairs. Negative capability occurs, he wrote, when we are "capable of being in uncertainties, Mysteries, doubts, without any irritable reaching after fact & reason." Negative space is the term that describes how a recognizable shape or form or image emerges when material "stuff" is scooped out, or clutter is cleared away. Negative capability makes empathy and compassion possible; negative space makes something *newly visible* real, present, and potent.

Negative capability and negative space come to focus in Christian ritual, especially in the celebration of Jesus' passion and cross. These are, after all, the realities that lie at the heart of our most important ritual, the Eucharist. Eucharist speaks not only the language of real presence, but also the language of *real absence.* I say real absence because at the center of the eucharistic sacrifice lies a cipher, a lack, an emptiness that *cannot—* indeed *must* not—be filled. Our liturgical and theological tradition calls Eucharist an *"unbloody* sacrifice," *worship without bloodshed,* as the Liturgy of St. John Chrysostom puts it. The key phrase here is "without blood-shed." The ritual of Eucharist *halts* the horrible human cycle of violence and bloodshed, brings it to a standstill. Never again, violence. Never again, victims or blood vengeance.[34] As Margaret Visser writes in her splendid book *The Rituals of Dinner,*[35] Christian Eucharist is a conclusive sacrifice; that is, it brings to a conclusion, to an end, the long human history of victimization and violence. No more killing, no more bloodshed. This *conclusive* sacrifice is what Eucharist embodies and enacts. Visser describes it this way:

> One past death ritually repeated leaves no excuse for any further violence or scapegoating. All the boundaries are crossed: between individual and group; death and life; spirit and body; meaning and fact; beginning, lasting, and ending; old and new; here and elsewhere; eternal and temporal; linear and cyclical time; host and guest; God and humankind. As a meal, the Mass spans all the meaning of eating at once—from cannibalism to vegetarianism, from complete fusion of the group to utterly individual satisfaction, from the breaking of the most fearful of taboos to the gentlest and most comforting restoration. All this and more is contained, expressed and controlled by ritual; dramatic movement and structure, song, costume, poetry, incense, gesture, and interaction; every one of the five senses is employed.[36]

As this passage suggests, ritual is our way of redeeming rage by means of rapture. In the rituals that stretch from Palm Sunday to Easter, the violent way of the cross becomes the nonviolent way of rapture. During Holy Week, we move ritually from place to place and scene to scene, "following Jesus' footsteps," not in order to "take possession" of those places, not in order to "retrieve" the past by imitating it, but in order to empty ourselves *so God can take possession of us*. The ceremonies of Holy Week are rituals of real absence, emptiness, surrender, silence and humility. They take us not to the top of the mountain but to the door of the tomb—a tomb that is *empty*. "He is not here. He has been raised" (Matt 28:6). "As we peer into that emptiness," writes Thomas Sheehan,

> the absence of the living Jesus and even of his dead body allows us to identify a unique form of seeking: the desire for that which can never be had. This unique kind of seeking is the experience that makes human beings different from any other kind of entity, and we see it exemplified in the women who actually found the tomb empty on the first Easter Sunday. Such seeking is not something we occasionally get caught up in; rather, it is what makes us human, constitutes us as the futile passion, the unfulfilled and presumably unfulfillable desire that we are....
>
> ...The meaning of the [empty tomb]...is an unsurpassable absence that cannot be changed into any form of presence. The absolute absence of [Jesus]...makes room at last for silent, unadvertised, and groundless mercy.[37]

Passion into compassion; murder into mercy; death into deliverance; blood into bread; rage into rapture; a corpse into a church; a cross into a tree of triumph—these are the mysteries Christians celebrate as night turns into day, and forty days of fast become fifty days of feast. An Easter homily given in the second century by Melito of Sardis highlights quite powerfully the paradoxical character of the mystery of the cross, with its power to transform death into life, disaster into victory. On the cross, Melito suggests, it is not only the body of Jesus that is lifted up. Rather, all humanity is lifted in him and so becomes an offering to God in spirit and truth. On the cross, Jesus embraces the whole world of human experience and lifts it in one redeeming act of sacrifice:

> [Here] is...One born as a child,
> led to slaughter as a lamb,
> sacrificed as a sheep,
> buried as a human being,
> raised up from the dead as God.
>
> Truly, this one is all things:
> as one who judges, the Law;

as one who teaches, the Word;
as one who begets, a Parent;
as one who is begotten, a Child;
as one who suffers, a Sheep
as one who is buried, a Human
as one who is raised, God.
This is Jesus the Christ,
to whom be glory for ever and ever. Amen![38]

NOTES

1. On Benedict of Aniane, see Allen Cabaniss, trans., *The Emperor's Monk: Contemporary Life of Benedict of Aniane by Ardo* (Devon: Arthur H. Stockwell, 1979), especially the introduction, 15–43. For the Cluniac customaries, see Kassius Hallinger, ed., *Corpus Consuetudinum Monasticarum*, 12 vols. (Siegburg: F. Schmitt, 1963–).

2. Critical Latin text and translation, with notes, in *Regularis Concordia: The Monastic Agreement of the Monks and Nuns in the English Nation*, ed. Thomas Symons (New York: Thomas Nelson and Sons, 1953).

3. Ibid., lii.

4. See ibid., ix–xxviii. In such arrangements, the cathedral community was ordinarily governed by a prior, with the bishop serving as titular abbot.

5. See ibid., xv for Latin texts; my translations.

6. *Regularis Concordia*, 43.

7. These same readings are found in the Roman Missal of 1570. Since Vatican II, the two readings are Isa 52:13–53:12 and Heb 4:14-16; 5:7-9.

8. The verses are from the hymn "Pange lingua." On its origins and influences, see Joseph Szoverffy, *Hymns of the Holy Cross: An Annotated Edition with Introduction*, Medieval Classics: Texts and Studies 7 (Brookline, Mass.: Classical Folia Editions, 1976), 7-27.

9. The *Regularis Concordia* also includes a third antiphon, "Dum Fabricator mundi," which did not survive in the Latin liturgy found in either the Missal of 1570 or the Missal of 1970.

10. *Regularis Concordia*, 44 in Symons edition, p. 43 (Latin text on facing page).

11. See, for example, the classic study by Karl Young, *The Drama of the Medieval Church*, 2 vols. (Oxford: Clarendon Press, 1933).

12. From "The Dream of the Rood," trans. Edmund Colledge, cited in *A Christian's Prayer Book*, ed. Peter Coughlan, Ronald C. D. Jasper, and Teresa Rodrigues (Chicago: Franciscan Herald Press, n.d.), 232.

13. Cited from Szoverffy, *Hymns of the Holy Cross*, 15. The author's dates are roughly 530 to 610 C.E., so the hymn probably dates from the second half of the sixth century. As the entry in the *Oxford Dictionary of the Christian Church* notes, Venantius Fortunatus was "the first Christian poet to express himself in terms of erotic mysticism" (2d ed., ed. F. L. Cross and E. A. Livingstone [New York: Oxford University Press, 1974], 1430–31).

14. Text cited in Szoverffy, *Hymns of the Holy Cross*, 79–80. The passage is from "Laus crucis" by Eckbert of Schonau; my translation.

15. Latin text in Migne, *Patrologia Latina* (PL) 184:657: "Sedes sponsalis crux erat, in qua verus sponsus sponsam suam Ecclesiam sibi copulavit, ipsam sibi proprii sacrati sanguinis effusione subarrhans. Exaudivit ergo Christus animam non jam Latronis, sed confessoris sui, sponsam suam, et orantem digna responsione confortavit: *Amen dico tibi*, vero dico tibi, *hodie mecum eris in paradiso*. Cur tibi? Tibi, qui me confessus es in cruce tormentorum: mecum eris in paradiso deliciarum. *Mecum*, inquit. Mira benignitas! Non dicit simpliciter, *eris in paradiso*; vel, cum Angelis eris: sed *mecum eris*. Satiaberis eo quem desideras: videbis in majestate, quem confiteris positum in infirmitate." My translation in text.

16. Latin text may be found in Migne, PL 184:727.

17. Text in Szoverffy, *Hymns of the Holy Cross*, 15.

18. In the *Regularis Concordia*, the communion appears to involve reception of the consecrated bread together with reception from a chalice of unconsecrated wine into which a particle of consecrated bread has been dropped ("consecrated by contact"). See the Symons edition, section 47, p. 45.

19. *Regularis Concordia*, Symons edition, section 46, pp. 44–45.

20. Ibid., section 51, pp. 49–50.

21. See the discussion in Nathan D. Mitchell, *Cult and Controversy: The Worship of the Eucharist Outside Mass* (New York: Pueblo, 1982), 129–36.

22. See Robert Taft, "A Tale of Two Cities: The Byzantine Holy Week Triduum as a Paradigm of Liturgical History," in *Time and Community*, ed. J. Neil Alexander, 21–41 (Washington, D.C.: Pastoral Press, 1990), 22.

23. It should be emphasized that the Jerusalem church did not single-handedly "invent" all the rites of Holy Week. Even Egeria notes that what she saw in the Holy Land often resembled "what we do back home." While Jerusalem's influence on the evolution of Holy Week was important, it was not always original, decisive or universal.

24. See James Burbank, "Catholics, Too, Venerate El Nino Fidencio," *National Catholic Reporter* (February 7, 1997), 3.

25. Ibid., 3–4.
26. Ibid., 4.
27. See Bob Haverluck, "Glory to God in the Lowest: Fragments for a Liberated Theology of Culture," *ARTS* 7/2 (1995), 15–19.
28. Ibid., 19.
29. Ibid., 16.
30. Ibid.
31. Ibid., 16–17.
32. See Simon Schama, *Landscape and Memory* (New York: Knopf, 1995), 263–76; 362–74.
33. Keith Thomas, "Review of Simon Shama's *Landscape and Memory*," in *The New York Review of Books* (September 21, 1995), 10.
34. See the comment on violence in culture in the work of René Girard, cited in the Introduction to this volume, p. 7.
35. Margaret Visser, *The Rituals of Dinner* (New York: Grove Weidenfeld, 1991).
36. Ibid., 36–37, italics added.
37. Thomas Sheehan, *The First Coming: How the Kingdom of God Became Christianity* (New York: Random House Vintage, 1986), 172, 173.
38. See Raniero Cantalamessa, *Easter in the Early Church*, trans. J. M. Quigley and J. T. Lienhard (Collegeville, Minn.: Liturgical Press, 1993), 42–43; text altered.

CHAPTER 4

Becoming Truly Human: Origen's Theology of the Cross*

Peter J. Gorday

By comparison with the work of the other Christian thinkers and writers discussed in this volume, the theology of Origen of Alexandria is not well known. However, it was not always so. In the third, fourth and fifth centuries of the Common Era, Origen enjoyed enormous popularity and influence in the church. At the so-called Fifth Ecumenical Council, the Second Council of Constantinople (553 C.E.), certain of his teachings became controversial, and as a result, his work fell under official condemnation. During the medieval period it was used mainly as a source for the "spiritual" exegesis of scripture by certain monastic writers; it then enjoyed an enthusiastic revival in humanist circles at the time of the European Renaissance in the fifteenth and sixteenth centuries because of its Platonic spirituality. Although official Protestant and Catholic reformers down to the present—all of whom have tended to be rigorously Augustinian in their constructions—have treated him with suspicion and disdain, some of his thought gradually found favor with writers who appreciated "Alexandrian theology" (John Henry Newman was one). As we will see in the next chapter, only in the twentieth century did he again become an important source for theology.[1] Even to consider him a significant voice in a discussion on the cross is remarkable, given this long history of official ostracism and rejection at worst, or of highly cautious and circumspect use at best. Perhaps our current examination of Origen's

---

*I wish to thank Eugene TeSelle of the Divinity School, Vanderbilt University, for substantial help in clarifying my thought in this essay.

understanding of the cross will allow us to draw some fresh and original inspiration from this neglected, even subversive, thinker, who worshiped God in Christ long before Augustine, Bonaventure or Luther had seen the light of day.

Since the cross is not a theme that was explicitly developed by Origen—a trait that is true for all of the patristic writers, including Augustine, as we shall see—and since his thought is scattered over a wide range of diverse writings, special procedures are required for this study. First, I consider exegetical and expository comments on scriptural passages in which Origen reflected on some aspect of the cross. I follow the chronological order of his writings and include as many texts as possible from his large exegetical corpus.[2] Second, I take note of some of the broader themes of Origen's soteriology and his understanding of redemption, partly as these are reflected in comments on scripture and scriptural themes, but also as they appear in the overall character of his theology. Third, I look at Origen's treatment of what he took to be the supreme example of practical discipleship in "bearing the cross"—the martyr's self-offering in accepting death as a confession of faith. Indeed, the theme of martyrdom will provide the bridge from this chapter into the next, where I delineate the constructive understanding and evaluation of Origen's theology of the cross by situating his thought in its context and then assessing its import for contemporary theological work.

Origen as Interpreter of Scripture

The twentieth-century scholarly consensus about Origen is that he was preeminently an exegete. From the beginning to the end of his career, he devoted himself to the interpretation of scripture and to the incorporation of this biblical work into his larger theological agenda. In various ways, that agenda always pointed back to a central question: How can Jesus Christ as the Logos of God be correctly and convincingly understood as possessing saving power for us? To answer this question, Origen grappled with a variety of matters that had become mainstays of the eclectic (Platonic-Aristotelian-Stoic) philosophical musings and debates of third-century Alexandrian culture.

One of these issues was how to bring a proper theory of interpretation to the decoding of classical and authoritative texts, particularly those of a religious nature. In Origen's earliest extant work, a commentary on Psalms 1–25 (preserved in fragments), this question of how to interpret the scriptures correctly concerned him. He wanted to find the key that would unlock the sealed writings in order to reveal their hidden truth and thereby lead the reader to true knowledge.[3] For Origen, scripture was a fabric of puzzles, enigmas and mysteries, all contained in the various linguistic and rhetorical forms of the text. He compared the task of interpreting scripture to a great combat in the arena—a pregnant image in light of his concern with martyrdom—or to the bewilderment faced by someone who attempts to penetrate a labyrinthine series of rooms, all intricately connected, with the keys scattered at random.[4] Understanding scripture correctly is a fine and mysterious art, in which every detail possesses its particular significance, because every detail or component of the text has been placed there by divine intention.

The discernment of this significance is an act of spiritual wisdom, reflective not only of the interpreter's level of maturity but also of God's providential revealing of precisely the right element of truth at the right time. This revelation happened for Origen through both the entirety of nature and the entirety of scripture, since he saw both as filled with what he called "obscurities"; that is, elements of contradiction and paradox that bring the interpreter into the ineffable and transcendent presence of God. A major implication of this view was that even the most repulsive or unseemly or nonsensical parts of scripture could be understood to manifest aspects of God's goodness—this being a line of thought with particular salience for Origen in his debates with the Valentinian Gnostics.[5] Thus, for Origen, the interpretation of scripture was part of a macrocosmic project, that is, understanding the fundamental modalities of divine action in the universe. We will see how this project plays itself out in Origen's understanding of the cross, particularly in its human dimension as *crucifixion*. For Origen, as for Paul (in Jerome Murphy-O'Connor's construal in this volume), the human reality and coarseness of the cross is essential to its meaning, although Origen had to struggle with this meaning in ways that were foreign to Paul, as we shall see below.

What we discover in the fragments of Origen's first exegetical foray is that he focused his attention on various formal aspects of the text—the singular or plural form of nouns, variant readings that emerged from comparing manuscript versions of the text, or different lexical meanings and associations for key words.[6] When he wrestled with the deeper significance of these details, however, he was constantly disturbed by the way in which mere surface meanings of the biblical text would not only be accepted as sufficient by simple believers, but, once accepted, would actually lead these sincere Christians astray.[7]

A case in point was the interpretation of Psalm 1:5, in which the Hebrew writer compared the destiny of the wicked with that of the righteous. He writes, "This is why the unrighteous will not rise in the judgment." At issue for Origen were differing views of the nature of the resurrection-body. Those whom he called "simple believers" took the verse to imply that the righteous will enjoy a literal, physical resurrection, while nonbelievers will have no resurrection at all, that is, will not rise in the judgment. When these simple believers were queried as to whether or not the actual substance of our present physical bodies is carried over into the resurrection life, they would reply ignorantly with an affirmation. Origen then responded to the crudity of this belief by pointing out that the earthly body is a constantly changing product of transformational processes, just as ingested nourishment is regularly turned into flesh and bone. The human body is in fact generated by the intake of vegetable and animal matter. The absurdity of imagining that these materials are taken up in the resurrection leads to the question: Exactly what body is it that is raised in the resurrection? The simple faithful would confess perplexity on the matter and appeal to the view that with God all things are possible, citing scripture texts in which God seems to promise the eschatological renewal of our actual physical bodies!

In order to counter this view, which he saw as grievously mistaken (because it would undermine the whole spiritual, that is incorporeal, character of a heavenly existence), Origen went to great lengths to develop an argument about the relationship between form and substance in the human body. Bodies, he suggested, are perpetually fluid, like rivers in motion, because of the indubitable fact that they rely on the regular intake of nourishment and the elimination of waste. But the form of our bodies remains constant. Like the river, this constancy is manifest in the stability of outward appearance—Peter and Paul are always recognizable as the persons they are—and it is on the continuity of this form that identity depends.

Our identities derive from this stability of *material* form as well as—in the more usual hylomorphic theory of Aristotle—from the stability and continuity of the soul within. It is this material form that will be wonderfully reconstituted in the resurrection to make the resurrection-body and not the perpetually changing material substance of the body on earth that is destined to fall away at death. Thus, the qualities of both continuity and change are preserved in the form of the human body as it makes the transition in the resurrection from earthly to heavenly existence. Origen pictured the soul as moving away from its service to an earthly body with its need for physical nourishment, toward service to a spiritual body that will require spiritual nourishment. The soul of a person serves the body whether in an earthly or heavenly state. In the latter, the body will require spiritual food so that with the help of the soul it will grow strong and healthy.

He then suggested that all the biblical texts in which persons in a resurrected state are depicted as having physical organs that endure suffering or experience pleasure, in fact refer to capacities of the soul. Thus, in the dress of its glorious body, the soul will be purified from sin and graced by God for its growth toward holiness and ultimate restoration. The implication of this argument for a correct view of Psalm 1:5 is, first, that all who die, not just the righteous, are raised, and, second, that the unrighteous will not be ready for judgment until their healthy growth is complete.[8]

This way of interpreting Psalm 1:5 expressed for Origen a fundamental principle: The surface or letter or outward "body" of the text can draw us into the truth contained therein but is not to be confused with it. The letter of the text, or its outward meaning, continues to exist in its physical contours but, through its obscurities, is also bound to the deeper, inner meaning that gives it life and reveals another order of reality. While simple believers misunderstand the verse of scripture to mean something contrary to its truth, mature believers take the same letter as a meaningful pointer to the authentic spirit contained within. In time, Origen would apply this understanding of the text to the meaning of the cross. In its literalness—its purely surface aspects, its human and corporeal crudity—it leads astray and confuses, but in its spiritual meaning it draws one to the truth about Christ.

This method of proceeding from the material presentation of objects to the elucidation of their inner dimension, without losing the connection between the two, is a master key to Origen's thought.

Origen's View of the Soul

A careful analysis of the relationship between body and soul, between the corporeal and the incorporeal, was virtually demanded by both the philosophical and the religious milieu in which Origen lived. For Christians, one particular aspect of this analysis involved serious reflection on the glorious or resurrection-body of believers after death. In turn, the question of a person's status after death entailed many of the issues at stake in the debates with Gnostic groups, particularly the Valentinians (see below), about the status of material, historical, embodied existence for human life and for the cosmos as a whole. Origen's concern, then, to work out a sound biblical hermeneutics was balanced by an equally strong desire to think through and elucidate for the Christian community a well-grounded view of human nature.

Origen's maturing thought came to its first comprehensive expression in the work *On First Principles*, composed about the year 229 in Alexandria. His central purpose was to explore a number of questions in which he could be loyal to the received creedal formulations of the church and move beyond these into speculative areas. In the course of this effort, he provided here-and-there a first look at how he understood the significance of Christ's passion and cross.

The background to his comments was supplied by his more basic need to clarify for intelligent Christians not only the nature of the soul, but more specifically, the nature of the soul of Jesus in the incarnation. As one might expect, Origen attacked those who understood the pertinent texts in a crudely literal, that is, in a corporeal and unspiritual, way. For instance, Jesus had indicated to the disciples that he would not drink of the cup of fellowship again until they were together in the Father's kingdom (Matt 26:29). Jesus was pointing to a spiritual gladness that he would share with his followers in heaven, not literally to some anticipated millennial kingdom with all of its earthly pleasures and rewards.[9]

In this context, Origen referred again to a central contention, that the soul is plastic, formable and transformable in its spiritual progress from earth to heaven (thus refuting the Valentinian notion of "fixed natures" in human beings, that is, that we are created good or bad from the beginning). When Peter swore to the maid that he did not know who Christ was (Matt 26:69–74, Luke 22:62, John 18:17), he revealed the fact that even a saint can fall into serious sin by the exercise of his own free will. He thereby showed that all rational creatures are capable of good and evil at any moment.[10] Origen also saw in Jesus' claim before Pilate that the latter would have no authority over him if it had not been given from above (John 19:11), an indication that the Father had intentionally given permission to the devil to inflict calamity upon him. This text thus demonstrated the watchful function of divine providence, since God structured earthly experience to contain that measure of suffering that would be conducive to the soul's education in virtue. The final purpose of such suffering would be the learning that prepares the soul for its return to the heavenly places whence it has come—a process that applied to Jesus as authentically human.[11] God is revealed to be providentially and paideutically in control of the final results of evil in the world.

Most important, however, was Origen's first mention of the crucifixion itself, when he cited Jesus' statement in Gethsemane, "My soul is sorrowful even unto death" (Matt 26:38, Mark 14:34). Origen noted "how at the last he was led to that death which is considered by men to be the most shameful of all—even though on the third day he rose again."[12] In the first of three references to this text in *On First Principles*, Origen marveled at the humanity of the Savior—how he "emptied himself" of majesty in coming to dwell among human beings—and he expressed astonishment at how the utter transcendence of the Word could be "believed to have existed within the compass of that man who appeared in Judea; and how the wisdom of God can have entered into a woman's womb and been born as a little child and uttered noises like those of crying children." Thus, we see in Jesus, said Origen, a remarkable combination of qualities, some that unite him with the common frailty of mortals, and others that remind us of his divine nature.

In his second use of the Gethsemane text, Origen made the particular christological point that it is the *soul* of Jesus that suffered during the passion, while his higher part, here called the spirit, remained unperturbed. As a result, Jesus could offer himself back to the Father in all calmness, while at the same time experiencing the pangs of distress with unbuffered sharpness. The third use of this text occurs in the context of Origen's claim that the soul of Jesus in its humanity truly suffered, but that the Word joined to it, because of its incorporeality, did not. No one, therefore, can claim that there was not a real union of the human and divine in Jesus, or that he did not really suffer in his humanity. Only as the Logos—that dimension of his being that was properly divine and perfectly joined to the Father—did the Son remain by nature immutable and untouched by pain.

In *On First Principles*, therefore, Origen revealed the seriousness with which he tried to develop a clear understanding of Jesus' human experience within the assumptions of contemporary views of the cosmos. In a way that is analogous to the complexity we saw in his understanding of the relationship between the literal and spiritual meanings of scripture, he argued for a comparable relationship between body and soul. The texts that suggest Jesus' genuine human distress fascinated him— "Now is my soul troubled" (John 12:27); "My soul is sorrowful even unto death" (Matt 26:38); and "No one taketh my soul from me, but I lay it down of myself" (John 10:18).[13] He saw these texts as particular demonstrations of how the soul functions in human nature as a medium between the "spirit," which is noble, and the "flesh," which is weak. The soul of Jesus was like the soul of every human being in that it preexisted the body, was joined with a material body at birth and then experienced the vicissitudes of that body—its passions and sufferings—in the course of a lifetime. As incorporeal, moreover, the soul can look to the realm of God and spirit, secure in this contemplation, while at the same time looking to the realm of matter and sharing its struggles. It is precisely here that Jesus shared the condition of suffering humankind, most notably in the agonies that led to the cross.

From this perspective, Origen claimed that Jesus was crucified in weakness, entered into the weakness of flesh, but was raised in power—in the power of the divine aspect of his soul completely united with the Word in eternal embrace.

From Theology to Practice

Therefore, having argued in *On First Principles* that in effect and by implication the cross of Christ in its human reality was the Father's means for launching sinful human beings on the way to salvation, Origen was in a position to tackle other Johannine and Pauline texts related to the theme of the cross. This took place in the earlier volumes of his commentary on the Gospel of John, written while he still resided in Alexandria and before his move to Caesarea in Palestine about 231 C.E.

For example, when Paul preached Christ crucified to the Corinthians, he had to speak to them on their level, for they were ready to know Christ only in a human, corporeal way, not in the form of the stronger, more spiritual food of the heavenly and resurrected Christ.[14] The cross of Christ—that is, the acting out of the vulnerability to human sin that the Son undergoes on behalf of sinners—is revelatory, for it is a portion of the larger dynamic of the incarnation in which the Son becomes many things for many people. In the John commentary in particular, Origen enlarged upon his view of the titles *(epinoiai)* of Christ; that is, the various aspects or concrete modes by which his power as the Word is concretely communicated to human beings. Some of these are the different images used by Jesus in the Gospel of John to describe his functions—for example, bread, vine, light, and so on—but most reflect a variety of terms found throughout scripture and applied as functional descriptors to Jesus. In every case, moreover, Origen tells us, these titles reflect the fact that Jesus was uniquely empowered through his intimacy with the Father to be the messenger of the eternal Word, to be the guide that we must have in order to share the life of the Father. For instance, because he reveals through his suffering on the cross more of the saving truth about God, Jesus can accurately be said to reign as a king during his crucifixion; in *this* sense, claimed Origen, the title of king for the crucified Lord has its profound truth.[15] "For we must dare say that the goodness of Christ appeared greater and more divine and truly in accordance with the image of the Father when 'he humbled himself and became obedient unto death, even death on a cross,' than when 'he had considered being equal to God robbery,' and had not been willing to become a servant for the salvation of the world."[16] The powerful truth of God could be revealed to mortal beings in no other way.

In the later volumes of the commentary on John, written in Caesarea, Origen continued along the same lines. In his discussion of Caiaphas's foretelling of Jesus' death (John 11:50), for instance, Origen argued that Jesus would die as a mortal creature and not as the Word of God, for as the Word he must be eternal. As a human being he will die in great humility for the sins of all people and thus accomplish on a far grander scale what others had done in a more limited way. Origen contended that there is nothing irrational in believing that Jesus died a propitiatory death. Since others are commonly thought by the pagans to have done the same thing for specific objectives such as defeating a plague, averting a famine, and so forth, the charge that Christians held irrational beliefs was refuted.[17] Thus it is clear again that the crucifixion of Jesus was for Origen an aspect of Jesus' historical and corporeal existence that made sense in human terms. The redeeming death of Jesus may look irrational, but—as with the connection between letter and spirit—the human and earthly qualities of the event point to the deeper divine truth contained within.

This connection resurfaced in Origen's return to reflection on Jesus' prayer in the Garden of Gethsemane. In the *Exhortation to Martyrdom*, composed sometime between 235 and 238, during a persecution under Maximin the Thracian, Origen argued that Jesus' words, "Father, if it be possible, let this cup pass from me," were not words of cowardice or lack of confidence (though they would appear that way). Rather, they were words of strength and power in relation to the Father. Jesus' request was that "this cup," that is, martyrdom as he, the Son, would embrace it, should give way to "another cup," that is, martyrdom as the Father would require it and as Jesus now indicates his willingness to undergo it. Thus, the conclusion, "Not as I will, but as you will."[18] Origen reminded us also that Jesus' willingness to endure the crucifixion was a truly voluntary laying down of his own life for others, an authentic act of virtue in purely human terms and an act that we are called to imitate in our own progress in virtue. This progress will entail martyrdom for us also.[19]

Closely related to this view of Jesus' prayer as a manifestation of his virtue (as well as to the teaching that believers share in Jesus' power precisely as they engage in similar acts) is Origen's argument in his work *On Prayer*. There Origen urged his readers to engage in prayer constantly, so that the combination of the daily practice of good works and set times of prayer would manifest a faithful following of the example set by Jesus when he prayed, "Our Father, who art in heaven." Such a sharing in the life of Jesus by entering into his prayer will do what true prayer is always intended to do. It will not change God, who is eternal and unchanging, always foreseeing our needs and the ways in which humans freely respond to grace, but rather, it will change the one who offers the prayer in the direction of virtue. Prayer rightly practiced moves us toward a deeper discernment of, and then a deeper obedience to, the purposes of God, which are heavenly and transcendent and thus prepare us for eternal life.[20]

In his *Treatise on the Passover*, written about the same time as *On Prayer*, Origen argued that the image of Christ as the Passover Lamb is easily misunderstood. Literalists refer the notion of passover to the passion and death of the Lord, but in fact it refers to the passing over in which through his whole life, as well as death and resurrection, Jesus makes a transit from preexistence to earthly and incarnate existence and back to heavenly existence. In this way, the Lord makes it possible for others to join him in his passing over to the Father.[21] Once again, the implication is that the earthly concreteness of things—in this last case a too literal likening of the details of the sacrifice of the Passover lamb to the details of the crucifixion—can lead astray, rather than, through correct exegesis, lead to the deeper, heavenly truth.

The homiletic literature of the Caesarean period contains many repetitions as well as enrichments of these themes. In the *Homilies on Ezekiel*, there is a particular emphasis on the human, physical reality of the incarnation. In connection with the use of the title Son of Man by Jesus, Origen advanced the notion that this title signified Jesus' real humanity in the crucifixion, but even more in the circumstances of his birth. Indeed, for Origen, the Platonist and ascetic, the facts of the Savior's human birth are even more of a scandal than those of his death—yet he is strong to affirm both.[22] In a famous passage, Origen took the view that all talk of the mercy of God makes sense only in light of this assumption of humanity by the Son. It is in this act that God proves to have a "sensible soul," a soul that can suffer our pain with us, and that allows us to say that God is moved by love.[23]

In the *Homilies on Leviticus*, the details of the Hebrew sacrificial offerings are related to the humanity of the Christ event. The holocaust of his flesh offered through the wood of the cross brings together the earthly with the heavenly and the human with the divine.[24] Commenting on Ephesians 2:19 and Colossians 1:20, Origen claimed that it is by the blood of Christ that the earthly and the heavenly are joined.[25] Numerous passages suggest parallels between the various sacrificial acts of the Old Testament and the Christian theme of "taking up the cross," although there is a real absence of typological connections with details of the crucifixion. It is generally the entire life of Christ, and the entire life of the Christian, that are envisioned by Origen in sacrificial terms.[26]

Further, in the *Homilies on Numbers,* Origen noted how the humanity of Jesus on the cross functioned simultaneously as a manifestation of his exercise of virtue through his own free will and as an active force by which the Father pulls us heavenward. Like the thief on the cross, the expression of faith is a real "passing through" to the river of paradise.[27] Finally, in the *Homilies on Jeremiah* we have an example of how Origen applied a prophetic text to the crucifixion of Jesus and used its problematic quality to smoke out a deeper meaning. The text, Jeremiah 11:19a, traditionally translated as "Let us put wood into his bread," is spoken by Jeremiah's detractors and follows Jeremiah's reference to himself as a lamb led to the slaughter. In Origen's view, the wood is the cross, but the bread is Jesus' teaching, which is now strengthened by the scandal of the cross so that it can take possession of the whole earth through the preaching of the gospel.[28] What is humanly disgraceful and was intended by persecutors to destroy the gospel will in fact lead to something that at first will seem to obscure the truth, but that will in the end create the conditions for its deeper apprehension.

The High Point

Finally, there is a gathering together of many of these themes in Origen's last, and arguably most mature, works—the commentaries on the Song of Songs and on the Gospels of Luke and Matthew, and the great work *Against Celsus.*

In a tradition that grew out of the rabbinic practice of seeing the lovers in the Song of Songs as an image for the relationship between God and the people of God, Origen applied the same idea to the relations between Christ and the church, as well as to the soul of the individual believer in its intimate and inward relationship with the Word of God. In this latter connection—using his notion that there is a spiritual, incorporeal vision of God enjoyed by the purified soul—Origen believed that those who witnessed the crucifixion were at first able to see Jesus only in the flesh. Only those filled with the Spirit of knowledge and wisdom were prepared to see the Word and Son of God in the crucified Jesus and thus be led to a higher awareness of the divine love.[29]

In commenting on Peter's confession of Jesus as the Christ in Matthew 16:16ff., Origen contended that the disciples were not yet ready to preach Jesus as crucified, that is, as the Christ, because he had yet to convince them that he must suffer. In order to proclaim him as Jesus the Christ, they must first "know" him as risen and victorious, something that will be possible only after his passion, in which the cross becomes essential to the "economy of salvation." This "showing" will be manifest to the reason or the inner spirit of the disciples, and not to outward sight. The cross will lead believers from the limitations of earthbound perception to the freedom of spiritual, rational perception.[30] The idea that the role of the cross is to lead those who contemplate the person of Jesus from false to true sight will dominate Origen's thinking on this subject in the huge apologetic work against Celsus.

In *Against Celsus*, Origen both honored the philosophical and theological concerns and assumptions of his own culture and simultaneously defended the particularity of the biblical revelation against them. The pagan philosopher Celsus had leveled the charge that Christianity turns people away from the best of morality, makes them superstitious and credulous, renders them disloyal and unproductive citizens and, most of all, roots them in a view of God that is absurd and blasphemous. In rebuttal, Origen marshaled all of his resources, including his understanding of the nature and meaning of the cross. The truth of Christianity, he claimed, is enshrined in the lived virtue of its practitioners, preeminently in the life and moral goodness of its founder. It is a remarkable thing, argued Origen, that the fact of Jesus' crucifixion has not taken away his fame and reputation.[31] Further, the integrity and zeal of his disciples suggest that claims for his resurrection are to be taken seriously, as well as the claim that he died willingly for the benefit of the human race.[32] Indeed, his death and the courage with which he faced it must be seen as testimonies to the genuinely human side of his "composite being." Thus, divinity could flow through him for the benefit of humankind.[33]

Origen makes this point repeatedly. It is by means of the human reality of Jesus, his human weakness, that the Logos speaks effectively to ordinary human sinners and thus produces conversion.[34] The resurrection itself can be claimed to be genuine only because the flesh and suffering that preceded were themselves genuine, since this suffering was the natural outcome of a life lived with moral steadfastness.[35] This argument for the moral strength of Christian witness became all-important for Origen precisely when he chose to emphasize the power of the cross:

> So Jesus did not cause difficulties for the Christian faith by the sufferings which he endured, but rather strengthened its cause among those who were taught by him that the truly blessed life in the proper sense of the word is not upon this earth, but in the world to come, as he calls it, and that life in what is called "this present world" is a calamity, or the first and greatest struggle of the soul.[36]

In addition, the passion of Jesus as a whole and in many of its details is a fulfillment of prophecy, and, therefore, by the criterion of ancient truth that both Origen and Celsus honored, itself a legitimate claimant for honor and respect.[37] One aspect of this ancient truth—the principle that absolute purity is required for the ascent to God—becomes blazingly and powerfully clear in the crucifixion, for it is here that the truth that our human nature must suffer and die in order to rise is incarnated for all time. For this reason, the death on the cross must be a real death that had to happen, not a charade or a mere appearing that the Word could have treated as optional.[38]

In fact, in a way that sets him apart from much of the early Christian use of proof-from-prophecy, Origen did not use Old Testament texts so much to argue for the truth of this or that detail of the life of Christ, but rather as a way of affirming that the essential nature of the Christ event—in this case the humanity of Christ—was necessary. Isaiah 53 is taken not as a foretelling of the crucifixion itself but as a reference to the human aspect of Jesus, that is, to the fact that a true man must suffer so that the life-transforming power of the Word can spread abroad.

> But in so far as he was a man, who more than anyone else was adorned by his participation in the Logos through wisdom and virtue, he endured as a wise and perfect man what must needs be endured by a man who does all in his power on behalf of the entire race of men and of rational beings as well. There is nothing objectionable in the fact that a man died, and in that his death should not only be given as an example of the way to die for the sake of religion, but also should effect a beginning and an advance in the overthrow of the evil one, the devil, who dominated the whole earth.[39]

Running throughout the last two books of *Against Celsus* is a steady argument that, by the character of their worship and belief, but especially by their virtue, Christians truly honor the incorporeality of the God of the universe.

To the charge that Christians engage in "body worship" by their belief in the incarnation, Origen responded that pagans, with their absurd worship of idols that in fact represent demons, fall into corporeality and materialism. The only true worship of God, Origen contended, is the exercise of virtue, just as the only true temple is the body of a virtuous and pure believer.[40] Pagan veneration of the demons, even by philosophers who should know better but lack the courage of their convictions, leads in fact to an unfruitful loyalty to the state. Thus, what is merely of the earth is wrongly and fatalistically exalted, while virtue, the thing most truly useful to the right ordering of society, is neglected.[41] Indeed, the Christian claim that what was crucified in Jesus was only his body and not the divine Word in him shows that it is precisely the triumph of virtue through his death that allows others to follow and so to serve the common good on earth.[42] The moral reform of society, including the rejection of all idolatry, is that for which Christians witness and for which they are willing to be martyrs, thereby following in the footsteps of Jesus and bringing the deepest significance of his crucifixion to light. By announcing the victory over evil in the cross of Christ, Origen brought the work *Against Celsus* to an end.

Moral Sacrifice

For Origen, the cross of Christ is the ultimate act of goodness and perfect virtue by the Logos-become-flesh, and hence by the only One adequately equipped to expose the full significance of faithful suffering and death. It is the goodness of this act, defined in terms of virtue and the human progress that precedes it, that gives the Christian gospel substance and credibility in the midst of history and of the world. The best way to develop this thesis is to consider Origen's understanding of the cross as sacrifice, and then to clarify his views on the witness of martyrdom as the practical enactment of the cross. I begin with his understanding of the concept of the spiritual sacrifice.[43]

Frances Young has argued convincingly that Origen's views on this subject are best placed against the background of the continuous critique of pagan sacrifice in late antiquity. Hebrew writers, at least since the time of the Babylonian exile, and then Hellenistic thinkers from the time of the rise of philosophical skepticism in the Greco-Roman world, contributed to the critique. Christian apologists were the heirs of both traditions, moving progressively toward more "spiritual" and "moral," that is, less crudely literal, understandings of the meaning of sacrifice.[44] In this development, Young distinguished between two views of sacrifice, that of the Hebrews, which was essentially expiatory, and that of the Greek world, which was aversive. The latter view came to predominate among Greek-Christian writers because of their assumptions about the nature of God as incorporeal and unchanging. While the expiatory view required that God's wrath against human sin be soothed and thus changed through the offering of sacrifices for forbearance and forgiveness, the aversive position looked to a deflecting of the power of evil spirits—incorporeal but not divine demons that corrupt and destroy the creatures of God.

Young believes that this context influenced Origen's emphasis on the power of the cross to change human beings, not God (already noted in the case of prayer), by subduing the forces that lead human beings to vice. Differently stated, the redemptive power of the cross lies in its ability to change human beings in the direction of virtue by freeing them from demonic powers. But at the same time, it does not work any change in God or God's dispositions. In Origen's words, the cross functions as central to God's educative therapy for the illness of the world.

As the preceding discussion shows, the meaning of Young's thesis becomes clearer when we remember that Origen's view of the cross is embedded in both his Christology and anthropology. That is, Origen's understanding of the nature and import of the incarnation, and his understanding of human nature and what it requires for transformation, provide the larger context for his soteriology of the cross. For Origen, the cross "fits" redemptively the space provided for it both by created and fallen human nature. This argument can be clarified and strengthened, I believe, by considering the moral thrust or moral valence given by Origen to his analysis of the processes of human transformation.

Henri Crouzel has emphasized the moral context of Origen's construal of the human constitution.[45] According to Origen, we are spirit, soul and body. Spirit is our highest and therefore essentially incorporeal dimension. Soul consists of a higher part, which is "mind" or "intellect" or the "ruling faculty," as well as a lower part, which is the sensory capacity of the bodily passions. Finally, the body is the physical, corporeal and earthly vehicle of soul and spirit. The purpose of describing this hypothesized structure of human beings as "moral" is to suggest that it provided a framework for the struggle that defines human existence. In that struggle, the soul, guided by the spirit, must exercise free will, that is, its rationality, in order to extricate itself as much as possible from *undue* adherence to the conditions of embodiment. By looking toward the incorporeal spirit, the soul makes itself available to that dimension of the universe to which God is most fully present and, by so doing, partakes of the nature of divine goodness. The soul's orientation toward God is thus tantamount to the free exercise of virtue and is the means by which the soul turns back toward its own origin in the realm of incorporeality. The soteriological question, then, is to discern what empowers the soul for the virtue that results in this reunification with God.[46] At this point, Christology, for Origen, sheds light on anthropology.

In its assumption of human finitude, it is the supreme task of the Logos to effect this return of the creature to the Creator. In the incarnation, the eternal Word of God, the eternally generated Son, joins with the soul of Jesus to become a human being who is in his humanity mortal and in his divinity immortal. As the Word, he is the perfect image of the Father and thus the source of saving knowledge, while as Jesus he must attain to this perfect knowledge by living out the conditions of earthly life, including the drama of his passion and cross. As we "enter into" this drama with our own dramas, our souls lay hold of their kinship with the soul of Jesus so that with him we may become spirits and as such present to God.[47]

Thus, we can see why Origen does not apply the title Lamb of God to Jesus primarily or only in his death, but instead uses it as broadly descriptive of his whole earthly career. Robert Daly has rightly emphasized that the notion of Jesus as the Passover Lamb, as Origen used it, is not cross-centered as such but relates to the whole event of Christ. It is descriptive of the entirety of Christ's "passing over" to the Father, because it applies to the entire course of human embodiment borne by the Logos in the temporal soul-drama of Jesus.[48] For Origen, the meaning of the cross must be set against the backdrop of the incarnation itself and the humanity of Jesus as the sacrifice or offering that the Word makes on behalf of the world by entering into the travail of mortality. At this point Origen's thought seems essentially in line with Murphy-O'Connor's understanding of the significance of the cross for Paul: the cross *means* a human Jesus, which *means* the infinite love that God has for us.[49]

In this discussion, one particularly important passage from Origen's writings has been his commentary on Ezekiel 16:4-5, in which Jerusalem is described by the prophet in the most physically graphic terms as an infant, vulnerable, uncared for and rejected by her parents. Origen argued that God showed mercy on Jerusalem by embracing her as this infant precisely through the incarnation, by entering into the passions of human corporeality, including the experience of the cross. In fact, in the nuance of the argument, and contrary to his usual assumption of the divine impassibility, Origen suggested that God felt pity for humankind before the incarnation, and then descended to flesh as an expression of that pity.[50]

It is important to note that in this moral soul-drama, the status of embodiment itself was called into question for Origen. Among modern critics, an older view saw Origen as purely and simply dualistic in his cosmology, with an absolute gulf between body and soul (and spirit). Views that are more recent emphasize the subtlety of his thought on this matter. We have seen, for instance, that his understanding of the resurrection-body contains an affirmation of some kind of corporeality as an essential dimension to the role of soul as the source of personal identity. Furthermore, since Origen believed that only God, strictly speaking, could be without a body of some sort, it would appear that all finite beings, whether heavenly angels or earthly human beings, need some vehicle as a basis for their mutability.[51] It has also been argued convincingly that Origen's very notion of human beings, as well as angels who possess rational natures, requires some form of embodiment as a full coming-into-being, as emerging, that is, into true subsistence.[52] This positive valuation of the bodily by Origen has also been noted by Peter Brown, who has interpreted Origen in terms of the iconic mentality of the Eastern church, in which the vital antithesis of flesh and spirit is manifested in the beheld spectacle of the soul's rational control of the body. This spectacle allows Origen to describe such a controlled body, as in the case of a "beautiful" virgin, as a truly resplendent temple of God.[53] In terms of the cross, we might say that Jesus as crucified bespeaks the glorious reality of God, because as the embodied Logos, he shows forth the moral journey of a corporeal realm that remains translucent to the incorporeal, as well as destined to rejoin it.

This moral journey of human existence, which is acted out in the incarnation and brought to a climax on the cross, began for Jesus even before he assumed earthly corporeality. Origen may well have applied the subject of the self-emptying of Philippians 2:5ff. to the preexistent spirit called Christ, but not to the Logos itself.[54] In this way Origen would have made the point that the incarnation, including death on a cross, was *willed* by the Son—a case made by Murphy-O'Connor in his interpretation of Paul's use of the Christ-hymn in chapter 1—and thus freely and virtuously embraced. There is, moreover, in a way peculiar to Origen, the further contention that the cross remains eternal and is not superseded, so to speak, by the resurrection. Even in his resurrected life, Jesus still hangs on the cross and continues to suffer for the sins of humankind, as long as one sinner has yet to repent and be saved.

This view, wrongly understood by Jerome,[55] was used as a charge against Origen in his condemnation in the sixth century. However, seen in the context of his theology of the cross as intrinsic to the saving work of the Word in Jesus' real humanity, it is more accurate to see it as a prime way of claiming the final and total efficacy of divine power in the cosmos as a whole. Origen did, of course, subscribe to the view that there will be a universal restoration in which all things, Christ included, will submit to the Father. The implication was that a particular event, in this case the cross, will continue to function forever both as the means of salvation for souls on earth but also for souls in heaven. The cross is both a contingent event on earth and a timeless reality in heaven.[56]

In terms of the pursuit of virtue, Origen sees Jesus' earthly life as an analogue to what the Son has accomplished in the incarnation. Jesus lived and died as a good and wise man, and his followers are to do likewise. Many passages in the work *Against Celsus* make this point. Since the cross is the high point of this pursuit of virtue, the proclamation of Christ without reference to the cross will always be inadequate, however much Origen understands the cross as belonging to the elementary stages of Christian faith. Consider Origen's comment on John 19:17,

"They took Jesus, and he went out, bearing his own cross," where he stated:

> Hence every thought and idea of ours, every word and deed in which we are involved should breathe our self-abnegation as we give witness about Christ and in Christ. For I am convinced that every deed of a perfect person is a witnessing of Jesus Christ, and that every rejection of sin is a denial of self which leads one in the footsteps of Jesus. Such a person is crucified with Christ (Gal 2:20), is someone who "takes up his cross and follows" (Matt 16:24) him who for us takes up his cross.[57]

Consequently, the folly of the cross (1 Cor 1:18) is central to the victory over the Prince of this world.

Finally, what carried the ethical example of Jesus beyond anything that the pagan world offered, in Origen's opinion, was its generosity in extending the love of God to all people and, most of all, its triumph over idolatry and over the compromise with true ethical goodness that all idolatry entails. In breaking the grip of idolatry, the cross as the center of Jesus' soul-drama and moral journey reveals its saving power for others. Here Frances Young's thesis about the *aversive* sacrifice of the cross comes home. For the moral sacrifice of the cross breaks the power of the demons who seduce people into worshiping idols and who then produce an abusive exaltation of the things of this world, including the authority of secular rulers. Because this demonic power is more than earthly, it requires that the death of Christ be a true breaking of the devil's power over humankind.

Origen's thought about the means of the defeat of the Evil One is usually treated under the notion of the ransom theory of the atonement. Hastings Rashdall has argued that the force of the theory in Origen is primarily ethical. In this view, Origen is preeminently concerned with the way in which Jesus' righteousness triumphs over demonic powers that are in league with unrighteousness of every kind and have thus robbed human nature of its God-intended capacity for goodness. For Origen, it is the freely willed obedience of Jesus, his won or attained sinlessness, that robs the demons of their power—though exactly how this happens remains obscure—and that restores a like capacity to his followers. What the ransom theory seems to convey, more than other theories of the atonement, is the way in which salvation has more to do with the nature of evil and of the human self than with the character of God as such.[58] Precisely because of his focus on free will and virtue in understanding the cross, Origen put himself squarely in the camp of such a moral theory of the atonement.

We see, then, why Origen can describe the cross as an "economy of salvation," for in many ways it serves as a focal point for a number of Origen's views about the fundamental relations between God, creation, human nature, evil and the unfolding of redemption. Consider the following:

> The suffering on the cross was the judgment over this whole world, for "having made peace by the blood of his cross, both for the things on earth as for those in heaven" (Col 1:20), and after triumphing on the cross, he disarmed the principalities and powers (cf. Col 2:15) and took his seat in the heavenly places (Eph 2:6) ordering each individual thing according to its fitting and proper end. Since, therefore, that which contained the judgment of each individual thing was the order of salvation on the cross, he said, as the time of this suffering drew near, "Now is the judgment of this world" (John 12:31).[59]

In such a passage, where so much is gathered, the significance of Origen's choice of the term "economy" (oikonomia–translated in the passage above as "order of salvation") to describe the cross is clarified. In other passages, the process of mortifying the flesh and being buried with Christ in his death through baptism is described as the "order of this way of salvation."[60] Jesus' preparation for washing the feet of the disciples, including those of Judas, is done so that the "economy" might be carried out.[61] It would not be too much to say that, as we grasp the meaning of the cross for Origen, we lay hold of the whole structure of his thought. The moral sacrifice, that is, the defining of the theology of the cross in primarily ethical terms, proves to be central and fundamental to Origen's entire theological project.

Martyrdom

In his convictions about the act of martyrdom, Origen gave practical expression to his convictions about the cross of Christ as the redemptive means of human transformation. In Exhortation to Martyrdom,

Origen told his readers that they must not deny Jesus but rather endure the cross and be seated with God as Jesus was. Such martyrdom is the renunciation of this world for eternity.[62] According to Eusebius of Caesarea's perhaps idealized account, Origen's exaltation of martyrdom came out of the cauldron of his own experience, beginning with the martyr's death of his own father and his mother's move to discourage him from rushing into the same fate by hiding his clothing. For many years, Origen also counseled fellow Christians as they approached martyrdom, and in the end, Origen's own death was linked to the sufferings he endured during a persecution.[63] It is quite striking that someone who easily can be pictured as a creature of study and the classroom was also, at least during times of high stress and genuine physical danger, a person of action and confrontation. This combination entitles him to be ranked with many of the genuinely heroic characters of Christian history.

The ideal of the martyr's death grew out of a long history of Jewish, then Jewish and Christian, persecution at the hands of Hellenistic and Roman overlords. Theofried Baumeister has suggested that in Christian tradition specifically, the call to martyrdom originated in straightforward imitation of, and unconditional obedience to, the charismatic leader, Jesus, who required that his followers practice radical renunciation of self for the sake of the gospel. This theme was then combined in various ways with the apocalyptic emphasis on the coming end of the age and the need for faithful preparation for divine judgment. Gradually this voluntary suffering in obedience to Jesus was understood as a personal communion with him and a primary way of extending his mission to the world. This apostolic suffering would then be a form of blessing for the whole community and, indeed, the highest form of sacrificial offering and a sign of God's favor. Martyred individuals were viewed as particular vehicles of grace.

The view of the martyr's death as a peculiarly powerful form of witness thus gathered a number of themes of diverse origin and came to hold great appeal for Origen.[64] By Origen's time, the particular context for the martyr's witness had come to be the judicial demand that loyal citizens make token sacrifices to the emperor and the divinities of the state cult as a mark of patriotism. When Christian leaders objected, claiming that an impious challenge had in effect been issued to the supreme lordship of Christ, the stage was set, as W.H.C. Frend has classically argued, for political martyrdom as an atoning sacrifice.[65]

For Origen, sanctity and purity attended the death of the martyr at a level with which nothing else could compete—either as an example of mature virtue, or as a spiritual power that benefited others. Prosper Hartmann calls the martyr in Origen a "soteriological mystery" in which there is a "mystical union with Christ through the baptism of a sacrificial death." For another commentator, the death of the martyr and the eucharistic sacrifice are viewed in tandem as perpetual, repeatable channels of new grace that serve to hold the devil at bay in the lives of faithful believers.[66] Virtually all interpreters of Origen have been struck by the way in which the martyr was the ultimate champion for Christ in a world that seemed utterly corrupted by idolatry.

Origen often sounded the note of dying with Christ in primarily ascetical terms, as the discipline of self-denial. In this connection he could call the preaching of Christ crucified an outward, carnal Christianity, since the emphasis was laid on visible and physical marks of renunciation rather than on the inward purification of the soul.[67] Elsewhere he appealed to doctrinal orthodoxy as a true walking with Christ, with the implication that those who preach heresy crucify Jesus afresh.[68] There are numerous passages in the commentaries and homilies of the Caesarean period in which he speaks of taking up the cross and following Christ (Luke 14:33 or Mark 8:34); of giving up our lives in order to lose them (Matt 16:25); and of being crucified to the world (Gal 6:14). These are passages in which he speaks of the cross as the priestly offering that all Christians make; as the ultimately personal and individual offering of one's own soul to God; as the giving up of one's soul so that an orientation to present fleshly satisfaction can be replaced by an orientation toward good works (*Commentary on Matthew* 12:26–27).[69]

Early in his Caesarean period, probably at the beginning of the persecution under Maximin the Thracian, Origen gave himself to more sustained reflection on the supreme importance of martyrdom.[70] In commenting on the variety of sacrifices offered by those who are holy, Origen noted that the supreme sacrifice is the assumption of humanity by Jesus as the Lamb of God, followed by the deaths of the martyrs in which the martyr is "associated redemptively" with the death of Christ. Through this association, the faithful are actually cleansed of sin,[71] given the powerful example of faithfulness to the truth, and benefit from the blunting of the power of the demons. In the commentary on John, he states:

> We must hold...that a dissolution of maleficent powers occurs
> through the death of the holy martyrs. The martyrs' zeal for godli-
> ness and endurance to the point of death blunt, as it were, the
> sharpness of the demons' treachery against the sufferer. Conse-
> quently, when their power is blunted and exhausted there are many
> others, in addition, who have already been conquered who are set at
> ease because they are freed from the weight with which the attack-
> ing evil powers were oppressing and harming them.[72]

In this last claim, Origen thought of the martyr's death as the draining
off of a serpent's venom by one who destroys the poisonous animal.[73]

In particular, it is the inner quietude of the faithful martyr, staunch
in the face of human reproach, that revealed his or her freedom from corporeality and readiness for the life of the spirit.[74] Indeed, the martyr is
prepared to claim the baptismal calling, even the priestly vocation, by
becoming a burnt offering and a living holocaust to God.[75] Martyrdom is
in fact a second baptism, a baptism of blood that unites the martyr with
Christ in his passion.[76] In encouraging resistance to the official require-
ment to offer sacrifice in the state cult, Origen could say: "Now let it be
seen whether we have taken up our own crosses and followed Jesus; this
happens if Christ lives in us. If we wish to save our soul in order to get it
back better than a soul, let us lose it by our martyrdom."[77]

The value of this martyrdom for others is constantly affirmed:
"Jesus laid down his soul for us; let us, then, lay ours down, not I shall
say for Him, but for ourselves—and, I think it may be also, for those who
will be built up by our martyrdom."[78] Indeed, martyrdom is a second
baptism that cleanses all sin.[79] By imitating these holy people, we may
"experience the heavenly dew that quenches every fire that arises in us
and cools our governing mind."[80] It is also true that in several famous
passages Origen cautioned against an excessive zeal for martyrdom and
the creation of unnecessary guilt for persecutors. Even Jesus himself had
avoided sacrifice that was not yet opportune.[81]

In the latter books of the work *Against Celsus,* in which he
mounts a sustained attack on the truth-claims of Hellenistic philosophical religion and popular cult, Origen developed his most sustained apology for martyrdom as a witness to truth. He carried out
this task by defending and exalting the principled, ancient monothe-
ism of the Jewish people. By their faith in the one, completely spiritual

God the Jews were faithful to the call to renounce worldly and material things for the pursuit of truth, thereby putting into practice an ideal that philosophers had always desired but failed to attain.[82] What derailed the philosophers was a variety of absurdities and superstitions, with the result that these thinkers failed to understand the Jewish and Christian scriptures correctly, weakening their ability to follow the truth that they knew. He developed a detailed comparison of biblical and pagan prophecy in order to demonstrate that the former has far more credibility in that it truly brings men and women to honor Plato's views about the incorporeality of God, while the pagans deny those views by their submission to corporeal idols.[83] He reminded his readers of the perfect virtue shown by Jesus in his suffering, virtue that had been discussed and proclaimed by many teachers but that had not affected hearts and lives with genuine efficacy until the coming of the gospel.[84] The only real image of God, said Origen, is a virtuous soul, since all agree that this is where life truly is to be found.[85]

In Origen's mind, purity of heart, mind and will are the only defenses against vice and the only real access to life with God, since all else is outward show, pretense, demonic charade and lies. The firm witness of the martyrs vanquishes these demons,[86] who represented the whole superstitious and ungodly dispensation of all that was worst in the ancient world—the submission to the passions, the materialism, the hypocrisy of the philosophers, and the vulnerability to absurd superstitions, including undue exaltation of the emperor.[87] Such was Origen's form of Luther's famous "Here I stand; I can do no other!"[88] It was his way of faithfully living out the theology of the cross.

Conclusion

I have shown that Origen made substantial use of the theme of the cross in his work by relating it to a great variety of scriptural texts. While his treatment of this theme was sometimes explicit, it was often implicit as well in the structure of his understanding of the moral journey of human life and of the drama of redemption. His concern for truth as moral and related to virtue led him to see the martyr as the supreme embodiment of the meaning of the cross.

For us, who struggle in our own time with the challenges to personal integrity and faithfulness and who wonder about the dynamics of, and resources for, human transformation, Origen's way of approaching the theology of the cross is instructive. What he helps us to rediscover is that the cross, like everything else about Jesus, is about being fully and completely human. In the next chapter, I argue that this claim does not mean that we can write Origen off as failing in the task of developing a real theology of redemption or accuse him of creating nothing more than an empty humanism. What the claim does mean is that the cross makes human nature complete and whole, revelatory of the glory and wisdom of God and God's intentions for the creation. Consequently, to talk about God, we must talk about the cross. And in order to talk about the cross, we must talk about the processes that build people up and make them brave in the face of the frightening forces of illusion—the demons.

Thus, with due allowances, Origen's theology of the cross is a kind of "great person" way of thinking. The modern neo-Freudian theorist Erik Erikson contended that the "great man" is the one who accurately grasps the tensions and contradictions of the age and wrestles them to a resolution in his or her life. Other writers have pointed, in more classically Freudian style, to the "autonomous superego," which represents the individual's freedom from the voracious infantile yearnings of neurotic conflict. Persons with a mature superego, or conscience, have been liberated to give away their life, not in submission to an external, constraining authority, nor in order to serve a need for self-glorification, but rather in faithfulness to an inner conviction. This conviction rests on the truth that has come to form the powerful radiating center of goodness for such persons. Such wholeness was what Origen believed he could see literally in the faithful martyr, whose soul was rapt in the spiritual vision of God through an act of self-giving, freely chosen and freely endured.

NOTES

1. There are many histories of the Origenist controversies and of the vicissitudes of Origen's thought and writings down through the centuries. One of the best recent analyses of this history for the early centuries is Elizabeth A. Clark, *The Origenist Controversy* (Princeton, N.J.: Princeton University Press, 1992). The most significant tracing of the entire history, especially in its

medieval and Renaissance forms, and with regard to its theological significance is Henri de Lubac, *Exégèse médiévale: Les quatres sens de l'Écriture* (Paris, 1959), and *Histoire et Esprit: L'intelligence de l'Écriture d'après Origène* (Paris: Aubier, 1950). A quick look at some of the Reformation and post-Reformation history, Roman Catholic and Protestant, is provided in the introduction to Walther Völker, *Das Vollkommenheitsideal des Origenes: Eine Untersuchung zur Geschichte der Frömmigkeit und zu den Anfängen christlicher Mystik*, Beiträge zur historischen Theologie 7 (Tübingen: J.C.B. Mohr, 1930). On John Henry Newman's fascination with the notion of "economy" in revelation, and thus the distinction between immature and mature believers, a distinction of central import for Origen, see Robin C. Selby, *The Principle of Reserve in the Writings of John Henry Cardinal Newman* (London: Oxford University Press, 1975), chap. I,1.

2. For the chronology of Origen's work, I follow Pierre Nautin, *Origène: Sa vie et son oeuvre* (Paris: Beauchesne, 1977), 409-13.

3. These fragments are gathered and edited, primarily from the *Philocalia* of Basil of Caesarea and Gregory Nazianzus and the *Panarion* of Epiphanius of Salamis, in a French translation by P. Nautin (*Origène*, 262-75).

4. Ibid., 264f.

5. Ibid., 266f.

6. Ibid., 267f.

7. What follows is based on Nautin's edited version (from the *Panarion* of Epiphanius of Salamis and the *De Resurrectione* of Methodius of Olympus) of the text, ibid., 269-72. Also relevant is the fragment printed by Nautin (274) and assigned by him to the early commentary on Psalms 1-25, from Rufinus of Aquileia's *Apologia pro Origène*, in which Origen makes a comparison between the relatively short pains endured by Christian confessors on earth, when the soul is still "dressed" in a physical body, and the relatively more agonizing purifications of life after death, when the soul will be wrapped in a more subtle body.

8. It should be pointed out that the interpretation of Psalm 1:5 was to have a long history in the evolution of doctrines about the afterlife, and, in particular, the doctrine of purgatorial fire. Cf. Henri de Lavalette, "L'interprétation du Psaume 1.5 chez les pères 'miséricordieux' latins," *Recherches de sciences réligieuse* 48 (1960), 544-63. Henri Crouzel has analyzed this text from Methodius of Olympus in "Les critiques adressées par Méthodes et ses contemporains à la doctrine origénienne du corps ressuscité," *Gregorianum* 53 (1972), 679-716, and summarized in *Origen: The Life and Thought of the First Great Theologian*, trans. A. S. Worrall (Harper & Row: San Francisco, 1989), 256. Crouzel contends that Methodius has misunderstood Origen's use of the concept of form by tying it too closely to mere outward appearance, but the key point is that the

concept allows Origen to "express the identity without neglecting the difference" between the earthly and the glorious bodies.

9. *On First Principles*, 2.11.2. For the English translation of texts from *On First Principles* I am using that of G. W. Butterworth (New York: Harper Torchbooks, 1966).

10. Ibid., 1.8.2.

11. Ibid., 3.2.6.

12. Ibid., 2.6.1; 2.8.4; 4.4.4. The citations in this paragraph are from 2.6.1-2 (Butterworth, 109).

13. In addition to Ibid., 2.8.4, and 4.4.4, for John 10:18 and John 12.27 and Matthew 26:38, this last text also appears at 2.6.2. Rowan Williams, "Origen on the Soul of Jesus," *Origeniana Tertia: The Third International Colloquium for Origen Studies*, ed. Richard Hanson and Henri Crouzel (Edizioni dell'Ateneo, 1985), 132-36, has noted Origen's use of this text as a witness to the subtlety of his picture of the *homo interior*, in which the soul, and not only the body, as in later Christology, actually suffers, despite its heavenly and incorporeal origin. Williams's specific contention is that this way of looking at the soul involved Origen's whole cosmic scenario of the preexistence of souls, such that in their embodied form they possess this bipartite character. Modern psychology provides us, however, with some other alternatives.

14. *Commentary on John* 1.43; 1.58, and often in Origen's work, for this is a frequent use of the "Christ crucified" texts of 1 Corinthians 1. (For English translation I am using *Origen: Commentary on the Gospel According to John, Books 1-10*, trans. Ronald E. Heine, The Fathers of the Church 80 [Washington, D.C.: The Catholic University of America Press, 1989], and *Origen: Commentary on the Gospel According to John, Books 13-32*, The Fathers of the Church 89 [Washington, D. C.: The Catholic University of America Press, 1993]).

15. Ibid., 1.278. Joseph Wilson Trigg, *Origen: The Bible and Philosophy in the Third-century Church* (Atlanta, Ga.: John Knox Press, 1983), 97-99, is particularly clear on the topic of the *epinoiai* in Origen: "The Son's *epinoiai* in the order of redemption are far more varied than in the order of creation. There need to be as many *epinoiai* here as there are needs which their fallen state imposes on rational creatures and as there are stages in the ascent of those creatures back to God" (98).

16. Ibid., 1.231 (Heine, *Origen, Books 13-32*, 80).

17. Ibid., 28.157-70.

18. *Exhortation to Martyrdom*, 28-29. (For English translation I am using *Origen: An Exhortation to Martyrdom*, trans. Rowan A. Greer [New York: Paulist Press, 1979].)

19. Ibid., 12-13.

20. See, for instance, *On Prayer*, 5 and 6, for a discussion of divine fore-knowledge and human freedom as they pertain to prayer, then 12.2, and 13.1, on the combination of set times for prayer with the active cultivation of virtue and the importance of following the example of Jesus in this regard.

21. *Treatise on the Passover* 1.1-2; 1.12-15. (For critical introduction and English translation I am using *Origen: Treatise on the Passover*, and *Dialogue of Origen with Heraclides and His Fellow Bishops on the Father, the Son, and the Soul*, trans. and ann. Robert J. Daly, S.J., Ancient Christian Writers 54 [New York: Paulist Press, 1992].)

22. *Homilies on Ezekiel*, 1.4.

23. Ibid., 6.6.

24. *Homilies on Leviticus*, 1.4.

25. Ibid., 4.4.

26. See, for instance, ibid., 9.9.

27. *Homilies on Numbers*, 20.3, on John 12:32, and 26:4.

28. *Homilies on Jeremiah*, 10.2.

29. *Commentary on the Song of Songs*, 3.12.

30. *Commentary on Matthew*, 12.18-20.

31. *Against Celsus*, 1.30, and *passim*. (For English translation I am using *Origen: Contra Celsum*, trans. Henry Chadwick [Cambridge: Cambridge University Press, 1965].)

32. Ibid., 1.31.

33. Ibid. 1.66. Cf. 2.36.

34. Ibid., 2.9.

35. Ibid., 2.17, 23.

36. Ibid., 2.42 (Chadwick, 99).

37. Ibid., 2.47-48; 6.81, and see the whole argument for the validity of Hebrew prophecy over against pagan oracles in 7.1-25. For discussion of this last passage, see Peter J. Gorday, "Moses and Jesus in *Contra Celsum* 7.1-25: Ethics, History and Jewish-Christian Eirenics in Origen's Theology," in *Origen of Alexandria: His World and His Legacy*, ed. Charles Kannengiesser and William L. Petersen (Notre Dame, Ind.: University of Notre Dame Press, 1988), 313-36.

38. Ibid., 2.68-69.

39. Ibid., 7.16-17 (Chadwick, 408).

40. Ibid., 7.48, and following, then 8.18-19.

41. Ibid., 8.70-75.

42. Ibid., 8.42.

43. In chapter 7 we will see how Augustine relates the cross to sacrifice, which he equates with compassion. Unlike imperial Rome, which saw sacrifice

as a way to earn praise, Christ's sacrificial act of mercy is disinterested, turned toward God.

44. Frances M. Young, *The Use of Sacrificial Ideas in Greek Christian Writers from the New Testament to John Chrysostom.* Patristic Monograph Series 5 (Cambridge, Mass.: Philadelphia Patristic Foundation, 1979).

45. Crouzel, *Origen*, 87–92. "The dominant context of this trichotomic anthropology is more moral and ascetic than mystical: it is the spiritual battle" (92).

46. Henri de Lubac, in his views on Origen, has emphasized very strongly this moral essence of spirit in the composition of human being, thus making it somewhat synonymous with conscience but at the same time insisting that it is more than conscience per se. De Lubac's real concern is to define spirit as the dimension of humanness that allows for, indeed requires, a real communion of human nature as such with God. See "Tripartite Anthropology," in *Theology in History*, trans. Anne Englund Nash (San Francisco: Ignatius Press, 1996), 136–44. See below for comments on how this way of reading Origen fits in with de Lubac's larger theological projects.

47. As background to this sketch, see *On First Principles*, 1.3.8; 2.6.3–5; 9.2, and 11.7. The best overall analysis in global terms of the character of this drama is still Hal Koch, *Pronoia und Paideusis: Studien über Origenes und sein Verhältnis zum Platonismus*, Arbeiten zur Kirchengeschichte 22 (Berlin and Leipzig: Walter de Gruyter, 1932), who conceived of it ultimately as a theodicy where the existence of undeserved suffering in the world must be reconciled by Origen with a view of God as supremely rational—again by the criteria of a Platonic view of the nature of God. Trigg, *Origen*, and H. S. Benjamins, *Eingeordnete Freiheit: Freiheit und Vorsehung bei Origenes*, Supplements to *Vigiliae Christianae* 28 (Leiden: E. J. Brill, 1994) are attempts in quite good but different ways to appropriate much of Koch's argument and make it more sympathetic with, and expository of, a biblical view of salvation history.

48. Daly, *Origen*, introduction. Daly emphasizes that Origen's insistence on a "passage" rather than a "passion" interpretation of the Passover sacrifice reveals his particular way of interpreting scripture, such that "the antitype of the Passover cannot be for Origen anything this-worldly....The true antitype, the that-to-which everything literal or this-worldly or historical points, must be fundamentally other-worldly....In this case it is the 'passage' of Christ (and, bound with this, the passage of the Christian) to the Father" (16).

49. Though he is more focused on the cross as such in his essay in this collection, Jerome Murphy-O'Connor has provided a broader background in *Paul: A Critical Life* (Oxford: Clarendon Press, 1996). There he makes it clear that in the letter to the Galatians Paul emphasized the humanity and human

faith of Jesus as the vital foundation of his Christology (203-5). This Christology of the human Jesus would allow Paul in his later letters to the Corinthians to highlight the human reality of the cross and its nature as "creative love."

50. The passage is *Homilies on Ezekiel*, 6.6. Ronald Heine has some helpful summary comments of different views as to whether Origen really countenanced the possibility of suffering on God's part (*Origen, Books 13-32*), 29f.

51. Eugene TeSelle has drawn my attention here to *On First Principles*, 2.2, and 3.3.

52. M. J. Edwards, "Origen No Gnostic; or, On the Corporeality of Man," *Journal of Theological Studies* n.s. 43 (1992), 23-37. After arguing a strong case for Origen's view of embodiment as necessary for subsistence for rational spirits, he concludes: "He does, perhaps, support an unwholesome dualism by teaching that the envelope of flesh in the present world is merely a fetter that we have forged by our own transgressions, rather than the provision of a benign and omnipotent will. Yet, unlike his docetic contemporaries, he could not disown the salvation of the body; and thus he was both a zealous counselor to the martyrs and a great theologian of the Incarnation (*De Principiis* ii.6 etc.), who, knowing how far man's permanent condition is from divinity, never ceases to wonder at the voluntary humiliation of Christ (*Contra Celsum* ii.23, iv.15, etc.)."

53. Peter Brown, *The Body and Society: Men, Women and Sexual Renunciation in Early Christianity* (New York: Columbia University Press, 1988), 160-77. At the end of the section—commenting on *Against Celsus* 4.23, where Origen cites Celsus's outraged frustration to the effect that Christians arrogantly place human beings and their welfare at the center of God's purposes—Brown makes the majestic statement: "Faced by such withering indignation, Origen, the Christian Platonist, made the *gran rifiuto* that separated him forever from the 'Ancient Wisdom' of his pagan colleagues. Christians, he replied, 'have already learned...that the body of a rational being that is devoted to the God of the Universe is a temple of the God they worship'" (177).

54. This would be a surmise based on one of the anathemas from the Second Council of Constantinople, printed in Butterworth's translation of *On First Principles*, 250 n.3.

55. Jerome, *Epist.* 124: *Ad Avitum* 11-12.

56. See the excellent treatment of Origen's Christology in J. A. Lyons, *The Cosmic Christ in Origen and Teilhard de Chardin: A Comparative Study* (London: Oxford University Press, 1982), and the treatment of the timelessness of Christ's sacrificial death, 139-41, with the citations from Origen's work.

57. *Commentary on Matthew*, 12.24 (my translation).

58. Young, *Sacrificial Ideas*; Eugene TeSelle, "Probing the Ransom Theme," *Journal of Early Christian Studies* 4 (1996), 147-70 and the portions of

his review of Elaine Pagels's *The Origin of Satan,* in *Religious Studies Review* 22 (1996), 3–9, that have to do with the concept of the "powers" that crucified Jesus (5–8). Hastings Rashdall's classic study is *The Idea of Atonement in Christian Theology* (London: Macmillan, 1919). With regard to Origen, Rashdall claimed that "every step in the rise of the soul must be due to its own efforts. It is a scheme contrived for the express purpose of persuading, without forcing, souls to make that free choice of good without which no true goodness, according to Origen, was possible. It is only by persuasion, example, moral influence that a soul can be made better even by the incarnate Word; and it is only so far as it is persuaded to repent, and so to become better, that God can or will forgive the sin that is past" (270–71).

59. This text is from one of the catena-fragments of Origen's commentary on the Gospel of John and is printed in *Origen, Spirit and Fire: A Thematic Anthology of His Writings by Hans Urs von Balthasar,* trans. Robert J. Daly, S.J. (Washington, D.C.: Catholic University of America Press, 1984), 348.

60. *Homilies on Numbers,* 12.6.

61. *Commentary on John,* 32.84, 86.

62. *Exhortation to Martyrdom,* 37.

63. Eusebius of Caesarea, *Ecclesiastical History* 6.1–2 on Origen's early life and the death of his father Leonidas; 6.3.13, to 4.3 on students whom he counseled as they approached martyrdom; 6.39, on his own death.

64. For all of this see Theofried Baumeister, *Die Anfänge der Theologie des Martyriums* (Münster: Aschendorff, 1980).

65. W. H. C. Frend, *Martyrdom and Persecution in the Early Church: A Study of a Conflict from the Maccabees to Donatus* (Oxford: Basil Blackwell, 1965).

66. Prosper Hartmann, "Origène et la Théologie du Martyre," *Ephemerides Theologicae Lovanienses* 34 (1958), 773–824; Willy Rordorf, "La 'Diaconie' des Martyrs selon Origène," in *Epektasis: Mélanges Patristiques offerts au Cardinal Jean Daniélou,* ed. Jacques Fontaine and Charles Kannengiesser (Paris: Beauchesne, 1972), 395–402.

67. For example, *Commentary on John,* 1.41 ff., though such texts are a commonplace for Origen.

68 Ibid., 1.72.

69. A good selection of these passages is contained in Balthasar, *Origen: Spirit and Fire,* under the theme of "Royal Priesthood," nos. 814–24.

70. In addition to the essay of Hartmann, see now Theo Hermans, *Origène: Théologie Sacrificielle du Sacerdoce des Chrétiens,* Théologie Historique 102 (Paris: Beauchesne, 1996), especially 196–205 on martyrdom as a suffering and dying with Christ and martyrdom as a collaboration with the redemptive work of Christ.

71. The famous passage is in *Homilies on Numbers*, 12.2.

72. *Commentary on John*, 6.281 (Heine, *Origen: Books 1–10*, 244).

73. Ibid., 6.282.

74. *Exhortation to Martyrdom*, 4.

75. E.g., *Homilies on Leviticus*, 9.9.

76. *Homilies on Judges*, 7.2.

77. *Exhortation to Martyrdom*, 12.

78. Ibid., 41. Cf. *Homilies on Numbers*, 27.12, where he used Ecclesiastes 10:4: "If the spirit of one having power rises against you, you will not leave your place."

79. *Exhortation to Martyrdom*, 30. The essay cited by Rordorf has a helpful discussion of the "second baptism" theme.

80. Ibid., 33.

81. E.g., *Commentary on John*, 28.192–201; *Commentary on Matthew*, 10.23; *Against Celsus* 8.65 (see Chadwick's editorial comment on this passage, *Origen*, 501 n.).

82. *Against Celsus*, 5.42–43; 6.4–5.

83. Ibid., 7.47.

84. Ibid., 7.55; 7.60.

85. Ibid., 8.17.

86. Ibid., 8.44.

87. Ibid., 8.58, 62, 66.

88. Actually, what Luther reported that he said to the pope's emissary at the Diet of Worms is, "My conscience is bound by God's words. Retract anything whatsoever I neither can nor will. For to act against one's conscience is neither safe not honorable." The passage is cited in Erik H. Erikson, *Young Man Luther: A Study in Psychoanalysis and History* (New York: Norton, 1993 [1958]), 47.

CHAPTER 5

The Martyr's Cross:
Origen and Redemption

Peter J. Gorday

In order to evaluate the theological viability and potential usefulness of
Origen's understanding of the cross, it is necessary to ask whether he has a
real place for redemption in his scheme. Does he believe that in the cross
of Christ, God does something that is historically decisive and ultimate for
the salvation of humankind? Or is the cross but window-dressing, an
accouterment, or even a convenient and useful sign of a naturalistic cosmic
drama that unfolds of its own inherent momentum? I pose this question
because many of Origen's critics have argued that in his statements about
the cross, he simply adhered to the apostolic kerygma and its traditional
mention of the death of Jesus. They contend that while he was a son of the
church and loyal to its creeds, he emptied these traditions of their real spirit
by substituting his own brand of philosophical idealism.

Origen's "Platonism"

The culprit here is usually Origen's Platonism, or certain affinities
in his thought with the Valentinian Gnosticism that flourished in his
context, both of which are viewed, for various reasons, as fundamentally
incompatible with a truly Christian theology. By Origen's "Platonism" is
usually meant his adherence to Plato's myth of the drama of the soul.
The incorporeal soul of a person preexists its embodiment in a timeless,
spiritual world of "intelligences" and then, in a kind of decline from this
higher state, "descends" for a time into the prison of human physicality,
only to "ascend" at death to the blessed place whence it has come. We

have seen that, indeed, Origen's version of this drama bears a striking resemblance to that of Platonic philosophy. For both hold what is found in all forms of idealism; namely, that the life of the mind transcends and has creative power over the life and very existence of the body.

By Origen's affinity to Gnosticism is usually meant some kind of adherence to the myth of the "redeemed redeemer," in which the Savior comes from the spiritual realm to earth, where he is devoured by the forces of darkness while also delivering a "saving knowledge" to those elect souls who share the divine spark with him, enabling them to pre-pare for return to the higher place. Contained in this myth is the idea that the progress from a life entangled with the passions and limitations of the body requires special, divine help that can come only in the form of One who identifies with our human state in all of its struggle—a view that Origen shared. The common assumption of both myths is that dual-ism of soul and body, of the incorporeal and the corporeal, underlies the tension and dynamic striving of human existence.

Many conclude that this dualism appears in the asceticism and extreme otherworldliness of Origen's views on the Christian life, making human redemption ultimately a matter of self-imposed purification from the body. This cleansing proceeds from a grasping with one's mind of the cosmic myth along with a self-imposed discipline over the body and a patient and faithful expectation of death in order that the soul may go home again from this earthly place of exile. In the Platonic myth, the cross would be only another example of human suffering and of the toll that virtue takes on a good person, much as in the death of Socrates. In the Gnostic myth, the cross is a mere way-station in the Redeemer's jour-ney back to his heavenly origin, in the course of which his suffering per-tains only to the contemptible and to-be-discarded body but not to the soul within.

Those who regard Origen as lacking any real theology of redemp-tion—that is, one in which there would of necessity be a real theology of the cross—usually claim that he over-identified either with the Platonism or with the Gnosticism of his cultural milieu. For example, Hal Koch con-tended that Origen's Platonism led him to a systematic use of the notion of a paideutic providence as the heart of his thinking.[1] Eugène de Faye[2] and Hans Jonas[3] contended that Origen's reliance on the notion of the titles *(epinoiai)* of Christ as the primary indicators of the means of salvation revealed his essential grounding in the timeless, ahistorical and world-denying Gnostic myth, in which the redeemer cannot be truly incarnate and the cross cannot be truly salvific.[4]

On the other hand, Roman Catholic apologists for Origen in the twentieth century, particularly the historians Jean Daniélou and Henri Crouzel, have argued forcefully that the effects of Origen's Platonism have been exaggerated from ancient times to the present. They suggest that he was much more a true son of the church than has been acknowledged, certainly by official authority.[5] More clearly revealing of what is at stake theologically in these diverse appraisals of Origen, however, has been the effort of two eminent Catholic thinkers who have attempted a critical retrieval of Origen for the present. It is helpful to consider and evaluate these reinterpretations, particularly with regard to the theology of redemption and of the cross.

Origen's Interpreters

Hans Urs von Balthasar

Hans Urs von Balthasar wanted to appropriate his fresh reading of Origen for his own theodrama of the glory of the Lord.[6] For Balthasar, and for reasons that reflect the inner structure of his massive theological enterprise, there is in the earthly career of Jesus a perfect unity of divinely given mission and divinely originated person. This means ultimately that the nature of the Trinity, indeed, the nature of being itself, is revealed as infinitely free love. Such love is in its innermost nature self-giving and self-emptying in a way that makes its manifestation in action beautiful, that is, morally good and intellectually true and thus aesthetically appealing. As a result, when persons are prepared by faith to "see" what is revealed, when their eyes behold the fair beauty of the Lord, they enter into the joy of their salvation.

In Balthasar's language, Christ is the "concrete universal," for he is a revelation of human nature as such. At the same time, in Jesus, he is a particular and contingent human being who lived out the polarities that make up the drama of human living. These are the polarities of body/spirit, man/woman and individual/community. All of this comes to complete expression in his death on the cross, the supreme moment of

the drama in which the inexpressible agony of human despair and abandonment is followed by the transformation of the resurrection. Thus the
beauty of the Lord becomes visible in the cross and brings to bear the
divine/human power of the paschal mystery.

The Johannine theme of the glorification of the Father in the Son
as the latter is lifted high on the cross is a central focus of this breathtak-
ingly vast, self-consciously christocentric theology, in which every dimension of Christian thought is freshly and creatively reformulated. The
spectacle of the crucified Lord is made to bear enormous weight, not,
Balthasar claimed, in Jürgen Moltmann's sense of the manifestation of a
timeless negative dialectics of the divine nature, but rather, in a dramatic
unfolding within the contingency of human existence of the realized possibilities of finite human spirit by One who combined infinite and finite
Spirit within himself. In other words, the event of the cross is God speaking the Word of love into the heart of humankind in a way that addresses
its deepest hunger and longing.

In the context of such a theological enterprise, then, Balthasar did
not hesitate to make Origen his ally. Balthasar argued that Origen's Platonism, and that of the Greek Fathers in general, was a great asset, precisely because of its dualistic view of the human constitution. While soul
and body together are a unity, the human soul nonetheless hungers for
freedom from its easily idolatrous immersion in the world of matter.
Insofar as the soul hungers for freedom and for its own natural breathing space, it also hungers for ascent from what is earthly. This ascent is
accomplished through an asceticism that masters the passions, and
through knowledge that focuses the mind Godward. Thus is transcendent communion with the Word established. For Origen, the Christian
Platonist, the instrument of this union is the Word in scripture, in the
church, in the sacraments, and above all, in the humanity of Christ. In
the last analysis, Christian discipleship would be a "Word-mysticism"
inflamed by a pure, burning passion of deep love in the soul for union
with the beloved Word or Logos.

Therefore, what Origen knew and continues to tell us, is that we
must learn to see with our spiritual senses, with the inner eye formed by
the aesthetics of faith, the breathtaking, truly redemptive beauty that
awaits us on the cross. This beauty beckons to us as the self-giving love
that shines from the Incarnate One, who is the Crucified One, who is

scripture and sacrament and neighbor. In this scheme, redemption entails a true descent of the Word into a true union with the flesh of the world, precisely so that the contemplative, mystical ascent can take place for us sinners.

On the other hand, because of Origen's Platonism, Balthasar doubted that Origen had arrived at a true incarnation of the Word, or that he had been able to articulate a valid theology of the descent of the Logos into flesh *(theologia descendens)*. Such a theology would be the indispensable presupposition for an orthodox understanding of the ascent of the Logos to heaven *(theologia ascendens)*. For in the final analysis, Origen left us in the lurch with his Platonizing devaluation of the world of matter and of its potential for a paradoxical vision of the glory of the Lord. Platonism does not allow that the temporal, finite order of things has its own proper being. Nor does it allow that the ultimate unity of the cosmos encompasses *both* the incorporeal and the corporeal without collapsing the latter into the former. Metaphysically, therefore, Origen's theology simply will not work—however correct its intentions and vision!

Balthasar claimed that only the Christian, biblical doctrine of creation, in which divine love empties itself in going over to the Other, and thus requires the Other as a completion of itself, could make room for a material world that is good and, as such, redeemable. Origen the Platonist was able to see the corporeal world only in terms of "fall," or at least decline, from a prior and higher state. It is here, says Balthasar, that Origen made the mistake of mixing the gospel with worldly philosophy—specifically idealism. Origen thus fell victim to all of the illusions of idealism from Plato—illusions that plague us down to the present (Hegel). Our fascination with abstract systems of logic and thought-structures must not blind us to the utter contingency and historical particularity of supernatural love:

> It is in the measure that Jesus' death is a function of absolute love—"he died for all"—that this death has, first and foremost, the validity and efficacious power of a principle. There is, of course, no question here of a "formal logic"; what is involved is a logic whose content is the uniqueness and personality of the eternal Logos become man, a logic created by him and identical with him....Of any other logic than this, the New Testament knows nothing.[7]

ORIGEN AND REDEMPTION

For Balthasar, there is no authentically Christian view of redemption in Origen, only the elements of such a view, or the straining after such a view. Origen saw that the theology of the cross required a theology of the Word-become-flesh, but the tools available to him for giving expression to his insight were not adequate.

Henri de Lubac

In view of Hans Urs von Balthasar's mixture of approval and critique of the Platonic context of Origen's theology of the cross, one is struck by the more unqualified endorsement of Origen in the theology of Balthasar's friend and contemporary Henri de Lubac.[8] Although he was not a systematic theologian, de Lubac sought to define through his historical and literary studies a sound basis for a modern theology of Christian knowledge and Christian mission in the world. Like Balthasar, he was convinced that such a theology requires a rethinking of the doctrine of human nature so that, in light of this revised anthropology, other aspects of doctrine could be similarly tested and adjusted. Unlike Balthasar, however, he turned to epistemology rather than metaphysics for his primary point of orientation. Consequently, we find him much less interested in Origen's Platonic cosmology and much more engaged with what Origen has to tell us about how we can know something of God and of ourselves so that personal transformation and spiritual growth can follow.

In this approach, de Lubac chose to emphasize especially Origen's views on the paideutic nature of human existence; everything is seen in terms of the soul's, or individual's, capacity for the acquisition of wisdom through experience. God, in de Lubac's reading of Origen, ceaselessly leads the soul forward through darkness and light to the spiritual contemplation that constitutes its destiny in the transcendent. This paideutic journey of the soul is at the heart of Origen's anthropology of body, soul and spirit, and it forms the basis for his theory of the spiritual interpretation of scripture.[9] It also reflects his particular way of adapting Plato's notion of the stages of knowledge to Christian ends. With this perspective on Origen, de Lubac was able to sidestep classic complaints about Origen's philosophical underpinnings. De Lubac did not prejudge him based on ancient dogmatic objections but rather was able to enjoy him as a practical and

mystical theologian. In quintessentially modern fashion, de Lubac substi-
tuted a hermeneutic approach for Balthasar's fixation on dogma as the ultimate measuring stick, thus shifting the angle of perspective from
Christology to anthropology.

Further, de Lubac was clear about what was at stake theologically in
making such a shift—the formulation of a sound view of the relationship
of created human nature, always reaching upwards for the knowledge of
God, and divine revelation always responding through Christ to that
hunger. In his central and controversial formulation, de Lubac settled on
an understanding of human nature in which—totally apart from any special infusion of grace—we are created absolutely by God to possess the joy
of the beatific vision. The import of this formulation is in its contention
that the desire for God is, so to speak, in our genes—not some kind of a
super-imposition from above as an antidote to sin. It is this naturally
graced relationship with God, obscured by sin and yet tending toward its
completion in the vision of God, that then can be allowed to define the
all-important modalities of the church's relation to secular culture. This
relation involves Christian faith's relation to scientific reason and the
spirit of modernity in all its forms; but, most important, it determines
the individual believer's faithful relation to the world in word and deed.[10]

Consequently, when he considered the theme of the cross of Christ
in Origen, de Lubac turned primarily to the Pauline texts of 1 Corinthians with their focus on the scandal, the mystery and the wisdom of
Christ crucified.[11] With Balthasar, he rightly denied that the crucified
Christ could be of central importance in Origen's thought only for simple and not mature believers. But unlike Balthasar, who wanted to see
the glory of the Lord manifested in the spectacle of the Crucified One,
de Lubac contended instead that the cross—the Pauline "wisdom of the
cross"—functioned for Origen intellectually as a formal principle of the
knowledge defined by faith. The cross is the lens of wisdom through
which the believer contemplates the world and by which deeper truth is
sifted from mere appearances or temporary uses. By means of the cross,
the "spirit" is discerned beneath the "letter," and the people of Israel
appropriate the "spoils of the Egyptians" for consecrated purposes. It is
by means of the wisdom of the cross that believers can accept all secular
knowledge as a "propaedeutic" to the teaching of the gospel. It is by
means of the wisdom of the cross that all of history can be perceived as

moving toward Christ. Since, moreover, it is the "wisdom of this age" that crucified Christ, that same wisdom is humbled, exposed as "demonic," when it is left to its own devices. Thus, it is the cross that judges, humbles, exposes the wisdom of the world. Thus for the Christian "there is no wisdom which may dispense with following him by bearing his cross."[12]

Most important, however, is the claim that for Origen the cross stands as the point where God's educative and illuminating grace draws human beings toward knowledge that is not, as Balthasar thinks, Gnostic and esoteric in its hiddenness, but rather invisible to persons whose eyes have not been opened by the "order of charity" revealed in Jesus Christ. Citing Romano Guardini, de Lubac claims that the cross is the "absolute symbol," for it brings together and literally constitutes as a modality of perception, the union of God with the human soul.[13] It is in the movement from carnal and literal knowledge to spiritual knowledge, from the "nude" cross to the "glorified" cross clothed in light, that our salvation happens, according to de Lubac's interpretation of Origen.

I contend that Henri de Lubac came closer to a sound interpretation of Origen's theology of the cross than did Balthasar, primarily because he is more genuinely empathic with the basic working metaphors of Origen's thought. He not only admired Origen as a great Christian and thinker, but he was also able to use him for a contemporary apologetic agenda in a more straightforward way. While Balthasar claimed that Origen shows us *what* theology is supposed to accomplish, but could not offer a valid means, de Lubac suggested that Origen speaks directly to the perennial problematic of Christ and culture. What Origen tried to say through his theology of the cross to both believers and skeptics provides lasting guidance for the church's care of souls in the present time. In the cross of Christ we see the standard, the criterion, by which faith both affirms as created, and critiques as fallen, the world that God loves and for which Christ died. The cross functions in this way because it is the definitive statement, deed and revelation of God's love as self-giving. It is this kind of love for which the human heart naturally longs, even when it finds itself inadequate to the task. Here is de Lubac's devotional language:

> This great Deed of Love, Jesus, it is You, Yourself. Perceptible to man, humble, dying in a corner of Judea, oh!, yes, You are a man!

Flower of Jesse, You are indeed the fruit of our earth, Born of woman, truly formed from her substance. You are not some sort of phantom come down from the clouds of heaven. You are deeply rooted in our earth. But in You, Jesus, as in no other child of our race, God showed himself. You were not merely His messenger, You are His living and substantial appearance. Through You, he has not only spoken. Or rather His language is an action, His word a deed: it is You Yourself. "Splendor, Verbum et imago Patris." You, Jesus, on your Cross, the act uniting earth to heaven.

In the accompanying note, de Lubac writes:

If it is true that the whole activity of Christ reveals it, can one not, however, think that through the Cross alone incarnate Charity is wholly revealed? This language alone communicates to us, along with the experience of Love, the knowledge of its conditions. With-out it, then, who among men would truly be able to understand the Gospel? "What makes us believe," says Pascal, "is the Cross."[14]

What is evident everywhere in de Lubac's work is that he wanted—with the help of Origen—to recover a theology of the cross that would not be, in his words, "rationalist, narrow and superficial."[15] He wanted the cross to function, in Newman's language *(The Grammar of Assent)*, as a source of real, and not merely notional, assent. He wanted the cross to capture and inflame the moral imagination of all who behold it and are prepared to act on what God teaches them there, by means of its right-ness and concord with human reality. Consequently, with de Lubac's work we move closer to a view of Origen's theology of the cross that defines it in more practical terms, because one has come to see that Christian faith is properly understood at least as much in terms of action and character as in dogmatic constructions.

An interesting convergence arises here in the way certain Protes-tant, as well as certain Catholic, interpreters construe Origen. Part of what is at stake is the clear recognition that Origen developed his thought, including that on the cross, in a context of ministry—in his case, teaching, writing and directing the practical living of a host of followers. This context has decisive significance and was, I think, not generally con-sidered by Balthasar and de Lubac, who were, after all, not so much his-torians as they were theologians concerned to retrieve tradition for a contemporary program. Consequently, the work of Walther Völker and that of Henri Crouzel adds essential historical perspective. Both scholars have focused on the ascetical, ethical and mystical dimensions of Origen's life and work in its broadly cultural, as well as more narrowly ecclesial, context.

Walther Völker

Contrary to a view popular among history of religionists at the time, Walther Völker saw that it was ridiculous to dismiss Origen as a rationalist, bookworm and dreamer, when, in fact, his writings are rich with practical devotion to Christ. There is a "religious-ethical" heart to Origen's work that Völker defined as the pursuit of the ideal of perfection, particularly in the form of a strong attachment to the person of Jesus and the imitation of his way.[16] In his concern for the history of Christian piety, Völker then contended that this perspective on Origen allows us to understand how his spirituality naturally evolved toward that of the monastic-ascetic ethos of the Eastern church with its strongly "mystical" orientation. However, Völker's treatment of Origen, while rich and suggestive, suffered from his need to set up a constant comparison of Origen's thought with the theology of the Augustinian-Reformation tradition of salvation by grace alone. He insisted, nonetheless, that there is a real theology of grace in Origen's views on the Christian life, and that dismissal of his thought as "works-righteousness" is egregiously in error.

Völker explicated a number of themes in Origen's work—all of which we have seen in passages relating to the cross. For example, salvation takes the form of the soul's acquisition of a properly intellectual communion with God, who is utterly incorporeal. Human free will, which is the mark of the rationality of the soul, is not radically compromised by sin and thus must be exercised through ascetic discipline so that the soul can disengage from its entanglements with the physical world. Bodily passions must be transcended by the soul so that, through practices such as virginity and the renunciation of earthly honors, a state of blessedness leading to the sweetness of mystical vision can be cultivated. Saving knowledge takes the form of a nonrational enlightenment of the soul in the enjoyment of "heavenly secrets" imparted to it by the Word (Origen's "spiritual exegesis" of scripture was a special form of this divine enlightenment of the believer). It is also clear that Origen held a view of the mystical union in which the believer "saw with the heart." Intellectualism alone is transcended, and there is a true "beatific vision" of the Godhead.

Especially important was Völker's claim that Origen modified the conventional Stoic-Platonic emphasis on the elimination of the turbulence of the passions as the ethical ideal. Mastery of the passions was not for Origen an end in itself. Rather, it served as the means by which the soul moved into deeper relationship with God and into a more immediate synergy with the divine purposes. Martyrdom as crucifixion with Jesus is the supreme example. In place of the pagan concern with the freedom and self-sufficiency of the wise man as the highest good, Origen focused instead on the self-giving humility of the spiritual man as the highest good. Martyrdom served as the arch-example of the spiritual person's decision to renounce everything for the service and glory of God. In his final section on the imitation of Christ, Völker was clear that following the Crucified One in martyrdom was for Origen the ultimate and "perfect" act of graced faithfulness: "Origen embraced all of life as one single martyrdom, as a being-crucified-with-Christ....Thus was the idea of a daily martyrdom, as it would later develop in monasticism, already anticipated."[17]

Henri Crouzel

In a lifetime of work on Origen, Henri Crouzel has also emphasized this mystical and ascetic view of Origen, though he has been careful (to say the least) to paint a picture in which Origen appears more a man of the church than in Völker's earlier work. Crouzel pays particular attention to the biographical sources contained in the sixth book of Eusebius of Caesarea's history of the early church, and he offers a sketch of Origen as a teacher, based on the thanksgiving discourse written by one of Origen's students, Gregory Thaumaturgos. What emerges from these sources is a view of Origen as a dedicated, subtle and highly disciplined spiritual master for whom the care and training of his students and patrons was the supreme value. In the curriculum of Origen's school at Caesarea, the capacity to engage in the spiritual exegesis of scripture and to have one's soul thus purified occupied the highest place. Thus, as Crouzel understands Origen, there was a gradual softening of Origen's somewhat rigorist early views on ascetical discipline.[18] What followed was a renewed sense that it is by means of a preeminently intellectual and inward communion with the Logos that persons grow in grace, both for this life and in preparation for the continuing process of purification in the resurrection-body.

Crouzel has been careful to view Origen's constructive theology in light of comments found in the preface to *On First Principles* and of the account composed by Origen's defender, Pamphilus of Caesarea. In Crouzel's view, Origen's work emerges as a "research theology," or a theology pursued for the sake of spiritual exercise and growth rather than dogmatic definition and comprehensive system building.[19] Origen was a theologian engaged in creative work for the service of the church, and thus he worked at the edges of Christian thought—where a thinker must be in order effectively to engage heresy and be a genuine teacher and director of souls.[20] Thus, more like de Lubac and less like Balthasar, Crouzel has seen that Origen's understanding of human nature and the inner processes that lead persons to God is essential to our reading of Origen.

Crouzel has written on Origen's view of the relations between theology and philosophy; on the nature of the mystical knowledge of God; and on the nature and implications of the concept of the image of God in Christology and theological anthropology.[21] In particular, we take away from Crouzel's masterful work a strong sense that all of Origen's thought and spirituality led, above all, to practice, to action, to ways of being and behaving in the world. The result is that others are "shown"—that is, have revealed to them—that which can only be known ultimately deep within, at first fragmentarily and finally in its fullness, the whence and wherefore and whither of human existence. The faithful life is thus a revelation of the mystery of things, of the mystery that we human beings are as we journey toward God.

I believe that the problematic aspect of Crouzel's way of seeing Origen arises from his need to retrieve him for orthodoxy—a particular concern of Origen's Roman Catholic apologists. Thus, there is a large temptation to assimilate him to later, safer models of Christian thought and witness as well as to look for ameliorating or balancing elements that tone down some of Origen's extremes. On the one hand, then, Crouzel sees clearly that Origen's thinking led him naturally to face the call to martyrdom. On the other hand, Origen was careful, we are told rightly, to resist any fanaticism.[22] As we have seen, Origen warns against creating guilt for the persecutors and taking unnecessary or ill-advised steps toward martyrdom.

The overall trend of Origen's understanding of the cross is, however, to push hard and straightforwardly toward the ethical act when the time is right and when truth demands it. We must not allow an emphasis on inwardness to obscure this simplicity. We must resist making Origen too much like the careful advisor of souls from the Golden Age of French Catholic spirituality.[23] If we were to compare Origen to figures from that time and place, I would liken him more to Fénelon, who eventually paid a humiliating price for conscientiously propounding heartfelt but risky and unpopular views, than to de Caussade, who walked the narrow line more skillfully but faded into relative and untroubled obscurity. I contend that one stays closer to Origen's treatment of the cross by focusing finally on the moral integrity of the martyr—particularly in the stand against idolatry—an integrity that he claimed to be the defining characteristic of the Christian mind and the Christian life. This behavior is seen as a particular kind of witness, the acid test for what constitutes a true theology of the cross.

Postmodern Interpreters

It has been the postmodern interpreters of Origen who have shown the least concern for his orthodoxy (or lack thereof) and the most sensitivity to the socially concrete aspects of his theology. These critics indirectly strengthen our awareness that Origen was a theologian for whom material things not only matter, but matter very much. In the preceding chapter, I noted Peter Brown's treatment of the importance of the possibilities and contradictions of embodiment in Origen's thought. Brown argues that Origen actually "sensualizes" the life of the spirit in human beings by inviting us to contemplate the way in which earthly pleasures echo in the mode of antithesis the higher pleasures of the heavenly places. In this view earth becomes a sort of photographic negative of heaven, in which the virgin, for instance, in the painful sharpness of self-denial, and like the martyr who is about to die, invites the kiss from us that would be the first taste of heavenly bliss. In this way, Brown tells us, Origen was reconciling bodily existence—from the ancient viewpoint—with its inevitable discontent, with "the unfathomable subtlety of God's justice."[24] In this perspective—which borders on an eroticism of physical pain—Brown has captured one dimension of the human reality of the cross.

Similarly, both Marguerite Harl and Patricia Cox point to Origen's capacity to capitalize on the scandalously physical nature of the incarnation.

Marguerite Harl

In her early study of Origen's understanding of the incarnation, Marguerite Harl showed that Origen labored long and hard to demonstrate that genuine saving knowledge, that is, spiritual knowledge, can be mediated or revealed to human beings through material things. This view was clearly contrary to the usual assumption in his day that only like could mediate like. Central to her thesis is the nature of language as Origen understood it, particularly in the biblical texts. There we see that words serve as concrete containers for the spirit of God, hidden under the form of the letter, but manifest through the various obscurities (that is, mysteries), puzzles and enigmas that point the reader to deeper, latent meanings in the texts. Through the patient search for understanding of these texts, the reader is led to illumination, that is, to the vision of a spiritual and transcendent order in the universe, which is also a vision revealed to corporeal creatures precisely in their corporeality. Jesus as the Word incarnate reveals God in exactly the same way. We are redeemed by the cross at the very moment when we allow ourselves, once scandalized by its shame and ugliness, to discern the logical chain that leads us from the letter to the spirit, from body to spirit.[25]

Patricia Cox

Finally, in her studies of the poetics and aesthetics of Origen's imagery, Patricia Cox has helped us appreciate, especially in his commentary on the Song of Songs, "the Origen who could find Wisdom herself in the sweetness of an apple." It was *this* Origen, not the Origen usually assumed to have a thoroughgoing repugnance for the flesh, for whom the natural world functions as a structure of significations waiting to be elucidated and enjoyed. From Cox's viewpoint, the cross can also become a concrete and physical thing that serves to signify more than is immediately apparent to the eye—more to be "enjoyed" than one would first suppose. This kind of aesthetic analysis of the concrete will often include, paradoxically, the enjoyment of a self-analysis that is painful, because it centers on the experience of discovering the darkness or "bestiality" of the human soul.[26]

The Human Reality of the Cross

I suggest, however, that we do not have to go to the extremes of postmodern critics and their dialectics, since something more straightforward is available. I refer to the sheer courage, the outright obedience and loyalty, that is, the virtue, that made the cross stand out for Origen as the saving moment of eternity thrust into the midst of human temporality. The great Catholic apologists for Origen have been right in one way, as are Origen's latest and most sympathetic interpreters in other ways. For Origen, the cross is the saving revelation of the divine presence redemptively manifested on the stage of history. And the cross is the "ascent," the self-transcendence, required for any ethic or aesthetic that would be a worthy human response to that manifestation. It is a critical principle given to us, by means of which faith can lay hold of, yet discerningly sift, that which is generated by human culture. It is an ascetic principle of self-denial in order to find the true self in loving union with the Word that informs all of life. It is a means of grasping within the parameters of embodiedness the disordered and unstructured dynamics of spirit in which another order somehow emerges through the unfolding of the soul's journey toward God.

But, as my emphasis on martyrdom suggests, it is above all the identification with truth in the face of lies and deception, that is, the rejection of idolatry even with the consequent danger of fanaticism, that most centrally characterizes Origen's theology of the cross. No one has seen this more clearly than Henry Chadwick. His various statements about Origen are in profound agreement with the picture that emerges of Origen's thought when we consider precisely those passages in which he speaks of the cross. It is not that Chadwick has been particularly interested in Origen's views about martyrdom. Rather, in a larger and more philosophical perspective, he has seen that it was Origen's task to argue the case for indeterminacy in a world committed to fatalisms of every sort. In thus arguing the case for indeterminacy, he made real free will, and thus real ethical striving, the point at which divine purpose and human possibility intersect.[27]

Though Origen has been, and still is, much criticized for his universalism—the view that, because of both human and divine freedom, all souls may finally be saved—his intention in putting forward this view was clear. He wanted to contend for a radically open-textured world and open-ended future for that world, with the goodness and trustworthiness of God as an absolute foundation. The alternative, in his view, was an impersonal, closed, ultimately static universe of endless repetition, in which there is no redemption because there is no creative goodness grounding and enlivening the processes by which growth, development and change can occur. Powerful ethical striving, then, is simply real life, life truly lived, for it is the mark of one who believes in, and has been grasped by, the truth of the nature of things—by the good God. Chadwick has argued that all of Origen's appropriation of classical philosophy alters its import in just this kind of ethical direction that I am describing. Origen's concern with Jesus' own human obedience in going to the cross may be seen as the definitive revelation of human reality and destiny—the touchstone, so to speak, of freedom in the empowerment of our conduct on behalf of God's purposes.

We must not, therefore, be misled by Origen's Platonism. While it is indeed the case that he saw this ethical striving worked out in the redemptive purification of the soul, through its liberation from the body and through an inward contemplation of the purely incorporeal God, it is also true that he saw in the success of this striving the transformation of life on earth, the institution of a more just, more godly, order of things. As the martyr seizes the wheel of history, it turns from the direction of lies toward the truth.

Eugene TeSelle has reminded us in an important but somewhat overlooked book that early Christianity brought nothing new to the ethical table of the ancient world.[28] As Origen himself noted (in a tradition extending from Justin Martyr to Augustine), the standards of truth and goodness for which Christians stood were largely identical with those of the best pagan thinkers of the day. What distinguished Christians from their pagan contemporaries was not the content of their ethics, but their insistence that consistency and rigor in living out these ideals form the criterion of truth, particularly when that witness leads to death and seems like a defeat. In what I have called in this study "the human reality of the cross," Origen claimed to see the "letter" that leads to the "spirit," the acted-out goodness of self-giving that leads to, and reveals, the presence of the living God. What we have in Origen's theology of the cross is the pattern of thought and action that grounded such living, made it possible. Through the cross of Christ, redemption was actualized for Jesus as a human being, at the same time that the mission of the Word in the incarnation was brought to its earthly completion. The confession of the martyr is the human way, because it is the divine way, for us too, who wish as disciples to be really human and really good.

My conclusion is that Origen did have a real theology of redemption in his understanding of the cross, that he did allow, with due qualification, for true incarnation in his Christology. And given his focus on the practice of faith—particularly in the idolatry-smashing power of the death of the martyr—it is best to look to the categories and modes of ethical reflection and action for understanding this great, but still to be fully reclaimed, Christian theologian of the cross.

NOTES

1. Hal Koch, *Pronoia und Paideusis: Studien über Origenes und sein Verhältnis zum Platonismus*, Arbeiten zur Kirchengeschichte 22 (Berlin and Leipzig: Walter de Gruyter, 1932), 74–77, where he takes the view that what happens on the cross is an illustration of the educative process by which human beings through the exercise of free will can follow in Jesus' footsteps. Thus the cross is a mere "annex" to Origen's real theology.

2. Eugène de Faye, *Origène, sa vie, son oeuvre, sa pensée*, 3 vols. (Paris: Ernest Leroux, 1923, 1927, 1928), 1:230, 2:234.

3. Hans Jonas, *Gnosis und spätantiker Geist. II, 1, Von der Mythologie zur mystischen Philosophie*, 2d ed. (Göttingen: Vandenhoeck und Ruprecht, 1966), 201–3.

4. Another form of this criticism is found in the many treatments of Origen as a mystic, as in William Ralph Inge, *Christian Mysticism* (New York: Meridian, 1956 [1899]), 89–91; or Charles Bigg, *The Christian Platonists of Alexandria* (London: Oxford University Press, 1886), 170–71. Both writers

emphasize that Origen assigns the cross only to the lower and inferior grades of the spiritual life.

5. See the conclusions in Henri Crouzel, *Origen: The Life and Thought of the First Great Theologian*, trans. A. S. Worrall (Harper & Row: San Francisco, 1989), 267–69, and Jean Daniélou, *Origène* (Paris: La Table Ronde, 1948).

6. For perspective on Balthasar's work, particularly his views on Origen, I am dependent on his introductory essay in *Spirit and Fire*; on Werner Löser, *Im Geiste des Origenes: Hans Urs von Balthasar als Interpret der Theologie der Kirchenväter* (Frankfurt am Main: Josef Knecht, 1976); and on Angelo Scola, *Hans Urs von Balthasar: A Theological Style* (Grand Rapids, Mich.: Eerdmans, 1995).

7. Hans Urs von Balthasar, *Mysterium Paschale: The Mystery of Easter*, trans. Aidan Nichols, O.P. (Grand Rapids, Mich.: Eerdmans, 1993), 54.

8. The principal source here is Henri de Lubac, *Histoire et Esprit: L'intelligence de l'Écriture d'après Origène* (Paris: Aubier, 1950). This is a very different work from Balthasar's *Spirit and Fire*. The latter is an anthology of selections from Origen's work, the selection being made according to Balthasar's criterion of how best to make sense of Origen for a larger theological enterprise—thus, a classically Germanic undertaking. De Lubac's book is an attempt to appreciate how Origen elucidated the "spiritual sense" of scripture for his own time and thus contributed to a better understanding of the textuality of scripture—a typically French undertaking.

9. See "Tripartite Anthropology: 2, II. *Origen*," 136–44, and "The Fathers and Christian Humanism: 2. Origenian Transposition," 34–39, in Henri de Lubac, *Theology in History, Part One: The Light of Christ*, trans. Anne Englund Nash (San Francisco: Ignatius Press, 1996).

10. See the excellent summary and discussion of de Lubac's theological project in Joseph A. Komonchak, "Theology and Culture at Mid-century: The Example of Henri de Lubac," *Theological Studies* 51 (1990), 579–602.

11. *Histoire et Esprit*, ch. II, 4, "La sagesse et la croix." Especially important is the 1950 essay on Origen in *Recherches dans la Foi: Trois études sur Origène, Saint Anselme et la philosophie chrétienne*, Bibliothèque des Archives de Philosophie 27 (Paris: Beauchesne, 1979), "'Tu m'as trompé, Seigneur': Le commentaire d'Origène sur Jérémie 20, 7," in which there is some contrasting by de Lubac of his way of understanding Origen's construal of this text and Balthasar's understanding of Origen. The essence of the contrast lies in Balthasar's way of finding fault with Origen, when he expounds the notion of "divine deceit" as a providential way of ushering believers into the mysteries of deep wisdom; Balthasar sees in this case only an unorthodox esotericism in Origen. De Lubac, on the other hand, while recognizing the element of Platonic philosophy in Origen, wished to congratulate him for recognizing that "the Word of God, in becoming human,

adapts itself to each of the degrees of existence and thus becomes all things for all people" (56; my translation).

12. Histoire et Esprit, 87 (my translation).

13. Ibid., 91: "Because, for those to whom the world is crucified, and who do not glory in anything more than in the cross, the end of the age has, so to speak, already arrived. Origen could have said, with Romano Guardini: 'The cross is the absolute symbol'" (my translation).

14. De Lubac, Theology in History, 211.

15. De Lubac, Histoire et Esprit, 434.

16. Völker, Das Vollkommenheitsideal des Origenes: Eine Untersuchung zur Geschichte der Frömmigkeit und zu den Anfängen christlicher Mystik, Beiträge zur historischen Theologie 7 (Tübingen: J.C.B. Mohr, 1930).

17. Ibid., 218f.

18. That a gradual "maturing" took place in Origen's views on ethics and ascetics, as his ardor lessened and he learned from experience over the years, is the argument of Henri Crouzel, "La Personnalité d'Origène," Origeniana Tertia: The Third International Colloquium for Origen Studies, ed. Richard Hanson and Henri Crouzel (Rome: Edizioni dell'Ateneo, 1985), 9-25.

19. Crouzel, Origen, 163-69.

20. Crouzel, "Personnalité," 22. It is useful to remember that this way of describing Origen came from his defenders, who, in the interest of orthodoxy, could have erred in claiming too much for Origen. The idea that Origen did theology in a research, investigatory mode is reflected in Athanasius, De Decretis 27, where he contended against his Arian opponents that Origen's statements were sometimes to be properly understood in their context of inquiry and not as reflecting his own settled belief (which was that of the traditional faith of the church).

21. These are his volumes: Théologie de l'image de Dieu chez Origène (Paris: Aubier, 1956), Origène et la "connaissance mystique" (Bruges/Paris, 1961), and Origène et la philosophie (Paris: Aubier, 1962), much of the results of which are contained in Crouzel, Origen.

22. Crouzel, "Personnalité," 13f.; also, less emphatically, Crouzel, Origen, 136.

23. Cf. Crouzel, "Personnalité," 13f., who cites Bernanos's rendering of an agonized director of souls from the time of the Revolution.

24. Brown, The Body and Society, 160-77. Brown speaks of Origen's profound ambivalence about the body, in that it produces torment but is at the same time the necessary vehicle for the education of the soul. "Thus, far from regarding the body as a prison of the soul, Origen arrived at an unexpected familiarity with the body" (165).

25. Marguerite Harl, *Origène et la fonction révélatrice du verbe incarné* (Paris: Éditions du Seuil, 1958), 16f., for the central problematic of Origen's thought, and 366ff. for the general conclusions. Some of her views on how Origen understands the nature of biblical texts as containing "obscurities" that point to the "mystery" are presented in the important essays, "Origène et la sémantique du langage biblique," *Vigiliae Christianae* 26 (1972), 161–87, and "Origène et les interprétations patristiques grecques de la 'obscurité' biblique," *Vigiliae Christianae* 36 (1982), 334–71.

26. Patricia Cox, "Origen and the Bestial Soul: A Poetics of Nature," *Vigiliae Christianae* 36 (1982), 115–40. In contrast to the Origen who was pictured by Jerome as understanding the "connections between soul and body to be distasteful and heretical," she asks "what of the Origen who could find Wisdom herself in the sweetness of an apple? What of the man who could use as figure for the entire cosmos an ensouled beast, immense and enormous?" (116).

27. Henry Chadwick, *Early Christian Thought and the Classical Tradition: Studies in Justin, Clement, and Origen* (New York: Oxford University Press, 1966). To be sure, Chadwick bases his views on the heart of Origen's thought on the *Against Celsus*, as I am doing here. Following the classically Anglican preoccupation (cf. Bigg, *The Christian Platonists of Alexandria*, mentioned earlier) with Origen's universalism—in the sense that Origen allowed for the possible salvation of all souls—Chadwick emphasized Origen's insistence against the Stoics on the divinely controlled rather than naturalist and materialist ending of the world.

Perhaps it is this insistence on freedom in God which most deeply marks Origen's theology with a Biblical stamp. We have seen that the main weight of Celsus's attack falls upon the Biblical doctrine of God. For Celsus there is an unbridgeable gulf beyond the God who is beyond being and this world of change and decay. He scorns the "personalism" of Biblical faith, and opposes to the Christian view a determinism which thinks of providence as simply the natural process at work. The nerve-centre of the debate between Origen and Celsus lies in the possibility of revelation in history: can there be grace?...For him [Origen] the ultimate question is whether God is goodness and love: if so, he cares for his creation and his goodness is the principle we are to discern throughout experience. (119f.)

28. Eugene TeSelle has argued that the massive christocentrism of many Christian theologies reflected the church's powerful, and then declining, relation to the state in post-Constantinian times, such that theologies of Origen's

type (that is, nonchristocentric, not yet wedded to the "archetype Christology" that eventually dominated much Christian thought) were largely superseded. In Origen's time, "the alternative position thrived as long as there was a situation of open encounter, in which one's claims had to be made good in the forum of reason even when it was clear that reason did not solve all problems, in which the gap between potentiality and actuality, demand and fulfillment, had to be closed by decision and enactment. This was the apologetic situation in the patristic age, when there were many philosophers and well-meaning pagans who agreed with the standards and goals taught by the Church, and the real question was where those standards were being taken seriously and those goals being approximated" (*Christ in Context*, 168).

CHAPTER 6

"The Tree of Silly Fruit": Images of the Cross in St. Augustine

John Cavadini

Augustine does not have a theology of the cross per se, if by that is meant a sustained devotion to the cross of Christ as an object of veneration or even as the focal point of a theological discussion of any considerable length. His comments about the cross itself are scattered amid his treatises and letters, sermons and commentaries, and need to be combed out and sifted through, connected and expanded, if we are to have anything like an Augustinian doctrine of the cross.

In another sense, however, Augustine has a very fully developed theology of the cross, if by that is meant a theology of the passion and death of Christ regardless of whether the cross itself is explicitly mentioned. In this chapter I delineate an Augustinian doctrine of the cross in both senses—first, by recovering some of the images and motifs that Augustine assigns to the cross itself, and then by attempting to correlate these images and motifs to Augustine's more expansive discussions of the passion and death of Christ, where, like as not, the cross itself is not mentioned or where a simple mention is left without elaboration.

The best place to begin may be with a discussion of the images for the cross found in Augustine's sermons, for it is in his sermons that we find the most frequent and most colorful references to the cross itself, though frequently they are left undeveloped and we are left looking for further explanation. After examining the images for the cross in the sermons, I will look more widely, examining not only sermons but Augustine's treatises and letters for help in drawing out more fully the meaning and intention of the vivid images Augustine used in preaching.

The Cross as Sign

Augustine frequently comments on the sign of the cross, sketched and fixed on the forehead of catechumens and the baptized. For Augustine, the sign of the cross replaces circumcision, the sign characteristic of and appropriate to the Old Testament.[1] Augustine reminds all Christians that, just as their foreheads have been signed with the cross, so their lives should be conformed to the mysteries that the cross represents, namely, the incarnation and passion of the Lord. They should avoid all behavior that would seem contrary to a life conformed to the cross. For example, should people who have had the sign of the cross fixed on their foreheads be going to the theaters and enjoying their characteristically lewd performances? he asks a congregation in the North African town of Bulla Regia.[2] His give-and-take answer to the congregation is typical of his style of preaching. He has just read a passage from the books of the Maccabees in honor of the seven Jewish martyrs and their martyred mother:

> The spectacle of the holy Maccabees...seemed to me to provide just the right opportunity for admonishing your graces about theatrical shows and spectacles. O my brothers and sisters of Bulla,...in practically all your neighboring towns, this kind of licentious civic piety has fallen silent. Are you not ashamed that among you alone obscenity has remained for sale?...Perhaps you're saying, "It's all very well for you to abstain from these things, you clergy, you bishops, but not for us lay people." So does that really strike you as a fair thing to say?...The apostle wasn't talking to the clergy, not to bishops and priests, when he said, But you are members of Christ [1 Cor 6:15]....A catechumen, perhaps, has a low opinion of his own worth. "I'm just a catechumen," he says. You're a catechumen? "Yes, a catechumen." Do you have one forehead on which you received the sign of Christ, and another which you carry along to the theater?...The sign of Christ's cross is sketched and fixed for you on your forehead![3]

In another sermon, preaching on the feast of the martyr Lawrence, Augustine commends to his congregation the martyr's disdain for temporal goods and temporal life itself in favor of eternal goods and eternal life. If it is objected that pagans and sacrilegious people sometimes prosper while Christians suffer losses, Augustine asks his congregation why they entered the catechumenate or became Christians in the first place:

> Can it be, brothers and sisters, that when we became Christians, we gave our name to Christ and submitted our foreheads to such a tremendous sign, simply in order to avoid [temporal] evils and obtain these [temporal] good things?

That is certainly not how the martyrs acted. Augustine reminds his congregation that they carry on their foreheads the sign of the cross of Christ. This mark or "character," stamped on their foreheads in the same way that recruits to the Roman army had the "character" of their unit tattooed on their bodies, should teach them what they should profess. They should delight not in the sign itself, but in the one who hung on the cross:

> When he was hanging on the cross—the cross you carry on your forehead; don't delight in the sign of the wood, but in the sign of the one hanging on it—so when he was hanging on the cross, he was looking round at the people raving against him, putting up with their insults, praying for his enemies....He said, you see, *Father, forgive them, because they do not know what they are doing* [Luke 3:24]. So here, brothers and sisters, is to be understood from this sign, from this stamp which Christians receive even when they become catechumens, here is to be understood why we are Christians; that it is not for the sake of temporal and passing things, whether good or bad.[4]

Christians place their hope in Christ, not in anything else, not even the sign of the cross in and of itself. Rather, the example of Christ forgiving his enemies, not seeking vengeance, tells us what kind of "character" we have been stamped with, and what sort of character (in the English sense) we are to embody. In deference to eternal goods, Christians are to endure persecution, if necessary, and not seek temporal retaliation against their enemies.

If Christians do not place their hopes even in the sign of the cross, much less should they place their hope in any other kind of sign, such as an amulet or charm for healing. Preaching another homily on the holy martyrs,

Augustine tells his congregation that even though they will probably not be asked to die for their faith, they can share in the heroic struggles of the martyrs in everyday life—for example, on the sickbed. Just as those who were put to death for their faith, the faithful sick who resist hanging amulets and charms dedicated to other gods around their necks are acting as "athletes of Christ," fighting with the cross of Christ that was signed on their foreheads.

> The one who says, "I won't do it; I'm a Christian....These are the sacraments of demons,"...says too "Even if So-and-so was saved that way, I for my part have no wish to be saved that way."...There you can see God's athlete, you can hear the voice of Christ's athlete. Someone indeed who's both sick and sound! Someone who's both weak and strong! A man who's lying on a sickbed and reigning in heaven!...The person who says that sort of thing...is a martyr on his sickbed....He will depart to his Lord, his forehead signed with the cross of Christ, whom he has not insulted with unlawful amulets.[5]

By placing their hope in Christ instead of in charms and amulets, Christians identify themselves with, and conform themselves to, the cross of Christ as fully as did the "athletes of Christ" of old.

In a fragment of a Pentecost sermon, Augustine comments that even highly educated and learned folk are no longer too proud to be signed with the cross, even though decades earlier it had seemed too disgraceful, too much a mark of the unlearned, uneducated disciples who originally preached Christ.

> It was men quite untrained in the liberal arts, and as far as secular disciplines go totally uneducated, unskilled in grammar, unequipped with the techniques of dialectic, it was fishermen whom Christ sent into the sea of the world with the nets of faith, and very few of them at that....And yet by their means he so filled the Churches with every kind of fish, that a great many even of the wise ones of the world, to whom the cross of Christ seemed so disgraceful, are signing themselves with it on the forehead, and setting up in the seat of shame the very thing they thought we should be ashamed of, and about which they used to taunt us.[6]

No Christian, learned or unlearned, should be ashamed of the cross. When Paul says, "Far be it from me to take pride in anything but in the cross of our Lord Jesus Christ"(Gal 6:14), Augustine takes it quite literally, reminding those whose "seat of shame" (forehead) has been signed with the cross that they should be proud, not embarrassed about being so marked. For as the sign of the New Testament, it is the sign of the "humiliation of the Most High," God himself, who accepted it without embarrassment. For us to be ashamed of it is to be ashamed of God's dramatic act of self-abasement, the very thing in which we should glory:

> This is Christian teaching, the rule of humility, the recommendation of humility, that we should not "take pride in anything except the cross of our Lord Jesus Christ."...Now let all our pride be in the cross of Christ, let us not be ashamed of the humiliation of the Most High.[7]

In another passage, Augustine dwells in almost loving detail on this humiliation, emphasizing that it involved the Creator's becoming a creature—and not one famous or celebrated but one rejected, dishonored and condemned to an especially hideous death:

> Among all kinds of death, there was nothing worse than that death. In short, that wherein one is racked by the most intense pains is called "cruciatus," which takes its name from "crux," a cross. For the crucified, hanging on the tree, nailed to the wood, were killed by a slow lingering death. To be crucified was not merely to be put to death; for the victim lived long on the cross....Death stretched itself out that the pain might not be too quickly ended.[8]

Augustine emphasizes that the Lord's humiliation is voluntary. He (in his preexistent state) not only chose to submit to death, but *chose* to submit to this particular kind of death, not a more honorable one. This choice, made in utter freedom of will, both human and divine, makes this death *significant*, makes it a sign. Continuing the homily just cited above, Augustine notes,

> He deigned to be crucified, became obedient even to the death of the cross. He who was about to take away all death, chose the lowest and worst kind of death....It was indeed the worst of deaths, but it was chosen by the Lord. For He was to have that very cross as His sign; that very cross a trophy, as it were, over the vanquished devil,

He was to put on the brow of believers, so that the apostle said, "God forbid that I should glory, save in the cross of our Lord Jesus Christ, by whom the world is crucified to me, and I to the world" [Gal 6:14].[9]

The relation between deliberate and free choice of death on the cross, and of its subsequent value as a sign of the humility of God—and also of the renewed Christian life—is emphasized in a more general way in a sermon preached on Good Friday, sometime before 420.

The fact is...that not even in his mortal flesh did he suffer anything out of necessity, but everything of his own free will. And so it may rightly be assumed that by every single deed that was carried out and recorded about his passion he also wished to signify something to us.[10]

In this sermon, every detail of the passion signifies an element of the Christian life. Christ could have chosen another sign to sum up what "belonging to Christ"—that is, the Christian life—means. But by choosing this death, he chose this sign.

If we are Christians, we belong to Christ. Upon the forehead we bear His sign; and we do not blush because of it, if we also bear it in the heart. His sign is His humility. By a star the Magi knew Him; and this sign was given by the Lord, and it was heavenly and beautiful. He did not desire that a star should be His sign on the forehead of the faithful, but His cross.[11]

Certainly a star on the brows of Christians as an indication of what "belonging to Christ" means would have a very different significance. In the end, those are true Christians who not only have the sign of the Lord's humility on their foreheads, but who bear it in their hearts, and so live lives conformed to the cross, or better, conformed to what the cross signifies, the humility of Christ and the humiliation of God. There is no reason to be ashamed of this, for it is not only a sign of victory over the devil, but even now the sign of the cross has gained such honor that this former instrument of torture is worn on the brows of kings and emperors, and the method of execution itself is no longer used by the Romans, since the guilty man would appear to be honored by being crucified. "What jewel in the crown of rulers is more precious than the name of Christ on their foreheads?" Augustine asks, pointing out that without army or sword the "absurdity" of the cross has triumphed over the whole world and its rulers.[12]

Ephesians 3:17–18 provides Augustine with one of his favorite opportunities for reflecting on the cross of Christ: "that Christ may dwell in your hearts through faith; that you, being rooted and grounded in love, may have power to comprehend with all the saints what is the breadth and length and height and depth." Augustine takes the "breadth and length and height and depth" as a reference to the cross and sees in the passage a description of the Christian life, "rooted and founded in love," as a life conformed to the cross. The *breadth* is the width of the cross on which the hands are outstretched, that is, the width of good works done in charity; the *length* is the length of the cross on which the body is stretched, signifying perseverance in the works of love; the *height* is the part of the cross above the head, signifying our performance of good works not for temporal benefits of goods or praise, but for God alone; the *depth* is the part of the cross buried in the earth, signifying the mystery of grace, in which the life of charity is ultimately rooted:

> If you like, you may fit this manner of life to the cross of your Lord. It's not for nothing, you see, that he chose such a death, seeing that it was in his power to die or not to die. If it was in his power to die or not to die, why shouldn't it be in his power to die this way or that way? So it's not for nothing that he chose the cross, on which to crucify you to this world [cf. Gal 6:14]. The breadth of the cross is given by the horizontal beam, where his hands are fixed, thus signifying good works. Length is given by that part of the upright which extends from the crossbeam to the ground; that's where his body is crucified, and in a manner of speaking stands, and this standing signifies perseverance. Next, height is given by that part of the upright which sticks up above the crossbeam to the head, so that it signifies expectation of the things that are above. And where do we have depth but in the part which is fixed in the ground? Grace, you see, is something secret, that always remains concealed. It can't be seen, but from it rises up what can be seen.[13]

Once again, for Augustine, the sign of the cross is a sign not only in the sense of the mark placed on the forehead, but in the deepest sense of the word, as indicative of the whole Christian life and its proper conformation to the humility of Christ. This exegesis of Ephesians 3:17–18 is one of the most characteristic Augustinian reflections on the cross.[14] It is poignant that in this age and in this world, such a life as Ephesians 3:17–18 describes, the life rooted in love, is the life of the cross.

The Cross as Mousetrap

Another image Augustine is fond of is the cross as a mousetrap:

> The devil was exultant when Christ died, and by that very death of Christ was the devil conquered; it's as though he took the bait in a mousetrap. He was delighted at death, as being the commander of death; what he delighted in, that's where the trap was set for him. The mousetrap for the devil was the cross of the Lord; the bait he would be caught by, the death of the Lord.[15]

This image is further elaborated in another sermon, where in addition to the image of the mousetrap, we find the image of a fishhook and a lion trap, and of the devil as the avid connoisseur of death, "greedy for death, a hoarder of death":

> Christ is life; why did life die? The soul didn't die, nor did the Word die; the flesh died, in order that in it death might die. He suffered death, he slew death; he put a bait for the lion in the trap. If the fish didn't want to swallow anything, it wouldn't be caught with a hook. The devil was greedy for death, the devil was a hoarder of death. The cross of Christ was the mousetrap; the death of Christ, or rather the mortal flesh of Christ, was like the bait in the mousetrap. He came, he swallowed it and was caught.[16]

The sermon goes on to cite 1 Corinthians 15:54 ("Death has been swallowed up in victory"), suggesting that this verse may have prompted Augustine's use of the trap metaphor (though he may have known earlier Latin use of a somewhat similar metaphor).[17]

In any event, the theory behind the use of the metaphor is that the devil justly puts to death those who, by original sin, have followed Adam in yielding to the devil. Thus we all have something belonging to the devil in us, that is, sin, by which he justly claims us. But in the devil's greed for death, in his joy at killing, he neglects to notice one thing—Jesus is sinless. So freely and so fully did the Word of God become one of us, so fully did he identify with our plight and enter into liability to death, that the devil did not recognize his compassion, mistaking it for the guilt that deserves death. He put the innocent one to an undeserved death. Now he is told, "You've put to death one who had no debt; now hand over the debtors."[18] In an odd way, the compassion of Christ would not have been disclosed apart from the devil's lust for killing, but once disclosed, the moving, persuasive force of the compassion of God renders the devil's blandishments impotent to persuade anyone who believes. The trap is sprung!

The Cross as Lampstand

Augustine uses this image for the cross as part of his interpretation of Matthew 5:15, "Nobody lights a lamp and puts it under a tub, but on a lampstand, so that it may shine on all who are in the house." In a sermon given in honor of St. Stephen, Augustine constructs a little allegory. The house is the world, the lampstand is the cross of Christ, the lamp shining from the lampstand is Christ hanging on the cross.[19] He uses the allegory as the basis for an exhortation against taking credit for any virtue or good deeds we have done, as though God's grace were not ultimately responsible. Earlier in the sermon, Augustine had observed that Jesus came into this world precisely as a lover of enemies, since indeed we, on whose account he came, were all of us enemies:

> After all, he came into the world as a lover of his enemies, he found absolutely all of us his enemies, he didn't find anyone a friend. It was for enemies that he shed his blood, but by his blood that he converted his enemies. With his blood he wiped out his enemies' sins; by wiping out their sins, he made friends out of enemies.[20]

Augustine goes on to point out how Christ was able to love his enemies even as he hung on the cross. He understood that it was their blindness that caused them to crucify him, and so he prayed for their forgiveness.

"Father, forgive them, because they do not know what they are doing" [Luke 23:34]; after all, it's blindness that is crucifying me. Blindness was crucifying him; and the crucified was making an eye-salve for them from his blood.[21]

That Jesus could forgive an act of violence against himself as gratu-itous as the crucifixion is a brilliant light, opening up the eyes of all to the love of God on the one hand, and to their own sinfulness on the other. It provides a place for all of us to stand and shine as Christ did.

The response of Augustine's congregation was to complain that for-giving one's enemies was all very well for the Son of God, but that they could never do what Christ did:

He could do that, as the Son of God, as the Only Son of the Father. Yes it was flesh hanging there, but God was hidden within. As for us, though, what are we, to do that sort of thing?

Augustine counters that Stephen, who was not God incarnate, was able to forgive his enemies even while he was being stoned.

Look, there's Stephen's light shining, that lamp shining; let's think about him. Nobody should say, "It's too much for me." He was human, you're human. But it wasn't from himself that he got the capacity to do it.[22]

In other words, there is a way in which the congregation is right; we can't conform our lives to Christ's without God's doing it (through grace). Augustine tells them that they, too, can drink from the same spring that Stephen did, and that they have only to ask. But when we do succeed in accomplishing a good work, like the forgiveness of our ene-mies, we must then confess the source of the deed in God's grace given through the one who suffered for us on the cross. That is what it means to shine from the lampstand of the cross.

It is Paul, once again, who provides the paradigmatic instance here:

From this very lampstand that man was also shining who first kept the coats of the stone throwers, Paul from being Saul, a lamb from being a wolf, both small and great; the robber of lambs, and the shepherd of lambs. He was shining from this very lampstand when he said, "Far be it, though, from me to boast of anything but the cross of our Lord Jesus Christ, through whom the world has been crucified to me and I to the world" [Gal 6:14].[23]

Doing deeds of virtue without acknowledging the cross of Christ would be to "boast" in ourselves and so to remain dark, unable to bear witness to the love of God shed abroad for all. Putting our actions on the lampstand, the cross of Christ, makes our actions light, makes them translucent to the love of God and so participatory in the revelation of God's love through Christ. In another sermon Augustine puts it more bluntly:

> Listen, so that you may understand that the lampstand is the cross of Christ. "Nobody lights a lamp and puts it under the bushel, but on the lampstand....So let your light shine before men, that they may see our good works, and glorify...your Father who is in heaven" [Matt 5:14-16]. Through your good works, may they glorify your Father. You were not able to light yourselves in order to be lamps, not able to put yourselves on the lampstand; let him be glorified who did all this for you. Glory in the lampstand. Always, lamp, preserve humility in the lampstand, so that you may keep your brightness; take good care you are not snuffed out by pride. After all, what were you, human?...Even if you were born a noble, you were born naked....At birth, poor and rich are equally naked.[24]

In Christ on the cross, God had laid aside all grounds for boasting, and in our devotion to God in his self-imposed humiliation, we too are laying aside all grounds for boasting except in the cross. Thus will our good works shine unto the glory of the Father (Matt 5:16), as though on a lampstand.[25]

The Cross as a Classroom

Contrasting the disciples' loss of hope after the crucifixion with the good thief's willingness to learn to hope from Jesus, even as Jesus was hanging on the cross, Augustine remarks that while the disciples had forgotten their teacher, the good thief saw the cross as a classroom: "That cross was a classroom; that's where the Teacher taught the thief; the tree he was hanging on became the chair he was teaching from."[26]

Also, Jesus' words from the cross to the Beloved Disciple and Mary are also of a "moral" character, as Augustine says, meant to impart instruction to us all.

> The Good Teacher does what He thereby reminds us ought to be done, and by His own example instructed His disciples that care for their parents ought to be a matter of concern to pious children: as if that tree to which the members of the dying One were affixed were the very Chair of office from which the Master was imparting instruction.[27]

The passage seems almost to trivialize Jesus' words on the cross, but Augustine rescues it, pointing out that Jesus did not give this instruction as God, but rather as a man and son, for the benefit of the mother whom he was now leaving behind. In other words, Jesus' instructions on the cross come from the vocabulary of the divine humiliation, of God's identification with our state and condition. Jesus' own family was as fragile as any other human family, subject to the disruptive power of death (even the premature death of a child before its mother). There is also, in the metaphor of the cross as a classroom or professorship, an echo of the contrast Augustine is fond of drawing between the educated elite and Jesus and (especially) the apostles as simple workmen, who nevertheless had a dazzling effect on the whole world, including (eventually) the learned. This connection moves us nicely to the next image to be considered.

The Cross as a Boat

Being stamped with the cross reclaims Christians from submersion in this world, so that in some sense they are now aliens here.[28] This is one of the most familiar and persistent images for the cross in Augustine's work, equally prominent in the sermons as it is in other works. This image of the cross is used especially in discussions of the learned, in particular those schooled in philosophical disciplines. Augustine cedes to them the status of spiritual adepts (so to speak). They had acquired contemplative skills, and had successfully ascended from consideration of created reality to the "vision" or direct awareness, however dim or intermittent, of God's eternal and incorporeal substance itself. In a typical passage, Augustine describes their astonishing spiritual progress:

But truly there have been some philosophers of this world who have sought for the Creator by means of the creature; for He can be found by means of the creature, as the apostle plainly says, "For the invisible things of Him from the creation of the world are clearly seen, being understood by the things that are made" [Rom 1:20]....Those, therefore, concerning whom he said, "Who, when they had known God" [Rom 1:21], saw this which John says, that by the Word of God all things were made. For these things are also found in the books of the philosophers: and that God has an Only-begotten son, by whom are all things.[29]

The philosophers had pierced through creation to see the essence of God so fully that, without scripture, they had been able not only to know God, but to see that God has an only-begotten Son (of course the philosophers would not have used the word *Son* to describe the second hypostasis emanating from the Father or the *One*). One would think, therefore, that Augustine would approve their spiritual advancement.

On the contrary, Augustine is rather dubious about it. He grants that they have seen the very essence of God, THAT WHICH IS. But without faith in Christ, the very vision of God is, in a way, useless, unassimilable. People who attain this vision without faith in Christ are like travelers who can see the destination they want to reach but have no way of reaching it:

Someone may have applied the strength of his mind to touch THAT WHICH IS, but how can he reach that which he may in any way have touched with his mind? It is as if one were to see his native land at a distance, and the sea intervening; he sees whither he would go, but he has not the means of going.[30]

Not only is this vision not useful, it is in fact dangerous without faith in Christ, an obstacle that must be overcome. It may be saying too much to call the vision of God an obstacle, but, for Augustine, it is at least a kind of temptation. Without faith in Christ, the very vision of God, however partial, is a moment of supreme temptation, a moment most vulnerable to the distortion that Augustine calls pride. It is tempting, indeed irresistible from Augustine's point of view, to avoid seizing the vision for oneself, to avoid calling oneself "wise" and wanting to be known as such.

They saw whither they must come; but ungrateful to Him who afforded them what they saw, they wished to ascribe to themselves what they saw; and having become proud, they lost what they saw....When they were proud, they said that they were wise.[31]

For to advance to the vision of God through what one assumes is one's own hard work tempts one to deny the distance between God and oneself, and so, in effect, to claim divine status. God, however, acts in an opposite way. The Word of God became incarnate and suffered on the cross precisely to provide a way to cross over the sea of worldly pride:

> That there might be a way by which we could go, He has come from Him to whom we wished to go. And what has He done? He has appointed a tree by which we may cross the sea. For no one is able to cross the sea of this world, unless borne by the cross of Christ....[The philosophers] were able to see THAT WHICH IS, but they saw it from afar: they were unwilling to hold the lowliness of Christ, in which ship they might have arrived in safety, at that which they were able to see from afar; and the cross of Christ appeared vile to them. The sea has to be crossed, and do you despise the wood? O, proud wisdom! You laugh to scorn the crucified Christ; it is He whom you see from afar: "In the beginning was the Word, and the Word was with God" [John 1:1]. But why was he crucified? Because the wood of His humiliation was needful to you....Believe in the crucified One, and you shall arrive thither. On account of you was He crucified, to teach you humility.[32]

In loving Christ, Christians are loving the humility of God (and the compassion behind it).[33] In loving humility, they have begun to renounce pride, and to undertake the journey—not literally from place to place but a journey of the affections,[34] a process of conforming loves and desires to the cross, or more precisely, to the Crucified. To believe in the Crucified is to embark on a journey of the affections in which one is "drawn" (or as Hill more dramatically translates it, "dragged") by the sweetness of the one in whom you have placed your faith. Commenting in a sermon on John 6:44, Augustine notes:

> *Nobody can come to me, unless the Father who sent me drags him* [John 6:44]. He didn't say "leads," but "drags." This violence happens to

the heart, not to the flesh. So why be surprised? Believe, and you come; love, and you are dragged. Don't regard this violence as harsh and irksome; on the contrary it is sweet and pleasant. It's the very pleasantness of the thing that drags you to it. Isn't a sheep dragged, or drawn irresistibly, when it's hungry and grass is shown to it? And I presume it is not being moved by bodily force, but by desire. In this way you, too, come each one of you to Christ; no need to plan long voyages. Where you believe, that's where you come. After all, to one who is everywhere one comes by loving, not by sailing. But even on this sort of voyage the waves wash over you and the stormy winds do blow of various trials and temptations; so believe in the one who was crucified, let your faith board the wood of the cross. You won't be drowned, but borne up by the wood instead. That, yes that is the way in which the multitudinous seas of this world were navigated by the one who said, "But far be it from me to boast, except in the cross of our Lord Jesus Christ" [Gal 6:14].[35]

Augustine finishes this passage with a favorite biblical verse about the cross. Paul's call to glory in nothing but the cross is fulfilled by one whose affections have been conformed to the cross, shaped by attraction to the God who out of compassion for us humiliated himself.

The Cross as a "Tree of Silly Fruit"

This image comes from *Sermon* 174.3, a commentary on the story of Zacchaeus the tax collector, who was so short he needed to climb a nearby sycamore tree to get a better look at Jesus in a crowd (Luke 19:1–10). Augustine remarks that the correct translation of the Greek word *sycamore* into Latin is "silly fig," so that a sycamore tree is actually a "tree of silly fruit." Armed with this (charming but false) etymology, Augustine finds that the sycamore Zacchaeus climbed to see Jesus better is a figure for the folly of the cross. In a way it *was* the cross. If the cross itself is not an end but a sign, a symbol for the humility of God, then who has embraced that humility—and so the cross—better than Zacchaeus? He wanted to see Jesus so badly that he was not afraid to admit it to the whole crowd by doing something silly in front of them all—climbing a tree. Zacchaeus is humble enough to stop relying on his own stature, his own *virtus* or strength, to attain the vision of God, and he doesn't care how silly he looks in the process. He is a model for Christians who have had the sign of Christ fixed on their foreheads and who should not blush out of shame[36] but instead rely on the cross to convey them to the vision of God. In his humility, Zacchaeus has actually climbed the cross of Christ, which, to the crowd, is only a sycamore, a "tree of silly fruit," a tree that bears folly.

> Climb the tree on which Jesus hung for you, and you will see Jesus. And what kind of tree did Zacchaeus climb? A sycamore....Sycamores are what a fruit is called that is like figs; and yet there's a definite difference, which those who've seen or tasted them can tell. However, as far as the meaning of the name goes, sycamores translate into English [Latin] as "silly figs." Now look at my friend Zacchaeus, look at him please, wanting to see Jesus in the crowd and not being able to. He was lowly, you see, the crowd was proud; and the crowd, as is the way with a crowd, was hindering itself from seeing the Lord well.[37]

Augustine constructs a little allegory on this passage. Literally, the short man Zacchaeus has done something laughable by climbing the tree to see Jesus. This turns the sycamore into a figure for the cross. But the crowd, too, takes on a role in the allegory. They become the worldly wise, who believe that those who worship God by bearing the character of Christ, forgiving their enemies, are foolish:

> The crowd, you see, says to the lowly, to people walking the way of humility, who leave the wrongs they suffer in God's hands, and don't insist on getting their own back on their enemies; the crowd jeers at them and says, "you helpless, miserable clod, you can't even stick up for yourself and get your own back." The crowd gets in the way and prevents Jesus from being seen; the crowd which boasts and crows, when it is able to get its own back, blocks the sight of the one who said, as he hung on the cross, "Father, forgive them, for they know not what they are doing" [Luke 23:34].[38]

Those who would forgive their enemies are just the sort of persons, the crowd decides, who would be foolish enough to worship a crucified God:

Finally, the wise of this world jeer at us about the cross of Christ, and say, "What sort of minds have you people got, who worship a crucified God?" What sort of minds have we got? Certainly not your sort. "The wisdom of this world is folly with God" [1 Cor 3:19]....The reason, after all, you can't see Jesus, is that you are ashamed to climb the sycamore tree.[39]

Zacchaeus, who "imagined it was a marvelous piece of luck, quite beyond words, to see Christ passing by"; who was not embarrassed to leave the crowd behind and climb a tree to see him, did something silly, was humble enough to do something silly, and found that he had thereby welcomed Christ into his home. Zacchaeus, the laughably short man, had in his very laughableness known the suffering of Christ, had climbed "the tree of silly fruit," and seen farther than the crowd into the very heart of the Wisdom that is wiser than human beings. The literal and the allegorical meld here in Zacchaeus's welcoming Jesus, true Wisdom, into his home and his heart.[40]

At this point we can use Augustine's exegesis of the story of Zacchaeus to integrate the various images from the sermons. Augustine began his sermon on Zacchaeus commenting that Christ is the "wisdom and power of God" (1 Cor 1:24)—"Wisdom," divine herself, "who orders all things sweetly" (Wis 8:1), the one "through whom the world was made" (John 1:10). Unfortunately, "the world knew him not." The blindness of the world is caused by pride, the desire to replace God's power with one's own power, *power* and *wisdom* to *order things sweetly* with ourselves at the center, the *power* to exact vengeance, to conquer enemies and make friends subservient, and the *wisdom* to know how. Or, when I turn away from such crude displays of power, still, I want my virtue praised, my justice recognized, my courage honored, my merits recognized and rewarded by God, as though the world were ordered and set up precisely to congratulate me. How do I break out of this failure of imagination?

It is God who does it, Wisdom herself, by becoming a human being.[41] A virgin conceives someone wholly untouched by the wisdom of the world. The man conceived, Jesus, did not merit his assumption into one person by the Wisdom of God: "It was an act of pure, gratuitous grace,"[42] an act, as Augustine characterizes it, of perfect *humanity* on the part of God:

After all, people are said in particular to be human who show some humanity, above all by giving hospitality to human persons. So if human beings are called human because they receive human beings into their homes, how human must that one be who received humanity into himself by becoming human?[43]

The Wisdom by which God ordered all, created all, is revealed as a perfect humanity—as grace itself, generosity itself, hospitality itself. The point is not lost on Zacchaeus, who returns the hospitality of God, inviting Jesus into his home. But there is more, for in the incarnation God's act of grace is also an act of perfect compassion or mercy toward those who were not simply nothing, as before creation, but had made themselves into enemies of God. This point is not lost on Zacchaeus either, who realizes he is a sinner, a tax collector, but he no longer cares. He has climbed the cross, where the humanity of God is most perfectly revealed as God's compassion in Jesus' forgiveness of the enemies, all of us, who killed him. Zacchaeus has seen the mercy of Jesus, and so he has, even before the crucifixion itself, in Augustine's phrase, climbed the "tree of silly fruit," which contradicts everything we might have expected about God and God's power. Climbing the cross with Zacchaeus, we see the Creator's intent, Wisdom itself, fully revealed as compassion.

Conclusion

The sign of the cross is the sign of God's compassion; the lampstand is that on which God's compassion shone forth; the classroom of the cross reveals its teacher as the one who teaches us the reality of his humanity, that is, his compassion, which cost Life itself his life; the boat that will take us back to Christ is the compassion of God revealed on the cross. Clinging to it, we will not be tempted to call ourselves "wise" because we have ascended to contemplative vision, but in our love for the compassionate Jesus, we find ourselves loving humility, hoping to set up all our virtues on the lampstand of the cross, where they will be so many testimonies to the one who has loved us with a perfect compassion. We have climbed the tree of silly fruit, where even forgiveness of our enemies is not an occasion of pride in spiritual accomplishment but a solidarity with the lowliness of God. In the process, we become more human, more humane, and thus become more Godlike, while our pride had made us both less like God and less humane. The cross enables us to see God's grace in the incarnation precisely as God's compassion. This is the truth that Augustine wants to illuminate through his use of these various images, including the image of the mousetrap. It was not the incarnation per se that trapped the devil, but rather the cross, which revealed a vulnerability the devil could not resist, for that is all that the devil could see in Christ's compassion.

Each of these images also calls for the Christian life to be conformed to the cross. The sign of the cross identifies Christian life as that conformed to the character of Christ, which is the humility of God. The cross as classroom and as mousetrap invites us to ponder the depth of the humility of God incarnate, and the cross as lampstand invites us to attribute even our most excellent, virtuous deeds to their source in the humility of the Lord, so that this wondrous character might shine through them. The boat of the cross invites us to travel a journey of the affections, where they are reshaped according to the compassionate humility revealed on the cross. And when we are finally conformed to the cross, we will have climbed that tree of silly fruit, which will be in the end our best vantage point for the vision of God.

NOTES

1. Sermon 160.6. Augustine says that the cross is signed on a place open to public view, the forehead, while circumcision is a sign not open to public view, just as the Christian dispensation was said to remove the veil from the revelation of the Old Testament (citing 2 Cor 3:18). The comparison is somewhat forced. Translations of texts from the *Sermons* of Augustine are taken from Edmund Hill, O.P.'s, translation in the various volumes of *The Works of St. Augustine: A Translation for the Twenty-first Century*, Part III, vols. 1–11, *Sermons* (Hyde Park, N.Y.: New City Press, 1990–97).

2. *Sermon* 301A.8.

3. *Sermon* 301A.7–8.

4. This and the previous passage are cited from *Sermon* 302.3 (cf. 302.10). See Hill's note on the "character" stamped onto Roman soldiers (8:312 n.6).

5. *Sermon* 335D.3.

6. *Sermon* 272A. The forehead is the "seat of shame" because it is where blushes first become visible.

7. *Sermon* 160.5, 7.

8. *Tractates on the Gospel of John* 36.4. Translations from the retouched homilies known as the *Tractates on the Gospel of John* are taken from John Gibb and James Innes, *Nicene and Post-Nicene Fathers*, First Series, vol. 7 (1888; reprinted by Hendrickson Publishing, 1995), though I have felt free to adjust these translations where needed.

9. *Tractates on the Gospel of John* 36.4.

10. *Sermon* 218.1.

11. *Tractates on the Gospel of John* 3.2.

12. *Sermon* 51.2.

13. *Sermon* 53.16 (dated 413-16). Augustine goes on to explain that the life conformed to the cross will grant the purity of heart of which Matthew 5:8 speaks, thus begetting vision of God. It is interesting to note that in a much earlier treatment of Matthew 5:8, the cross has not yet achieved the prominence in Augustine's thinking that it has here. In *Our Lord's Sermon on the Mount* (393-96), the person who is pure of heart and sees God is the one who rises above human praise and looks only for divine approval, that is, looks at God alone. By the time we get to *Sermon* 53, it is the cross of Christ that effects this purification.

14. See, for example, especially *Sermons* 53.15-16; 165.2-5, 9 (sec. 9 emphasizes the rootedness of this life in grace and not in our virtue); *Letters* 140.26.64; 147.13.34; 55.14.25; and also *De Doctrina* 2.41.62; *Tractates on the Gospel of John* 118.5; *Ennarationes in Psalmos* 104.14. Letter 55 contains the earliest instance of this exegesis of Ephesians 3:17-19, and it is interesting to note that here, ca. 400, and thus eleven years before the Pelagian controversy begins, the depth is faith, not grace. Note the exegesis of Ephesians 3:17-18 in *Tractates on the Gospel of John* 118.5, where Augustine explicitly unites the two major senses of the cross as a sign, namely, as that to which the Christian life is conformed, and as a cross mark traced out on the foreheads of believers and over baptismal water and chrism.

15. *Sermon* 263.2.

16. *Sermon* 265D.5.

17. See Rufinus, *Commentary on the Apostles' Creed* 14.

18. *Sermon* 265D.4.

19. *Sermon* 317.4. Cf. *Tractates on the Gospel of John* 97.3.

20. *Sermon* 317.2.

21. Ibid. Cf. the imagery of the "medicine of his blood" at *Sermon* 302.3 and elsewhere.

22. *Sermon* 317.4.

23. Ibid.

24. *Sermon* 289.6.

25. It is interesting to note that in *Our Lord's Sermon on the Mount*, written much earlier than the sermons we have been studying here, Augustine does not mention the cross at all in connection with Matt 7:18 (see *Our Lord's Sermon on the Mount* 1.7). Augustine does comment that in saying Let your works shine..., the Lord is admonishing his disciples not to seek praise for themselves, but for the Father; still it does not occur to Augustine that such a sacrifice of praise is patterned after the cross, and made possible only by the cross. The Pauline connection between grace and the cross lies mostly unexamined in Augustine's work until the Pelagian controversy.

26. Sermon 234.2.

27. *Tractates on the Gospel of John* 119.2.

28. *Sermon* 75.2.

29. *Tractates on the Gospel of John* 2.4. See also the famous passage at *Confessions* 7.9.13.

30. *Tractates on the Gospel of John* 2.2. See also *Confessions* 7.20.26.

31. *Tractates on the Gospel of John* 2.4.

32. Ibid.

33. A common theme in Augustine, but see, e.g., *Tractates on the Gospel of John* 11.2, "It was because of his compassion, then, that he suffered."

34. *Tractates on the Gospel of John* 36.8. A famous Augustinian motif (see, e.g., *On Christian Doctrine* 1), which is taken up by Bonaventure, among others.

35. *Sermon* 131.2.

36. *Sermon* 174.3. "Let Zacchaeus grasp the sycamore tree, the humble person climb the cross. That's little enough, merely to climb it; we mustn't be ashamed of the cross of Christ, we must fix it on our foreheads, where the seat of shame is; yes, there, there above all where our blushes show, that's where we must firmly fix what we should never blush for."

37. *Sermon* 174.3.

38. Ibid.

39. Ibid.

40. There is one other relatively minor image for the cross in Augustine's preaching, which I note here for the sake of completeness, and that is the image of the cross as key, which opens things that were closed and so reveals things

that were hidden. Augustine has in mind the completion of the figurative revelation of the Old Testament (*Ennarationes in Psalmos* 46.1).

41. *Sermon* 174.1.
42. *Sermon* 174.2.
43. *Sermon* 174.1.

CHAPTER 7

Jesus' Death Is Real:
An Augustinian Spirituality
of the Cross

John Cavadini

The cross and the passion of Christ were not always important to Augustine's theology or spirituality. Neither is mentioned in his earliest works, but they begin to appear very early in the 390s, even before his ordination as priest. The earliest elements of an Augustinian spirituality of the cross are anti-Manichaean in provenance, since they are found in dialogues and treatises written against Manichaeism, the dualist religion that Augustine saw as a Christian heresy, and to which he himself had belonged before his conversion.

The Manichees in Northern Africa professed many familiar beliefs from other Gnostic religions. They did not, for example, believe that the sufferings of the historical Christ were real, but rather that the Savior had come in the likeness of human flesh to symbolize the vicissitudes of the soul. According to Manichaean doctrine, the soul was a fragment of the luminous divine nature, alienated from, and in the captivity of, the kingdom of evil and darkness. Trapped in a material body by the forces of the kingdom of darkness, the soul had forgotten its origin. The Savior descended from the heavenly realms not actually to enter a body and to suffer (for that would be to involve himself in the same plight of mortality and forgetfulness that the soul is in), but to reveal to the soul that it too had descended hither and would return to the fullness of the kingdom of light once it was freed from the body. In other words, the Manichees believed that Christ the Savior did not suffer, because he did not really become entrapped in a body, but the divine nature in effect could suffer and did in the many fragments that had actually become entrapped in a body.

Writing in 392 against Fortunatus the Manichaean, Augustine argues that it is a serious error to believe that the divine nature can suffer in any way:

> First of all I regard it as the height of error to believe that Almighty God, in whom is our one hope, is in any part either violable, or contaminable, or corruptible. This I know your heresy affirms, though not indeed in the words I now use.[1]

Fortunatus was apparently no match for Augustine in this debate, as he is virtually converted by the end of it, but he did protest that he did not exactly believe that God is violable or corruptible, but that the alienation of fragments of the divine nature—of "souls"—came about willingly. The divine nature let part of itself be fragmented into "souls" and as such captured by the darkness, so that there would be a limit to the kingdom of evil:

> Fortunatus said: We have already said that God can in no way suffer injury, and we have said that the soul is in a contrary nature, therefore that it imposes a limit on the contrary nature....For He Himself said, "I have power to lay down my soul and power to take it. The Father gave to me the power of laying down my soul, and of taking it up" [John 10:18]. To what soul, therefore, did God who spoke in the Son refer? Evidently our soul, which is held in these bodies, which came of His will, and of His will is again taken up."[2]

God is "incorruptible"[3] in this view because the souls that are the entrapped fragments of divinity are not destroyed, though they are submerged in evil so fully that their free will is compromised and they are impelled to sin by the evil forces entrapping them.[4]

Still, the original "will" that prompted the souls to submit to the kingdom of evil does in fact set limits to evil, since the soul is not destroyed, and since the sins it commits cannot be attributed to the soul but rather to the usurpation of the kingdom of darkness that compels it to sin. The Savior comes to remind the soul of its origin and destiny:

Fortunatus said:..."Let this mind be in you that was also in Christ
Jesus, who when He had been constituted in the form of God,
thought it not robbery to be equal with God; but emptied Himself
receiving the form of a servant, having been made in the likeness of
men" [Phil 2:5-8]. We have this in mind therefore about ourselves,
which we have also about Christ, "who when he was constituted in
the form of God, was made obedient even unto death" that he
might show a similitude of our souls. And like as He showed in
Himself the similitude of death, and having been raised from the
midst of the dead showed that He was from the Father, in the same
manner we think it will be with our souls, because through Him we
shall have been able to be freed from this death.[5]

The Savior does not die; he simply reveals a similitude or likeness
of our death, rising from which he shows us that we are not destroyed by
death because we, like Christ, are from the Father. The soul must act on
the knowledge that is revealed in the "similitude" of Christ's death and
resurrection, which serve as an instruction for souls to repent of the evil
they have done unwillingly, and to segregate themselves from the forces
of evil by practicing good deeds and so obtaining reconciliation and
eventual reunion with the rest of the kingdom of light.[6]

Augustine continues to object that the Manichaean doctrine
involves God in corruptibility and suffering. He counters Fortunatus's
frequent query as to how the soul became involved in suffering and misery in the first place—and answers that the soul's free choice turned it to
evil, and that God's grace can free it. But Augustine, though he chides
Fortunatus for not answering his questions, seems himself unable to
counter or to match Fortunatus's reflections on the cross or the passion.
Augustine seems not to have reflected theologically on the cross or the
passion of Christ, or, for that matter, on any sort of redemptive suffering,
while Fortunatus has.

Fortunatus's position on the inviolability of the divine nature is
not simply metaphysical—namely, that the soul is divine so that no matter how mixed up it gets in the doings of evil against its will, it cannot
be mutated or changed into evil—it is also in the "will" to lay itself
down to fragmentation and alienation so that the goodness of the
divine nature is especially revealed and shown to be inalienably good,

John Cavadini

the evil forces being vanquished by this voluntary "passion"[7] or suffering of God's nature.

However, this position has changed by 400, the time of Augustine's debate with Faustus the Manichaean. I bring up for discussion here only a small part of the massive *Reply to Faustus the Manichaean*, a passage in which Augustine discusses one of the most famous Manichaean doctrines, that of the "Jesus patabilis" (the "mortal" Jesus, the Jesus "susceptible to suffering"). Apparently, the Savior's "similitude" or enacted likeness to our soul's plight extended not only to fragments of divinity/light entrapped as souls in human bodies, but to fragments of the divine light entrapped elsewhere, such as in the bodies of fruit hanging from trees. Augustine objects to the sheer materialistic dimensions of this doctrine (the idea that physical light was part of God's nature), continuing to object that it means that the divine nature has suffered.

Fortunatus states his position as follows:

By the influence and spiritual infusion [of the Holy Spirit], the earth conceives and brings forth the mortal Jesus, who, as hanging from every tree, is the life and salvation of humans. Though you oppose these doctrines so violently, your religion resembles ours in attaching the same sacredness to the bread and wine that we do to everything.[8]

The Savior's passion and suffering, even though not true suffering but rather a representation of the passion of the fragmented divine nature, still gives the key to the interpretation of nature and of the cosmos; it is a place defined by the suffering of the divine nature, which, by its willingness to suffer, has placed a limit on the kingdom of evil. In a sense, every tree is the cross, and every cross begets life.[9] Every cross except, that is, the cross of Christ, which simply represents, and so reveals, the world as a place redeemed by the suffering of God, but which, strictly speaking, itself plays no salvific role.

In Augustine's refutation of this position we can see how much his theology of the cross of Christ has developed since his earlier work. Augustine insists that the Manichaean system is in effect a return to the mythological religion of the pagans. The suffering of light contained in fruit, the idea that the earth and its vegetation can conceive the Divine

172

nature under the influence of the Holy Spirit, and so on, are simply myths.[10] Any doctrine implying the suffering of the divine nature cannot but fragment into mythology. If Jesus' death on the cross is only a kind of virtual suffering presented by a spiritual presence, a similitude of the plight of the fragmented divine nature in ourselves and in the rest of the cosmos, it is merely the revelation of a myth.

But Augustine appears to have absorbed something from Manichaean teaching in his polemical encounter with it, and that is the value of a doctrine of salvation focused in some sense on the suffering of God, and eight years after his dialogue with Fortunatus, he emphasizes the sacrifice of the Mediator, who is both God and human[11] and who suffers in his human nature.

> We believe and confess Christ the Son of God, and the Word of God, to have become flesh without suffering defilement, because the divine substance is not defiled by flesh.[12]

The divine nature does not die: that would be mythology; but rather God the Word becomes flesh, is truly born of a mother, suffers, and dies as flesh, not as divinity. Augustine comments later in the treatise,

> We believe, then, that Christ was born of the Virgin Mary, because it is so written in the Gospel; we believe that He died on the cross, because it is so written in the Gospel; we believe that both His birth and death were real, because the Gospel is no fiction. Why he chose to suffer all these things in a body taken from a woman is a matter known only to Himself.[13]

Augustine presents Catholic Christology as a way to describe God's involvement in our human plight, which is not a myth but real, and real in the only way that suffering can be real as we know it, that is, as the suffering of a historical person. Anything less is a fiction:

> A mere spiritual presence could not have made him liable to these sufferings, and in his bodily presence he could not be at the same time in the sun, in the moon, and on the cross.[14]

For Augustine, the problem with the specifically Manichaean version of this doctrine is that it makes the suffering of God into a myth, an unreality, a "fable" or a fiction. The suffering of God is mythic unless it is somehow the suffering of a historical person.

But as the suffering of a historical person, it is the suffering of the Mediator, his sacrifice, and, far from its being a similitude of the suffering of the divine nature in the cosmos, all other sacrifices are prefigurations (Old Testament sacrifices), imitations (pagan sacrifices) or continuations of it (the Eucharist):

> The typical rite of blood-shedding in sacrifice dates from the earliest ages, pointing forward from the outset of human history to the passion of the Mediator.[15]

Again,

> Before the coming of Christ, the flesh and blood of this sacrifice were foreshadowed in the animals slain; in the passion of Christ the types were fulfilled by the true sacrifice; after the ascension of Christ, this sacrifice is commemorated in the sacrament.[16]

In other words, he has reversed the Manichaean paradigm. Where they saw in the suffering of Jesus a simulated representation of the suffering and destiny of the fragmented divine nature, Augustine sees in the cross of Jesus the reality of God's gracious identification with our plight, the true sacrifice to which all other sacrifices are in some way conformed. This sacrifice is an act of the will of a historical person even as it is an act of the Word of God, who chose to become flesh and suffer in the flesh. Against the Manichaeans, who see in the Eucharist a veneration for bread and wine similar, though narrower, than their veneration for all light-bearing produce, Augustine sees the Eucharist as a memorial and a participation in the sacrifice of Christ. Thus by hearing the gospel preached and participating in the Eucharist, we do not come to a saving knowledge of our own true nature and destiny as fragments of the divine nature entrapped in matter, but we discover what God did to "reconcile us to Himself in the remission of sins through our Lord Jesus Christ."[17] Our task, in faith, hope, and love, is to be conformed to this gracious act of God, at once the act of a human being, and "to present [our] bodies as a living sacrifice, holy, acceptable to God" (Rom 12:1).[18] Augustine has in a way turned the Manichaean soteriology inside out by insisting that the suffering of God is not real if it is the (mythic) suffering of the divine nature, but only if it is the suffering of a historical person. Augustine's focus on Christ's suffering as the suffering of God made real in a historical person enables the theology of the cross embodied in the images examined in the last chapter to arise. And during the course of writing his two great treatises, *On the Trinity* and *City of God*, he returned to develop the themes he first explored in his anti-Manichaean literature.

On the Trinity

In the treatise *On the Trinity*, Augustine takes up in detail the question he could not answer for Fortunatus, namely, why the Word chose to suffer in a body taken up from a woman. Without asking the question explicitly, he begins to answer it in Book 4:

> First we had to be persuaded how much God loved us, in case out of sheer despair we lacked the courage to reach up to him. Also we had to be shown what sort of people we are that he loves, in case we should take pride in our own worth, and so bounce even further away from him and sink even more under our own strength. So he dealt with us in such a way that we could progress rather in his strength; he arranged it so that the power of charity would be brought to perfection in the weakness of humility.[19]

Augustine cites Romans 5:8 in support:

> God shows the quality of his love for us in that Christ died for us while we were still sinners. Much more being justified now in his blood shall we be saved from the wrath by him. For if while we were enemies we were reconciled to God by the death of his Son, much more being reconciled shall we be saved in his life.[20]

Augustine goes on to explain how the incarnation, passion and resurrection of Christ accomplish this through a kind of salvific "harmony" of correspondence:

> The only thing to cleanse the wicked and the proud is the blood of the just man and the humility of God; to contemplate God, which by nature we are not, we would have to be cleansed by him who became

what by nature we are and what by sin we are not. By nature we are not God; by nature we are humans; by sin we are not just. So God became a just human being to intercede with God for sinful humans....So he applied to us the similarity of his humanity to take away the dissimilarity of our iniquity, and becoming a partaker of our mortality he made us partakers of his divinity. It was surely right that the death of the sinner issuing from the stern necessity of condemnation should be undone by the death of the just man issuing from the voluntary freedom of compassion, his single matching our double.[21]

Augustine is explaining that God is not bloodthirsty, but rather the blood, meaning the death, of the just man is necessary because only a death that is not absolutely owed but rather offered in perfect freedom makes the "love" that God wants to demonstrate to us visible and so available for contemplation. The death of the just man is a "single" of perfect freedom exercised in love. It is the "humility" of God, God's willingness "to become our friend in the companionship of death."[22] But following the principle demonstrated in *Against Faustus*, this cannot mean any suffering of the divine nature, for that would be a myth, but rather the true and perfect exercise of a human freedom, the choice of one who did not have to die to submit nevertheless to death. The suffering of God can only be in a historical person, whose "intercession" for us is in his solidarity with us, an identification with, and complete acceptance of, our lot despite his immunity from it.

Augustine explains the mediatorial role of Christ as an "application" of his "single" of perfect freedom to our "double" of necessity or unfreedom, in the death of the body and of the soul.

The single of our Lord Jesus Christ matches our double, and in some fashion enters into a harmony of salvation with it. We, for a start,...were dead in both body and soul—in soul because of sin, in body because of sin's punishment; and thus in "body too because of sin" [Rom 8:10]....To balance this double death of ours the savior paid in his single one, and to achieve each resurrection of ours he pre-enacted and presented his one and only one by way of sacrament and model.[23]

The Lord's death on the cross is "single," that is, it is *only* the death of the body, not of the soul, but as such it becomes a "sacrament" for our inner life and an "exemplum" or model for the "outer man."

The crucifixion of the "inner man" is the sorrow of repentance and the self-discipline involved in "stripping off the old and putting on the new" (Eph 4:22). This renewal of the inner self (from 2 Cor 4:16) begins with the faith by which one "believes in him who justifies the ungodly" (Rom 4:5). The death of the Lord is a model for the outer self by showing us how to be ready for death—that we "should not fear those who kill the body but cannot kill the soul" (Matt 10:28).[24] In other words, the Lord's death is not a divided reality, as ours is, the result of a disintegration of the person—body from soul—and of alienation—the soul from God—but is rather a single and perfect act of the will, where the outer is perfectly expressive and transparent to the inner. Anyone given the grace to consider in faith "him who justifies the ungodly," who sees in faith the "blood of the just man," sees not just a death but a death that is a "model," courageously undertaken under no compulsion, the expression of a soul perfectly united to, not alienated from, God. As this death is considered in faith, it begins to mediate an interior transformation that corresponds to this model, the beginning of interior renewal, for which the one death of Christ has thus become a "sacrament." As we discover the love of God in Christ, we are prompted to inner renewal. This is the *harmonia* of the one that balances two, the "curative accord or symmetry" of mediation.

The same is true for the resurrection of Christ. It is a "model" of the resurrection promised our outer self, and, in faith and hope, it becomes a "sacrament" of the interior resurrection; in a perfectly loving and obviously lovable human choice, we find not a similitude "seek the things that are above, where Christ is seated at God's right hand" (Col 3:1). Thus, the inner life of transformation and renewal is a life conformed to the cross in the hope of the resurrection:

> So then, the one death of our savior was our salvation from our two deaths, and his one resurrection bestowed two resurrections on us, since in either instance, that is, both in death and in resurrection, his body served as the sacrament of our inner man and as the model of our outer man, by a kind of curative accord or symmetry.[25]

The "Rights" of the False Mediator

Augustine contrasts this death with that of the devil, whose death is also "single," but it is the death of the soul rather than of the body, and it mediates to us nothing but death. He uses his immunity from bodily death to appeal to our pride, desiring to be worshiped in place of God and so exercising his primal preference for "power over justice."[26] The devil's appeal is very effective. We are easily impressed by his immortality, and by contrast, Christ's death looks like a very ungodlike weakness:

> The truth is, people were more inclined to avoid the death of the flesh which they could not avoid, than the death of the spirit; that is, they shrank more from the punishment than from what deserved the punishment. Few, after all, care—or care very much—about not sinning; but they make a great fuss about not dying, though it is in fact unobtainable....The devil falsely presents himself to his followers as a mediator offering purification by his sacred rites, but in fact giving them only addiction and ruin; and then he easily persuades the proud to despise and scoff at the death of Christ, and to regard him, the devil, as all the more holy and divine for being immune from any such thing.[27]

Our willingness to be impressed by the immortality of the devil, stemming from our desire for immortality at all cost, gives him what Augustine calls "property rights" over us. The expression should not be interpreted in an overly legalistic sense, for Augustine is at pains to show that these rights represent a privilege that we ourselves have ceded to the devil by the conformation of our wills to his in fear and pride. But as such the rights of the devil are indeed an expression of the justice of God, where the unjust preference of power over justice cannot but result in a worse rather than a better state, a state of subjection rather than freedom, of "addiction" rather than poise and self-possession. If it were otherwise, then God would not be God, the highest good and source of all happiness.

But what if the same justice that gives the devil "rights" over us were presented to us in a form that is obviously lovable? What if it were shown that the greatness of God is not in God's power conceived simply as the ability to dominate and control, but rather in God's love? What if God, in order to show us that it is his love that is the greatest reality, were willing to take on a vulnerability to suffering without reserve, becoming, though no power constrains him, our "companion in death"? Here the justice of God, God's stature as the greatest reality to which worship alone is due, becomes visible as the "humility" of God, the "suffering" of the Word of God, not in myth but in the reality of a historical person,[28] our "companion in death," whose choice to die is a fully free, human choice to be in complete solidarity with his friends, not by constraint— since he has no sin—but out of love ("for greater love has no one than to lay down his life for his friends" [John 15:13]).[29]

Christ's death is not a similitude of a mythic suffering of divine nature. Rather, in Christ's perfectly loving and obviously lovable human choice, we find the actual solidarity of God with us through which the spell of the devil over the human heart is broken. The mousetrap—to use the imagery of the sermons—is sprung. The devil's rights are abrogated when his killing of Christ reveals his own impotence and deceit, since the greatness of God's love shines out in the death he so greedily caused. We are persuaded of "how much God loves us" in the loving choice of Jesus, and the devil loses the subjection that gave him his right over us.

> Being avid for human death in any shape or form he turned his attention to procuring the only death which he was able and permitted to [by Christ, who resisted his temptations], the death of that mortal element which the living mediator had received from us. And precisely there, where he was able really to do something, was he well and truly routed; and by his receiving the exterior authority to strike down the Lord's flesh, the interior authority by which he held us captive was itself struck down....As he was able not to die if he wished to, it follows since he did die that it was because he wished to; and thus...by his death he offered for us the one truest possible sacrifice, and thereby purged, abolished, and destroyed whatever there was of guilt....In being slain in his innocence by the wicked one, who was acting against us as it were with just rights, he won the case against him with the justest of all rights, and thus "led captivity captive" [Eph 4:8, Ps 68:19].[30]

We may still be afraid of death, but we have faith that the love of God is greater. Thus begins the inner death and resurrection by which we can make loving, progressively more free choices, as Jesus did. The renewal of the image of God within, its "repair," its reformation as the image of God, is conformed to the death and resurrection of the Lord and yields a life which is Christlike in its determined preference for justice over power.[31]

City of God

The second great treatise that develops a theology of the cross and salvation in response to the question Augustine left unanswered in the *Against Faustus* is the *City of God*, and to this treatise I now turn. Begun in the aftermath of the sack of Rome in 410 by Alaric, *City of God* responds to criticisms lodged against the regime of the Christian emperor Theodosius, who had enacted laws prohibiting divination and pagan sacrificial practice. The empire was in decline, the pagans alleged, because the gods who made Rome great were no longer being worshiped, and the ethos they represented no longer cultivated. Nor were these worries limited only to pagan Romans; Christians wondered why their persons and property had not been immune to injury and damage during the sack, since they worshiped the correct God.[32]

Augustine responds in two converging discussions: one in Book 5, about what made the Roman Empire great; the other in Book 10, about what true worship is. The discussion in Book 5 proceeds along the lines of what one might call the demythologization or demystification of empire building. To whom or to what is the growth and extension of the Roman Empire due—to the ancient gods? to fate or destiny? The true answer is actually not very complicated. One need only look at the Roman character to explain the growth and duration of the empire. The Romans had an imperial character and so built an empire—they *deserved* an empire, and God would not have given them their appropriate reward had he not granted it.[33]

Using a phrase of Sallust, Augustine characterizes the Romans as "greedy for praise." Augustine describes the lust for praise or passion for glory as the essence of the Roman character:

> They were "greedy for praise, generous with their money, and aimed at vast renown and honorable riches" (Sallust, *Catilina* 7.6). They

were passionately devoted to glory; it was for this that they desired to live, for this they did not hesitate to die.[34]

This passion gave rise to the wondrous, almost miraculous achievements for which the Romans are so deservedly famous. For the lust for praise occupies a curious niche in the ecology of morals—it is a vice, but it is a vice that suppresses all other vices such as avarice and sexual lust:

> This unbounded passion for glory, above all else, checked their other appetites....They took no account of their own material interests compared with the common good...; they resisted the temptations of avarice; they acted for their country's well-being with disinterested concern; they were guilty of no offense against the law; they succumbed to no sensual indulgence. By such immaculate conduct they labored toward honors, power and glory.[35]

Augustine goes on to explain that the Romans' lust for praise had such salutary consequences partly because they wanted glory in the eyes not just of anyone, but of enlightened judges:

> Those who long for true glory, though it be the glory of merely human praise, are anxious for the good opinion of enlightened judges.[36]

For example, Augustine has in mind the philosophers who recognize and extol the desirability of the virtues (*virtutes*, which one might translate the "strengths" or "excellences" of human beings) and of justice in particular.

Augustine himself seems to have admired the virtues or excellences that the Roman character achieved at its best, and he provides the reader with examples of the Roman heroes and their virtuous behaviors. Brutus, Torquatus, Furuis Camillus, Curtius, the Decii, Cincinnatus and others are uplifted for admiration and even emulation.[37] Augustine has a special regard for Marcus Regulus, who was a prisoner of war captured by the Carthaginians. When they sent him on an embassy to the Roman Senate to argue for a prisoner exchange, they made him swear an oath to return. In Rome he argued that the exchange was not in the best interest of the Roman republic, and then, having secured by his actions the certainty of

Carthaginian retaliation against him, his fidelity to his oath compelled him to return as a prisoner to torture and death:

> After the success of his plea he was not forced by his countrymen to return to the enemy, but since he had taken an oath, he voluntarily fulfilled his obligation and the enemy put him to death with every refinement of dreadful torture. They shut him in a narrow box, where he was forced to stand upright, and sharp nails had been fixed on all sides of it, so that he could not lean in any direction without the most horrible suffering; thus they dispatched him by keeping him awake.[38]

And if fidelity to the ancient gods can result in such a fate, then no one should taunt Christians who suffered in the sack of Rome despite their piety. Of course Augustine is implying that if there were a few more Reguluses around now—if the critics of the Christian Roman order were more like Regulus—maybe the empire wouldn't be failing after all:

> Now how are we to cope with men who are proud to have had such a fellow-citizen, but afraid to belong to such a community?[39]

But Augustine implies more. There is more to the fall of Rome than the present regrettable absence of the imperial virtue, and his analysis here verges on the poignant. In the very passion that was the greatness of Rome was also the seeds of its destruction. For the Roman cultivation of praise and glory meant that even the virtues themselves ultimately became a function of opinion, no matter how exalted that opinion:

> It is most improper that the Virtues...should be the servants of Glory. For then Prudence would exercise no foresight, Justice make no dispensations, Fortitude show no endurance, Temperance impose no moderation, except so far as to win human approval, and to serve the ends of Glory and her inflated conceit.[40]

In other words, it would (and did) become a virtue *not* to rise above opinion. Augustine claims that ultimately Rome failed because it had become a society closed in on itself, unable to rise above the prevailing opinion on what was just, temperate, courageous and prudent behavior. In its fixation on its own virtue precisely as its own, that is, precisely as a pattern of behavior and accomplishment meriting praise, it in the end squelched its own imagination by rendering it unable to allow for self-criticism. For example, perhaps the whole premise on which the empire was founded, namely, domination—by means however virtuous and glorious—was wrong. But such a thought could not be admitted, for it would seem to destroy the empire, leaving nothing in its place.

True Worship

But how does one rise above the domination of the imagination that the empire represents? Where is there revealed an Archimedean point outside the sphere of imperial opinion from which it can get a perspective on itself? In the true worship of God, of course. But that answer has its own problems. Once again taking up where the *Against Faustus* left off,[41] Augustine goes on in Book 10 to analyze what true worship is. *Latreia*, the true worship due only to God, is sacrifice, Augustine claims, for "no one would dare to assert that sacrifice is due to any other being than God."[42]

Augustine then goes on, beyond the *Against Faustus*, to develop an analysis of the inner meaning of sacrifice. The essential act of sacrifice is not the slaying of an animal or any external action at all. The outward act is actually the sign of the true, inner sacrifice:

> Thus the visible sacrifice is the sacrament, the sacred sign, of the invisible sacrifice....Hence the meaning of the text, "I desire mercy rather than sacrifice" [Hos 6:6] is simply that one sacrifice is preferred to another; for what is generally called sacrifice is really a sign of the true sacrifice. Mercy is, in fact, the true sacrifice.[43]

The true sacrifice, Augustine says, is mercy or compassion, and true sacrifices are "acts of compassion"—*opera misericordiae*—"the works of mercy" (10.6), though they are such only when they are directed to no ulterior motive but to God alone:

> For that reason even an act of compassion itself is not a sacrifice, if it is not done for the sake of God. For sacrifice is a "divine matter," in the phrase of the old Latin authors, even if it is performed or offered by a human being. Hence a man consecrated in the name of God, and vowed to God, is in himself a sacrifice inasmuch as he

"dies to the world" so that he may "live for God" [cf. Rom 6:11]....So then, the true sacrifices are acts of compassion, whether toward ourselves or toward our neighbors, when they are directed toward God.[44]

It is necessary for Augustine to emphasize that works of mercy or acts of compassion not directed to God are not true sacrifices, not only because of the essential idea of *latreia* as directed only to God, but because of the ethos or character of the Roman Empire, for did not the Romans know compassion or mercy? In fact, was it not virtually the imperial motto, as expressed by Virgil and repeated by Augustine, "to spare the conquered and beat down the proud"?

> For the King and Founder of this City [of God] which is our subject has revealed in the Scripture of his people this statement of the divine Law, "God resists the proud, but he gives grace to the humble" [Jas 4:6]. This is God's prerogative; but man's arrogant spirit in its swelling pride has claimed it as its own, and delights to hear this verse quoted in its own praise: "To spare the conquered, and beat down the proud."[45]

Was it not the hallmark of Roman imperial character, even as Augustine describes it, that in their lust for praise they had mercy, that is, they "spared" those whom they conquered? This is the ultimate perversion—the exercise of sacrificial mercy, the veritable worship of God, only for the glory and praise it can accrue.

That is why Augustine must go on to qualify his description of true worship even further. *Latreia* is not only the inner sacrifice of mercy or compassion. The "true sacrifices are acts of compassion, whether towards ourselves or towards our neighbors, when they are directed towards God." Augustine adds that "even an act of compassion itself is not a sacrifice, if it is not done for the sake of God."[46] And this is where the cross comes in, for only Christ has accomplished a perfect sacrifice, a perfect work of mercy, wholly directed not toward any ulterior gain, praise included, but toward God. In Christ, God makes the ultimate sacrifice, the sacrifice of the right to be praised by the highest form of praise, reserved for God—sacrifice itself. Christ's sacrifice on the cross is God descending into shame and death; it is the cross that reveals the specific character of the incarnation as God's "stretching out of a hand to the helpless,"[47] a perfect act of compassion rather than just another bid for praise. Here is true compassion, and it is not a "virtue" or "power" or "excellence," but precisely the renunciation of "virtue" or "power" or "excellence," an act of humility that renders the Word less glorious than even the demons whose airy bodies are immortal and so superior to the mortality of Christ.[48]

No one of us, fallen as we are, can enact a perfect work of compassion with absolutely no ulterior motive. That is why we have the Eucharist, for in celebrating the memory of Christ's death at the Eucharist, we are formed into this very renunciation. We are formed by the sacrifice represented and enacted in the Eucharist, formed into the mortal body of Christ, which is the compassion of God:

> This being so, it immediately follows that the whole redeemed community, that is to say, the congregation and fellowship of the saints, is offered to God as a universal sacrifice, through the great Priest who offered himself in his suffering for us....This is the sacrifice of Christians, who are "many making up one body in Christ" [Rom 12:4]. This is the sacrifice which the Church continually celebrates in the sacrament of the altar, a sacrament well-known to the faithful where it is shown to the Church that she herself is offered in the offering which she presents to God.[49]

By this sacrifice we are no longer "conformed" to the world but are "reformed in newness of mind" (Rom 12:2).[50]

Vision and Critique

In the eucharistic life, we have climbed (to return momentarily to the imagery of the sermons) onto the lampstand of the cross, where our virtues themselves can no longer blind us because they too are conformed to the sacrifice of Christ, "given" to us as such, testifying not to our own glory but to the glory of pure Compassion.[51] When conformed to the sacrifice of Christ, our lives and deeds of virtue, our acts of compassion or works of mercy, are so many acts of devotion to Christ crucified and so exhibit to everyone Christ's assessment of things, the assessment of things in the original order of creation as reflecting God's goodness and wisdom, not the glory of the empire.

When we act out of compassion toward a neighbor, and our compassion is progressively formed by our participation in the Eucharist, we are reclaiming that neighbor from the identity the empire would impose, as simply another vehicle for its glory. We are reinvesting the world, and each creature in it, with the glory of God, and so the character of compassion as *latreia* or worship of God is vindicated. Our devotion to Christ, visible outwardly as works of mercy, becomes a practice of critique, a dismantling of the body politic's hegemony over meaning or, at least, over opinion. In the eucharistic life, one has climbed the "tree of silly fruit," our vision progressively restored and progressively able to help restore that of others, assisting them to recover their birthright as made in the image of God, not in the image of the state.

An Augustinian spirituality of the cross, then, is above all a spirituality founded on the Eucharist and issuing in a practice of mercy or compassion. It is a spirituality of progressive interior renewal according to the sacrifice of Christ, and on the basis of that renewal, a spirituality of revisioning, of breaking open circles of meaning and reference that had seemed closed. The cross is a sign in which we begin to see the original meaning of things, of God's creative speaking forth of the world in love, precisely because it entails the dismantling of received meanings that have for so long been taken for granted, though they obscured the glory of God in favor of the glory of the empire.

Insofar as we are conformed to the compassion of Christ in the Eucharist, we are conformed to the preference of justice over power, and so a true Augustinian spirituality of the cross is one that enables us to revision the world in terms of justice, that is, in terms of the glory of God over all, and so to see through and dismantle the claims of power over justice, whatever form they may take. Devotion to the cross reinvests the imagination with a whole new paradigm of power by which to measure all the kingdoms of this world.

NOTES

1. *Against Fortunatus* 1.1 (translated by Albert H. Newman, in the *Nicene and Post-Nicene Fathers*, series 1, vol. 4).
2. Ibid. 2.32.
3. Ibid. 1.3, Fortunatus's speech.

4. Ibid. 2.21, Fortunatus's speech (cf. ibid. 2.20, Fortunatus's speech).

5. Ibid. 1.7.

6. Ibid. 2.21, Fortunatus's speech; 2.20, Fortunatus's speech.

7. Ibid. 2.22, Fortunatus's speech.

8. *Reply to Faustus the Manichaean* 20.2, cf. 20.11.

9. Ibid. 20.11.

10. Augustine's insistence that Faustus's position amounts to mythology runs throughout Book 20 (for example, at 20.11: "Finally, as in Faustus's statement, in which he alludes in the briefest manner possible to the lengthy stories of Manichaean invention, the earth by the power of the Holy Spirit conceives and brings forth the mortal Jesus, who, hanging from every tree, is the life and salvation of human beings,...if you mean that the Jesus on the trees, and the Jesus crucified under Pontius Pilate, and the Jesus divided between the sun and the moon, are all one and the same substance, why do you not give the name of Jesus to your whole host of deities? Why should not your World-holder be Jesus too, and Atlas, and the King of Honor, and the Mighty Spirit, and the First Man, and all the rest, with their various names and occupations?").

11. *Reply to Faustus the Manichaean* 22.40.

12. Ibid. 20.11.

13. Ibid. 26.7.

14. Ibid. 20.11.

15. Ibid. 22.17.

16. Ibid. 20.20; cf. 20.18, 22.

17. Ibid. 20.22.

18. Ibid.

19. *On the Trinity* 4.2 (translations taken from Augustine, *The Trinity*, trans. Edmund Hill, O.P. [Brooklyn: New City Press, 1990]). I have not noted those places where I have diverged slightly from Hill's choice of words.

20. Ibid.

21. Ibid. 4.4.

22. Ibid. 4.17.

23. Ibid. 4.5-6. Note how, in a way, this is a transmogrification of the Manichaean doctrine. For Fortunatus, the death of Christ was a similitude of something that happens in us, but Christ's death was not a real death, and that of which it is a similitude, the suffering of God in us, is not free on our parts but something given. In Augustine's version, the suffering of God is a real, free, historical choice truly to die, and this act not only signifies as "exemplum" but mediates as "sacramentum" a renewal of our own freedom not as God but as God's created image.

24. These various scripture citations are given by Augustine at *On the Trinity* 4.5–6.

25. Ibid. 4.6.

26. The devil "holds human beings in subjection by his swollen self-esteem and his determined preference for power over justice" inasmuch as we have become complicit in this same preference (*On the Trinity* 4.13).

27. Ibid. 4.15, 18.

28. Augustine is very clear that it is the Word who suffers. The fault of the prideful is that they think there is no way for God to suffer. Pride here is a fault of the imagination, which constructs the perfection of God in a way that cannot imagine any suffering: "They are not prepared to consider how it can be that the Word of God abides totally unchanged in himself and yet by taking on a lower nature can suffer what is proper to that nature, which an impure demon cannot suffer because he does not have an earthly body" (*On the Trinity* 4.18). Seen from this perspective, the taking on of an earthly body is God's taking on the vulnerability to suffering.

29. Ibid. 4.17.

30. Ibid.

31. The theme of the renewal of the image of God is taken up in Books 13 and 14. As part of this treatment of the renewal of the image, Augustine returns to the theme of redemption, this time explicitly asking and answering the question that he said he could not answer in the *Against Faustus*, namely, why God chose to become incarnate of a woman and suffer in human nature, death, and so on: "We must show, not indeed that no other possible way was available to God, since all things are equally within his power, but that there neither was nor should have been a more suitable way of curing our unhappy state. Nothing was more needed for raising our hopes and delivering the minds of mortals, disheartened by the very condition of mortality, from despairing of immortality, than a demonstration of how much value God put on us and how much he loved us. And what could be clearer and more wonderful evidence of this than that the Son of God, unchangeably good, remaining in himself what he was and receiving from us what he was not, electing to enter into partnership with our nature without detriment to his own, should first of all endure our ills without any ill deserts of his own" (*On the Trinity* 13.13). In the course of the discussion Augustine reiterates the notion of the rights of the devil, but once again interprets this in terms of our choices and our own self-willed restriction of freedom. The sin of the devil is pride, the desire to replace God with himself, and in this he has lapsed from justice, since God is in fact greater than the devil and ought to remain God. Pride is thus a disordered preference, once again, for power over justice, and our complicity with the devil is

our complicity in this disordered preference of power over justice. Simply put, we would rather be powerful than just (*On the Trinity* 13.17).

How then does God act? By a display of strength, overmastering the devil and ourselves with him? But that would only be to confirm our worst suspicions, we who are complicit with the devil and addicted to power, that God shares this addiction. Augustine then tells us what this means: "The devil would have to be overcome not by God's power, but by his justice. What, after all, could be more powerful than the all-powerful, or what creature's power could compare with the creator's? The essential flaw of the devil's perversion made him a lover of power and a deserter and assailant of justice, which means that human beings imitate him all the more thoroughly the more they neglect or even detest justice and studiously devote themselves to power, rejoicing at the possession of it or inflamed with the desire of it. So it pleased God to deliver man from the devil's authority by beating him at the justice game, not the power game, so that humans too might imitate Christ by seeking to beat the devil at the justice game, not the power game" (*On the Trinity* 13.17).

For Augustine, this explains why Christ had to be both God and human. For, unless he were human, he could not have been killed, but unless he were God, we would not have believed he was preferring justice over power, but simply that he lacked power like the rest of us (13.18). When the devil claimed Christ in death, as though swallowing the bait in a trap, he lost power over us, "turned out of power and out of the hearts of the faithful," for the death of Christ revealed the incarnation—itself an act of justice as described—as also an act of love. Augustine speaks in the strongest terms possible of the suffering and humiliation of God undertaken for us—not, again, the suffering of the divine nature, for that would be a myth, but the real suffering of a historical person: "As it is, however, he suffered human pains for us because he was man, though if he had not wanted to he would have been able not to suffer so, because he was God. In this way the justice of humility was made more acceptable, seeing that the power of divinity could have avoided the humiliation if it had wanted to; and so by the death of one so powerful we powerless mortals have justice set before us and power promised us....What could be more just than to go and face even death on a cross for justice's sake?" (*On the Trinity* 13.18).

32. See, for example, the complaints reflected in the charges made at *City of God* 1.10–16 (translations are taken from Augustine, *City of God*, trans. Henry Bettenson [New York and London: Penguin, 1972], sometimes slightly modified).

33. *City of God* 5.15.

34. Ibid. 5.12.

35. Ibid. 5.12, 15.

36. Ibid. 5.19.

37. Ibid. 5.18.

38. Ibid. 1.15. See also the treatment of Regulus at 5.18.

39. Ibid. 1.15.

40. Ibid. 5.20.

41. *Against Faustus* 20.21 discusses the true worship called *latreia*: "What is properly divine worship, which the Greeks call *latreia*, and for which there is no word in Latin, both in doctrine and in practice, we give only to God. To this worship belongs the offering of sacrifices." Augustine explains that Hebrew and pagan sacrifices are, respectively, foreshadowings and imitations of the true sacrifice that Jesus alone accomplished and that is commemorated and continued in the Eucharist. But he does not develop the inner meaning of sacrifice as mercy and compassion (apart from a hint at the beginning of 20.20).

42. *City of God* 10.4.

43. Ibid. 10.5. The word translated "mercy" is *misericordia*, and it is just as accurately translated "compassion."

44. Ibid. 10.5, 6.

45. Ibid. 1.Prologue, citing *Aeneid* 6.853.

46. Ibid. 10.6.

47. Ibid. 10.24.

48. See *City of God* 10.24, remarking on Porphyry: "It was of course his pride which blinded Porphyry to this great mystery, that pride which our true and gracious Mediator has overthrown by his humility....It was because they were free from that mortal condition that the false and malignant mediators vaunted their superiority, and deluded unhappy men by false promises of assistance, as immortals coming to the aid of mortals."

49. *City of God* 10.6.

50. Ibid.

51. This is another reason why the Manichaean soteriology must be rejected and modified from Augustine's point of view. If the suffering of God is not real in the sense of a choice of a historical person, our virtues are not contextualized as conformed to and empowered by *this* perfectly free and loving choice, at once human and divine. Otherwise our virtues are not put into perspective. So neither is the sway of opinion, and thus the source and possibility of cultural renewal, compromised. The vulnerability of the nature of God is a myth; it leaves our virtue and its status as merit completely unaffected. Note, too, how in the *Lord's Sermon on the Mount* Augustine says mercy cleanses the eye of the mind; yet in sermon 103 it's the cross that does this purifying. In terms of the concerns raised by the texts we have been considering from *City of God*, one can see that this is an important shift. It is

AN AUGUSTINIAN SPIRITUALITY OF THE CROSS

God's mercy, not our merciful deeds, that are praiseworthy; to consider our deeds of mercy as cleansing is to subject them without recourse to the stream of opinion, and as desirable because we can be praised for doing them (a danger Augustine articulates in the text of the *Lord's Sermon on the Mount*, where he had no solution to it).

CHAPTER 8

A Condescending God:
Bonaventure's Theology of the Cross

Elizabeth A. Dreyer

Bonaventure's Christocentric Theology

As background to a discussion on Bonaventure's theology of the cross, it is helpful to examine Bonaventure's understanding of theology as both a speculative and a practical science.[1] These two aspects of theology are ordered, with the speculative aspects subordinated to the practical. For Bonaventure, the ultimate goal of theology is not understanding—as important as this is—but holiness—one does theology "so that one can become good" (*ut boni fiamus*).[2] Theology is a "slow yet sure orientation towards beatitude through the mediatorship of Christ."[3] Since Bonaventure's own life experience encompassed the roles of both theologian and university professor, as well as pastor and general of the Franciscan order, he was in a good position to understand the importance of both formal theological reflection and its practical effects in the Christian life. Thus, his theological thought provides a metaphysical foundation for, and is in harmony with, his understanding of the spiritual life. Zachary Hayes writes about Bonaventure's work: "The imitation of Christ and the ascent of creation to God which constitute the saving realization of human perfectibility are not only a mystical or spiritual theme. It is grounded in the metaphysical teaching of trinitarian theology and the theology of creation."[4]

Bonaventure inherited from Neoplatonism a cosmology that saw everything as coming forth from God and returning to God. God is the source and fullness of all reality. Bonaventure also makes use of the Neoplatonic idea that reality is a shadow—a vestige, image, or similitude of ultimate reality, which is God. As a result, the universe has a pervasive sacramental character. The trinitarian God is the exemplar for the human person and for all of creation. Bonaventure's trinitarian theology flows less from Augustine and more from Richard of St. Victor, who speaks of the three Persons as three modalities of love. Bonaventure's understanding of God is founded on and grounded in love. And Christ is the primordial exemplar of that love, the reality in light of which we model our lives and understand God and the world.

Hayes places Bonaventure's soteriology on the larger canvas of the tradition. He outlines three approaches to soteriology—all of which are reflected in Bonaventure's theology. The first and most enduring is that of Anselm, in which Christ's death signifies a sacrifice, an offering to God necessary to pay the debt for sin. This view is prominent in Bonaventure's theology. The second view, common in patristic authors, views the incarnation as a mystery of redemption that consists in the union of the human and the divine. Bonaventure emphasizes this strain by giving Christ the role of mediator, the one who links these two seemingly disparate spheres. Hayes calls the third "personalist," which reflects the exemplarism so prominent in Bonaventure's system. Christ's life and death show others the way by which they too can return to the Father.[5] Christ has a commanding role for Bonaventure: "Christ is the purest actualization of a potential that lies at the heart of the created order."[6] Hayes further reminds us that "regardless of any specific interpretations of the textual tradition, it is fair to say that for Bonaventure, the meaning of Christ should never be limited to the overcoming of sin." The incarnation is the highest act of God's creative work and the fitting completion of the cosmic order. "In a positive sense, salvation is the actualization of the potential which God placed in the world through the act of creation."[7]

In 1247, Bonaventure wrote a theological work that he describes as "a brief summary of true theology," entitled the *Breviloquium*.[8] In this work, Bonaventure establishes the basis upon which one can say that Christ suffered. Christ assumed in his body, hunger, thirst and fatigue, as well as sorrow, anguish and fear in his soul. He did not assume physical disease either by ignorance or the body's war upon the spirit. He accepted the necessity of suffering, but no pain touched him against either his divine or rational will, which he freely aligned to the will of the Father. The passion did do violence to his sensorial and carnal will

(*Brev.* IV.8.1). He suffered against his instinctive will, that is against the sensible impulse and desire of his flesh. This is evident in words of Jesus such as "Not as I will, but your will be done" (Matt 26:39) and "Let this cup pass away from me" (Matt 26:39). These wills were not opposed to each other, for in his divine will he wished what was just; in his rational will, he consented to justice; and his natural instinct, while averse to pain, did not contest justice. There was, therefore, in Christ, no struggle or conflict but peaceful order (*Brev.* IV.8.5).

For Bonaventure, Christ's suffering functioned to provide a model of virtue—to restore God's honor and to respect the harmonious functioning of the universe. Of the first he says, "Now, nothing could show humans the way to virtue more clearly than the example of an agonizing death endured for the sake of divine justice...and nothing could move humans to virtue more strongly than the benignity with which the most high Son of God laid down his life for us who were undeserving" (*Brev.* IV.9.2). It is fitting, he says, that our evil should be healed through its opposite. Our death is overcome because Christ's physical death could not bring death to his person, who never ceases to live (*Brev.* IV.9.8).

The utter centrality of Christ in Bonaventure's theology is the crucial backdrop for his understanding of the cross, indeed of all of reality. One can say that, for Bonaventure, the person of Jesus provides the most adequate form of revelation.[9] The poverty and humility of Jesus and the mystery of the cross form a further centerpiece of this theology, but never in isolation from Jesus' life and resurrection. It is a commonplace that Bonaventure's understanding of the cross stems from Francis. Hayes writes, "Bonaventure was deeply impressed by the spiritual reality that Francis lived....For years he wrestled with the mystery of Francis and with the enigma of the Order that claimed Francis as its founder....The consistent Christocentrism of the Seraphic Doctor's theology can be seen as nothing other than an elaborate theological explication of the Christ-piety of the Poor Man of Assisi."[10]

And the culminating event in Christ's life that reveals the meaning of this exemplar is the cross and resurrection. In the cross, God in Christ overcomes pride by being humble, disobedience by being obedient, destruction as the final word through forgiveness, illness through healing and death through life.[11] I cite Hayes again: "In a special way, the passion that ended the life of Jesus is exemplar of the necessity to die to sin in all its forms, while resurrection is the exemplar of glory in which the world in humanity will be brought to completion. Reconciliation is not only moral, but cosmic as well."[12] In a work entitled *Collations on the Six Days*, written toward the end of his life, Bonaventure again locates the center of reality in Christ, which when lost can be found by "tracing two lines that intersect at a right angle," that is, the cross (*Hex* 1, 24).[13] The cross thus reveals the truth about reality, about the nature of God, as well as the nature of our human reality and the "fundamental law of the spiritual journey to God."[14] As Christians today, we continue to explore how the cross of Christ shapes our present cosmological under-standings, taking into account, of course, current scientific understand-ings of the origins and makeup of the universe.[15]

I would like to examine Bonaventure's theology of the cross with two questions in mind. First, given this basic structure of his theological system, how does Bonaventure speak about the identity and activity of God? Second, how does he envision the human response to this God? In particular, we will focus on poverty and humility.

Who Is Bonaventure's God?

Condescending Love

I think that, for Bonaventure, one of the primary meanings of the cross is the image of God it reveals. In *The Mystical Vine: A Treatise on the Passion of the Lord*, Bonaventure writes, "The Just One fell in love with the iniquitous, the Beautiful One with the vile, the only Good and the Holy One with the sinful and unholy. Oh, tremendous condescension! See now how much he loved us. Who could explain it well enough?" (VM XVI.1).[16] For Bonaventure, the term *condescension* connotes God's overwhelmingly generous love and willingness, as Creator of the universe, to enter that cre-ation in a most complete way. There is no hint of arrogance or a disposition to "look down" on others—meanings that we might associate with the term today. Rather, it points to God's humbleness and meekness.

Bonaventure is not the first Franciscan to emphasize the conde-scending nature of God revealed in the cross. Inspired by Francis's stigmata, Clare of Assisi understood mystical prayer as being united to, and transformed into, Christ crucified. For Clare, the crucified Christ, the mirror of the invisible God, becomes the center of her spirituality. Ingrid Peterson writes that "Clare found the core of her spiritual understanding of love in gazing on the visual image of the crucified Christ."[17] For more than forty years, Clare meditated on the cross at San Damiano, the very cross that, according to legend, told Francis to "go and repair my house" (2Cel 5). Clare links the humbleness of Christ's birth; of his blessed poverty in life; and above all, of his suffering on the wood of the cross. Christians are to imitate this Christ in his poverty, his humility and his charity.[18]

For Bonaventure as well, it is God's nature to be self-communicating love. In Jesus, God shows Godself to be not only a mystery of love, but a mystery of humble love. In a very particular way the mystery of the cross offers insights into the mystery of divine love as well as the dynamism of the spiritual way to God.[19] God takes the human community so seriously that God assumes even the pain and death of our existence. For Bonaventure, it was appropriate for the Redeemer to have the natures of both God and humanity, the two parties estranged by sin. But it was also necessary for the redeemed to share in the particular circumstances of humanity as well (*Brev.* 4.8).[20] It was therefore necessary for Christ to share in the wretchedness of human life after sin—pain, suffering and death.[21]

In his *Commentary on the Sentences*, Bonaventure offers three principal reasons why Christ assumed a nature capable of suffering. First, since sin flows from pride and the misuse of the human will, redemption must also flow from the human depths of humility and loving obedience. Second, Christ's example of humble, loving obedience unto death gives humans a model to follow. And third, by assuming our weaknesses, Christ thereby more effectively encourages humans to try to live a life of true faith, hope and love.[22] When Christ took on human sinfulness, thus becoming capable of suffering and death, he showed the genuineness of his human nature, allowing both his body and his spirit to become vulnerable. The incarnation was no docetist ploy in which Christ pretended to enter fully into human pathos. In fact, because he was God, he was supremely susceptible to pain and suffering. "Thus Bonaventure provides a systematic basis for the image of the suffering Christ which plays so important a role in his spiritual and mystical writings."[23]

This condescending love is visible in a number of ways, according to Bonaventure. First, it is evident in God's choice to enter history. This love is further evident in the assumption of the flesh, which is more alien to God than is spirit. Bonaventure tells us that God assumed the more expressive medium of the flesh to indicate "a greater humiliation and a deeper condescension." Thus we call this work not "in-animation but in-carnation" (*Brev.* IV.2.4). God's condescension is also visible in the poverty and humility of Jesus' life and especially in the cross. Zachary Hayes writes,

> For the simplicity and poverty of the life of Jesus, and especially the tragic outcome of his ministry on the hill of Calvary, can be seen as a statement about the nature of divine love. In the context of the poverty controversy, Bonaventure develops this issue extensively into a theology of divine condescension and compassion. Seen from this perspective, the divine compassion becomes the archetype for the form of love to which human beings are called.[24]

Bonaventure tries to hold in tension both the glory of a transcendent God and the poverty and humility God assumed in the incarnation and the cross. For Bonaventure, these choices do not tarnish divine glory but rather enhance it. The incarnation says something about God's love—that God can condescend to the weak without impinging on the divine perfections. It is precisely in this act of condescension that God's true dignity and nobility are revealed. Bonaventure writes, "While remaining most high in Godself, God became humble for us" (AP 1.10).[25] For Bonaventure, God is self-diffusive goodness, revealed in a startling and paradigmatic way in the cross.[26] And since humans are made in the image and likeness of God, this aspect of God's innermost being will have ramifications for Bonaventure's anthropology. Each Christian is to live in imitation of the poverty and humility of Christ, as we will see in more detail later.

The Cross Reverses Expectations

This condescending and merciful God revealed in the cross upsets expectations. Instead of a symbol that repulses and points to evil, Bonaventure sees the cross as a gift of truth and love. He sees the cross as the way to truth because one can't love the good without knowing it, and the cross teaches us the truth about God (*Sol* 1.33; and DTV 3.3).[27] The cross reveals everything; it is the key to all knowledge; the one who contemplates the cross is in the truth, possesses the truth, is possessed by the truth. The cross is the key, door, way and splendor of truth. One who contemplates the cross no longer walks in the shadows but in the light of life (DTV 3.3; and *Itin.*, 7).[28]

Each detail of the passion is given a meaning that is a reversal of what appears. For example, Christ was flagellated so that we could be free from eternal suffering; he underwent an unjust trial so that we could be saved from a just condemnation; he immersed himself in a sea of suffering so that we would be free from our passions; he allowed himself to be abandoned for the good of the church; for us he yielded to vileness and scorn. In the *Soliloquium* he writes, "Look and consider the marvelous things the Lord has done on earth. God is derided, so that you, O soul, might be honored; flagellated so that you might be consoled; crucified so that you may be liberated; the immaculate lamb slaughtered so that you might have a banquet; the lance made blood and water to flow from his side so that you may drink" (*Sol* I.33).[29]

Maurycy Suley notes that these reversals stem from Bonaventure's theological fascination with the particular strategy of the divine action, so different from the human way of valuing and acting. Bonaventure defends the cross by pleading that God's strategy, so different from our own, is a most effective way to convince us of God's love.[30] In every age, theologians revisit the meaning of the cross—most recently, searching for its source not so much in God's plan, but rather as an inevitable consequence of Jesus' actions in his particular community. But the scandal of the length to which Jesus was willing to go out of commitment to his mission and love of the world perdures.

This reversal of expectations as to the meaning of the cross is perhaps most dramatically presented in *The Mystical Vine*. This work was probably a sermon delivered in northern Germany.[31] Bonaventure turns to the wound of love from the Song of Songs (4:9) to explicate the meaning of Christ's wounds on the cross. He says, "For one who ardently loves is wounded by love. How could Christ better show us this ardor than by permitting not only his body but his very heart to be pierced with a lance? The wound of the flesh reveals the wound of the spirit....Who indeed, would let his heart be wounded for the sake of one beloved if he had not first received from her the wound of love?" (VM III.5).[32] He goes on, "Who could fail to love the heart that bears such a wound? Who could fail to return the love of such a Lover?" (VM III.6).[33] Bonaventure's understanding of the cross gives us some clue about why he insists that the friars—and by extension, all Christians—have affection for the cross, a seemingly scandalous juxtaposition. How is one to have affection for, to cling to the cross, unless one meets there the individual who offers ultimate, unconditioned love and acceptance of our worst selves?

As we will see, for Bonaventure "the most intimate and personal levels of spiritual theology correspond fully with the metaphysical and universalist dimensions of speculative Christology; for both spirituality and speculative theology reflect the true character of the world and of human existence." God chose to become a pilgrim on this earth. Thus, we too must become "pilgrims and strangers" (1 Peter 2:11), existing in the world ultimately so that we may undertake an exodus into God.[34]

Human Response: Poverty and Humility

Let us now inquire into two of the primary virtues that Bonaventure links with the cross—poverty and humility. The cross reveals a most profound truth about the identity of God—God's love is a humble, condescending love. And since we are made in God's image and called in faith to be imitators of God in Christ, we are called to become like the poor one, stripped of all material, physical and spiritual comforts, because he chose to live a life of love. For Bonaventure, the model for his own life, for the lives of the friars and even for the lives of all Christians, was Francis.[35] In *The Life of St. Francis*, Bonaventure links Francis with a long line of the poor and lowly—the Suffering Servant of Isaiah, John the Baptist and Jesus (LM, Prol. 1).[36] Poverty—Francis's mother, bride and lady—was a centerpiece of the Franciscan Order (LM 7.6). And Bonaventure relates that it was the sight of a poor man that caused Francis's own heart to be filled with compunction (LM 7.6).

In part because Bonaventure had to defend poverty against its adversaries, it became for him a comprehensive theological category. Humans are doubly poor. They are poor in their very being because their existence depends on God's love. Spiritual poverty stems from an awareness that everything in the universe has been created by God from nothing. Without God, humans are nothing. Humans are also morally poor because in spite of God's infinite goodness they turn away from God, rejecting the uprightness and clear vision of salvation in favor of being bent over and blind. Like the prodigal son of Luke's Gospel, humans are sinners, unworthy of God's goodness and gifts. But admitting our poverty gives rise to humility. Next to God, we are nothing, but in the spirit of Francis, Bonaventure encourages sinners to pray for forgiveness because God is a God of mercy.

In a sermon on gratitude (1 Cor 1:4-5), Bonaventure says we need to acknowledge that to the extent we are separated from God, we are poor (RF 4). Our lives are filled with failure, foolishness, blindness and nakedness. It is Christ who provides the remedy. Repentant sinners are gifted with compassion; the blind who pray are offered wisdom; the naked receive grace; the foolish receive glory. For Bonaventure, our poverty takes on dramatic proportions because it is seen in contrast to the generosity and riches of Christ.

Experiencing our poverty is the first step toward a contrite heart. Whether it is moral, intellectual, spiritual or physical poverty, we all stand poor before God. As we reflect on these truths today we ask: Are there specific ways in which we experience ourselves as "poor ones" in the desert? Examples include our inability to simplify our consuming ways; to heal intractable problems in relationships; to protect ourselves against illness and death; to abandon petty personal concerns. There is little hope that our hearts will be pierced unless we become aware of our own and the world's poverty. Only when we stand together in solidarity as "the poor ones in the desert" will we be moved to address the ills of our own time.

Linked to poverty is the virtue of humility.[37] Humility presents a distinctive set of issues in a society that is fueled by images of "manifest destiny." This virtue is also problematic from the perspective of gender studies. Many Christian men simply exempt themselves from this virtue, while women see themselves as oppressed rather than freed by preaching that establishes a special female link—through Mary—to humility. An initial response is to discard it, relegating it to the dung heap of patriarchal detritus. But that is to throw the baby out with the bath. Instead, theologians, ethicists and specialists in spirituality need to reflect on the virtue of humility in the context of recent discussions of virtue and the feminist critique. We need to reflect on how we experience genuine humility and find language that will serve to nurture rather than stunt the spiritual life. One aspect of this retrieval will be to examine the tradition for possible insight. What does Bonaventure say about this virtue?

As pride is at the top of the list of vices, so humility forms the foundation of the virtues as pride's antidote. In the *Disputed Questions on Evangelical Perfection*, Bonaventure speaks of humility as (1) holding oneself in little esteem; (2) giving due honor and worship to God; (3) bearing with one's neighbors; (4) the gateway to wisdom; (5) the abode of grace, thus constituting humility as the summit of the whole of Christian perfection. It involves giving what is due to both God and human beings. Thus Bonaventure links humility with justice (EP 1; V, 122).[38] Following in Christ's footsteps, Francis is seen as an exemplar of humility. Bonaventure says, "St. Francis was a servant of God humble in his reverence for him, more humble still in caring for his neighbor and most humble of all in despising himself. I admire the humility of Francis more than all his other virtues" (LM 6).

In a sermon on the verse from Matthew's Gospel, "Learn from me, for I am meek and humble of heart" (Matt 11:29), Bonaventure examines humility in his usual threefold way: (1) the fruits that make it so attractive; (2) the manner in which it is acquired; (3) the means by which it is maintained (DM, 73f.). His first point is an important one that we often forget. That is, humility can only be acquired through meditation on the goodness and the judgments of God. Too often we think of our sinfulness and our human frailty exclusively within the horizon of human existence, and shrink from it. The point of humility is not to "dump on" or belittle ourselves. Rather, humility is simply the truth of our condition *over against* the infinitely generous and unconditional love of God. Bonaventure calls to our attention that unless we gaze on this goodness, the truth about ourselves will never become evident and exhortations to compunction will fall on deaf ears. Only when we keep God's love before us—symbolized by Christ on the cross—will we open ourselves to this gift.

As a university professor, Bonaventure offers a special word about intellectual hubris resulting from a lack of humility. Toward the end of his life, in the *Collations on the Six Days*, Bonaventure criticized severely what he considered to be the errors of Christian professors at Paris, whom he perceived as embracing Aristotle at the expense of gospel humility. Without humility these so-called lovers of wisdom embraced a false human wisdom. Thus they lost track of the hermeneutical key to all knowledge, that is, Christ the center (*Hex* 1.10–17).[39] The text reads in part: "Opposing the concelebration of divine praise, we have the spirit of presumption and curiosity, in the sense that the presumptuous one does not glorify God but praises himself, while the curious ones are lacking in devotion. There are many men of this kind, empty of praise and devotion although filled with the splendours of knowledge. They build wasps' nests without honeycombs, while the bees make honey" (*Hex* 1.8).

Truth demands that humans admit their sinfulness and the transient nature of human life. The ashes of Ash Wednesday remind us that we come from dust and return to dust. When we keep before us the truth that our lives are but a moment in time, we are less likely to "sweat the small stuff." As Bonaventure reminds us, "Today you are alive, tomorrow you may be dead; healthy and strong today, sick and weak tomorrow, today a rich man, tomorrow perhaps a beggar; wise today, possibly you will become foolish tomorrow" (DM, 77). It does not follow that we think less of, or denigrate, the lives we are given. Rather, the daily material and spiritual aspects of existence become ever more precious, deepening our sorrow whenever we prove ungrateful or indifferent. Feeling truly wretched, poor, blind and naked are genuine and valuable feelings that result from our growing love affair with the world and with the God who created it.

Finally, humility involves respect for others. Bonaventure captured Francis's "persona" as one who had a deferential demeanor toward all other persons, toward animals and all of creation (LM 8.6; 12.3). If we see ourselves rightly, it is unlikely that we will see ourselves as better than, and privileged over, others. Humility nurtures a profound reverence for creation, and to the extent that our love for the world grows, to that extent are we devastated when we or others act to destroy it.

Bonaventure can be quite concrete when he speaks about how to maintain the virtue of humility. This is accomplished by having sorrow for one's sins; by being silent about one's virtues; by hard work and discipline; and by despising honors (DM, 79). Humble persons keep the commandments and attribute nothing of God's glory to themselves.

Bonaventure cites Bernard of Clairvaux: "You are indeed a faithful servant of the Lord when nothing of the Lord's abundant glory, which does not come from you but is channeled through you, remains clinging to your hands."[40] The result of putting oneself at the service of others in humility is to experience the joy of friendship with God and to be invited to "go up higher" (Luke 14:10; DM, 129).

How can we understand Bonaventure's reiteration of Francis's advice to strive to be considered worthless by others? Can we read chapter 6 of the *Life* and not conclude that Francis was a crazy man, and that Bonaventure must have been like him to praise such behavior—for example, Francis asking the friars to drag him naked through the streets; saying things like "the more contemptible the superior the more pleasing is the humility of the one who obeys"; comparing a humble person to a corpse; commanding friars to insult him. What is one to do with these texts? Bonaventure suggests that it is easier to admire Francis's humility than to imitate it (LM 6.2), but today, do we even admire it? I don't know.

Bonaventure also raises the question whether the act of humility seems to be out of harmony with humans' natural instinct to seek the good for themselves. Here we find ourselves in more accessible territory. He answers in the negative, since it benefits humans to realize that one is dependent on God and to root out vanity and pride. Humility transcends and perfects nature, but it is not against it (EP 1.1 ad 1).[41] Rather, humility is a way to oppose hypocrisy; it is the mean between cowardice and stubbornness or arrogance, which give rise especially to pride. Humility instructs followers of Christ to despise the fame of transitory praise and to "suppress the arrogance of bloated bragging and reject the lies of deceptive pretense" (LM 6.2). One should take less account of oneself, not because one knows oneself to be of less account than another in some absolute sense, but rather because one is more certain of one's own defects than of another's.[42] We are asked not to judge, because we cannot know either the reasons for another's sin or the fullness of a person's perfections. While accounts of Francis's behavior certainly get our attention, and while few will aim to imitate Francis in a literal sense, Bonaventure helps us to probe further by inviting us to ask how we can free ourselves from a pseudo-humility that is a cover for self-preoccupation, insecurity and self-hate.

A final foundational truth about humility that is implicit in Bonaventure's spirituality of the cross is that one cannot command it. One can only approach it indirectly, for to set out to be humble is already not to be. It is a gift for which we pray, a gift that emerges when we see truly the awesome beauty and goodness of God, others, ourselves and the world in their light.

Bonaventure: Resource for Today

I would like to offer three suggestions as to how Bonaventure's approach to the cross can be helpful today. The first has to do with his invitation to gaze on the cross in and through his words. This means allowing Bonaventure's language of metaphor and image to draw us into the existential reality behind it. This does not mean that we should try to have Bonaventure's experience, but rather that we use his evocative and provocative language to lead us into our own experience of the Cruci-fied. How, when, where do we meet this poor, condescending God? What is the effect of allowing this truth, put forth so eloquently by Bonaventure, to penetrate our beings? What is the relationship among the poverty and humility of God; the poverty and humility of those around us; and our own openness to be poor and humble?

Second, Bonaventure's focus on the cross invites us to grapple with the meaning of the cross for our own time, and this means, in part, from a psychological perspective. A contemporary theologian who has something to offer us in this vein is Sebastian Moore. In his 1977 book, *The Crucified Is No Stranger*, Moore suggests that we see the cross as a symbol of our refusal to become our true selves, that is, selves characterized by freedom and identity. Like Bonaventure, Moore suggests that we see Jesus as the rep-resentative, the symbol, the embodiment of the fullness of humanity—"of this dreaded yet desired self of each of us, this destiny of being human, this unbearable identity and freedom."[43] The evil that crucified Jesus is the same human evil that takes shape in our refusal to embrace the fullness of life for which we were intended. It is the desire to kill that which is good and full of life in ourselves and others—the good that is the evidence that we are indeed called to full personhood, to be imitators of God in Christ.

When we gaze at the Crucified, can we see all the evil of our lives become explicit and concrete in the man on the cross—an evil that is, happily, "resolved in the forgiveness of God of which the crucifixion thus becomes the symbol and sacrament"?[44] Moore sees the cross as the sym-bol that transforms evil into sin and sin into sorrow and forgiveness.

The paradox of the cross is this: When persons of faith gaze on the cross, they discover a God who loves and a self who crucifies. The sources of evil in us become conscious and personal in the face of the Crucified, as we discover the worst dimensions of ourselves, and yet know, as if for the first time, a total acceptance. "That which we kill, in ourselves and in each other, in vicarious and clandestine ways, we have killed once clearly and in the light of day....Love is experienced in the vision of the Crucified."[45] God convinces us of our acceptance in the cross, because it is at that point that we see ourselves at our worst, as crucifiers of life, of the innocent one. The cross makes explicit our sin. Jesus' death is the effect of sin. It is also the healing of that sin. As we come into the fullness of the self, in and through the cross, we can either take credit for it (allowing the ego to prevail) or we can sit in silent contemplation, in humility and gratitude.[46]

As helpful as such psychological analyses are, we need to link them to our present world, filled with agony and suffering. Liberation theologians remind us to link our "theologies of the cross" to the suffering of humanity. Too often theology does not lay open the utter dread and terror of the cross, or the death that one encounters in solidarity with the poor. One wonders whether Bonaventure ever experienced this kind of terror. It certainly is not strikingly evident in his texts. One does get a glimpse of it in the work of a contemporary of Bonaventure, Jacopone da Todi, who writes in a quite different genre—the poetic "laud." He writes,

> I flee the consuming cross and its fires;
> Their heat drives me back and I flee from Love.
> Nowhere can I find refuge—
> The flames continue to blaze in my heart and mind.
> ...
> I am in flight, Brother, because I have been wounded,
> And wounded close to the heart;
> You know nothing of such pain.
> I pray you, say no more.
>
> I find [the cross] full of arrows
> That speed from the side,
> Piercing my armor and my heart.
> The archer aims them straight at me.[47]

It strikes me that one does not "decide" to feel the terror of the cross. Certainly Jesus did not. It is not a "skill" of the spiritual life that one cultivates. Perhaps all one can do is to pray to learn how to love well, to open oneself to God's tender and terrifying love. For genuine love inevitably leads to taking a stand, and in the darkness that follows, all one can do is choose to endure, to follow, to be faithful, to forgive, to do the right thing, to speak the truth—in other words, to model ourselves on Jesus.

But ultimately, I think Bonaventure's theology of the cross invites us to hope. His work is a valuable hedge against the modern tendency to see the cross either as the act of a vindictive God, in which Jesus is the victim of divine wrath or dissatisfaction—or as an act of masochism. For Bonaventure, the cross is the ultimate revelation of a humble, condescending God. In today's understanding, this approach can support the contemporary soteriological shift from a God who orchestrates the event of the cross to one who chooses rather to participate in the pain of the world. The cross was the result of love, a love that led to behaviors that eventually threatened the status quo enough to bring about conviction and death. The cross is our assurance that God is mysteriously, unpredictably, but nevertheless certainly present, especially where we might least expect it—among the disinherited and the brokenhearted.[48] And although Bonaventure did not have the sense of historical consciousness that is ours today, I think he can still help us to recognize the cross as a way in which God draws near to us in the midst of suffering and war, violence and destruction on all levels, from the individual to the globe. A theology of the cross points to the wager that death and suffering are not the final words. Ultimately the cross bears the seeds of new life and resurrection—a promise that is trusted only in faith.

I close with one of Bonaventure's many soaring passages. This one is from *The Mystical Vine*:

> Be strong, then, my weak and wretched soul, and rise aloft; on the wings of faith and hope, fly to this garden of love; concentrate the scattered vision of your mind, and follow the zeal of the bee in gathering for yourself the honey of devotion. Rise to the paradise of love—rise, I say, to the heights of the heart; behold, the One you seek has been lifted up.

But have no fear: being exalted, he was humbled. For he was not lifted up on the cross to show himself less accessible to those who seek him, but in very truth to make himself more accessible to all. And as you approach this paradise with trusting heart, feel the love of the crucified expressed by the open arms, feel the embrace of him who offers himself to you and calls you, and who, wondrously combining misery with mercy, exclaims; "Turn, turn, O Sulamite, turn, turn, that we may look at you" (Ct 7:1; VM XXIV.1).

NOTES

1. For a general discussion of the medieval emphasis on the Passion, see Ewert Cousins, "The Humanity and the Passion of Christ," in *Christian Spirituality II: High Middle Ages and Reformation*, ed. Jill Raitt. World Spirituality Series (New York: Crossroad, 1987), 375-91.

2. *1Sent Prooem.*, q.3, 1–3 (I, 12). References in parentheses refer to volume and page number in *Opera Omnia* (Quaracchi, 1882–1902), 10 volumes. Abbreviations for all the works by and/or related to Bonaventure, Francis and Clare cited in this chapter and the next are as follows:

Commentary on the Sentences (I–IVSent)
Breviloquium (Brev.)
Collationes on the Six Days/Collations in Hexaemeron (Hex)
The Mystical Vine/Vitis mystica (VM)
Second Life by Thomas of Celano (2Cel)
The Defense of the Mendicants/Apologia pauperum (AP)
The Triple Way/De Triplici Via (DTV)
The Journey of the Mind into God/Itinerarium (Itin.)
Soliloquium (Sol)
The Major Life of St. Francis/Legenda maior (LM)
Bonaventure: Rooted in Faith: Homilies to a Contemporary World. Trans. Marigwen Schumacher [Chicago: Franciscan Herald Press, 1974] (RF)
Disputed Questions on Evangelical Perfection/Quaestiones disputatae de perfectione evangelica (EP)
The Disciple and the Master, trans. Eric Doyle [Chicago: Franciscan Herald Press, 1983] (DM)
The Tree of Life/Lignum vitae (LV)
The Office of the Lord's Passion/Officium de passione Domini (OPD)
On the Perfection of Life for Sisters/De perfectione vitae ad sorores (DPV)
The Legend of St. Clare (CL)

The Acts of the Process of Canonization (Proc.)

The Testament (TestC)

Letters to Blessed Agnes of Prague (1–4LAg)

3. George H. Tavard, *Transiency and Permanence: The Nature of Theology According to Bonaventure* (St. Bonaventure, N.Y.: The Franciscan Institute, 1954), 114.

4. Zachary Hayes, *The Hidden Center: Spirituality and Speculative Christology in St. Bonaventure* (New York: Paulist, 1981), 143.

5. Ibid., 94.

6. Ibid., 87.

7. Ibid., 100.

8. Prologue 6.5 (V, 208). English translation, *The Works of Bonaventure*, trans. Jose de Vinck. Vol II (Paterson, N.J.: St. Anthony Guild Press, 1963).

9. Zachary Hayes, "Bonaventure: Mystery of the Triune God," In Kenan Osborne, ed. *The History of Franciscan Theology* (St. Bonaventure, N.Y.: The Franciscan Institute, 1994), 83.

10. Ibid., 45.

11. For a study of the narrative paintings of the passion of Christ in thirteenth-century Italy, see Anne Derbes, *Picturing the Passion in Late Medieval Italy: Narrative Painting, Franciscan Ideologies, and the Levant* (Cambridge: Cambridge University Press, 1996).

12. Hayes, "Bonaventure," 96.

13. (V, 333). In this text, Bonaventure uses the six days of creation as a literary and symbolic framework to explicate his theological ideas. A primary aim of this work was to refute what he saw as an excessive dependence on reason due to the reliance on Aristotle's philosophy as a basis for doing theology at the University of Paris.

14. Hayes, *The Hidden Center*, 214.

15. See articles on the relationship of theology to cosmology and physics by Lyndon Harris, James Studer, Elizabeth Newman and Huston Smith in "The Matter of Matter." *Cross Currents* 48/1 (Spring 1998): 3–60. For an analysis of how union with the Crucified is the key to cosmic harmony in Francis's *Canticle of Brother Sun* and in the works of Bonaventure, see Ilia Delio, "The *Canticle of Brother Sun*: A Song of Christ Mysticism," *Franciscan Studies* 52 (1992): 1–22; and *Crucified Love: Bonaventure's Mysticism of the Crucified Christ* (forthcoming). See also Alexander Gerken, *La théologie du verbe: la relation entre l'incarnation et la création selon S. Bonaventure*, trans. Jacqueline Greal (Paris: Éditions Franciscaines, 1970); and Dominique Gagnan, "La croix et la nature," *Antonianum* 57 (1982).

16. (VIII, 159-189). Using the theme of the vine from John 15:1, Bonaventure compares the cultivation of the vineyard to the spiritual life. The work concludes with a prayer filled with references to the passion of Christ.

17. Ingrid J. Peterson, *Clare of Assisi: A Biographical Study* (Quincy, Ill.: Franciscan Press, 1993), 290; and "Images of the Crucified Christ in Clare of Assisi and Angelo of Foligno," in *That Others May Know and Love: Essays in Honor of Zachary Hayes, O.F.M.* (St. Bonaventure, N.Y.: The Franciscan Institute, 1997), 167-92.

18. Peterson, *Clare of Assisi*, 293.

19. Hayes, "Bonaventure," 85.

20. (V, 248).

21. Hayes, *The Hidden Center*, 124.

22. *III Sent.* D. 15, a.1, q.1, resp. (III, 330-31). In Hayes, ibid., 124-25.

23. Ibid., 127.

24. Hayes, "Bonaventure," 86-87. See Bonaventure, AP 7, 7-8 (VIII, 274-75) and 1, 10 (VIII, 238-39).

25. Hayes, *The Hidden Center*, 136.

26. Ibid., 137.

27. (VIII, 39b) and (VIII, 3-27).

28. (VIII, 14a) and (V, 312). For a new edition of the *Itinerarium*, see *Bonaventure: The Journey of the Mind to God*, trans. Philotheus Boehner. Ed. Stephen F. Brown (Indianapolis/Cambridge: Hackett Publishing Company, 1993).

29. (VIII, 396b).

30. Maurycy Suley, "La Croce Nella Vita Del Cristiano Negli Opuscoli e Sermoni Di S. Bonaventura." *Miscellanea Francescana* 96/1-2 (1996): 117.

31. See E. Longpre, s.v. "Bonaventure" in *Dictionnaire de spiritualité*, I, 1771, note 1.

32. (VIII, 164).

33. Ibid.

34. Hayes, *The Hidden Center*, 214.

35. See "The Passion of Christ in the Life of St. Francis of Assisi: A Comparative Study of the Sources in the Light of Devotion to the Passion Practiced in His Time" by Octavian Schumuck. Trans. from the German (1960) by Ignatius McCormick. *Greyfriars Review* 4/Supplement.

36. (VIII, 505-64). English translation. *Bonaventure: The Soul's Journey into God; The Tree of Life; The Life of St. Francis* (New York/Mahwah: Paulist Press, 1978), 177-327.

37. See John Francis Quinn, *The Historical Constitution of St. Bonaventure's Philosophy* (Toronto: Pontifical Institute of Medieval Studies, 1973), 833-35.

38. (V, 122).

39. (V, 330–32).

40. Bernard of Clairvaux, *On the Song of Songs*, I, 13.3. *The Works of Bernard of Clairvaux*, vol. 2. Cistercian Fathers Series 4 (Kalamazoo: Cistercian Publications, 1971), 90.

41. (V, 122–23).

42. See John Francis Quinn, *The Historical Constitution of St. Bonaventure's Philosophy*, 833.

43. Sebastian Moore, *The Crucified Is No Stranger* (London: Dartman, Longman & Todd, 1977), x.

44. Ibid.

45. Ibid., 2–3.

46. Ibid., 11.

47. Jacopone da Todi, *The Lauds*, No. 75.1–4; 9–12; 17–20. Trans. Serge and Elizabeth Huges (New York: Paulist Press, 1982), 225–26.

48. Elizabeth Johnson, "Jesus and Salvation." *CTSA Proceedings* 49 (1994): 9, 15.

CHAPTER 9

Mysticism Tangible through Metaphor: Bonaventure's Spirituality of the Cross

Elizabeth A. Dreyer

It's All in the Image

In this chapter we continue to probe the rich and diverse imagistic language employed by Bonaventure when he writes about the cross. We move now from Bonaventure's Christology, with its dominant image of God in Christ as condescending lover who does not cling to divinity, to an exploration of several major images he uses to speak about the cross. We begin with some reflections on how to approach medieval images in general. Then we proceed to six specific images Bonaventure linked with the cross—fire, tears, nakedness, the tree of life, the vine, and "marked with the cross."

Scholars continually explore the methods, benefits, and risks involved in retrieving medieval texts. Russian literary theorist, Mikhail Bakhtin, warns against isolating texts from their broader sociocultural matrix and from the long trajectory of history in which any given text must be situated. Language must be understood in a dialogic fashion; that is, the complex elements that impinge on both the reception and the creation of language must be seen in relationship to each other. The basic image through which he understands all language is two people talking with each other—each in the fullness of her or his specific time and place. He writes, "There is neither a first nor a last word and there are no limits to the dialogic context (it extends into the boundless past and the boundless future). Even past meanings, that is, those born in the dialogue of past centuries, can never be stable (finalized, ended once and for all)—they will always change (be renewed) in the process of subsequent development of the dialogue."[1] Such an understanding of the never-ending flow of language gives us courage to try to understand and relate to our own time Bonaventure's language of the cross. Elements of this retrieval include the understandings of the cross that were passed down to the Middle Ages; how the medieval community saw the cross; and how the symbol of the cross functions for us now, which meaning will, of course, lead into future understandings.[2]

In particular, I focus on the imagistic language of the cross in Bonaventure's works. Bonaventure is an apt subject for such an approach, for his distinctive penchant for image-filled language is well documented. Our recent, renewed appreciation of the role of image and metaphor in literature can lead us, I believe, to a greater appreciation of Bonaventure's use of these literary devices, even though his context and ours differ markedly.

How does imagery function for Bonaventure? Regis Armstrong notes how frequently Bonaventure uses the phrase "from the visible to the invisible." This movement is part of the very structure of *The Soul's Journey into God*, and, in the *Life of St. Francis*, Bonaventure says of Francis before his conversion that he "did not know how to pass from appearances of visible things to the contuition of the truth of the invisible" (LM, T. 3).[3] While we do not share the Neoplatonic worldview of the Middle Ages, which sees the material world as but a pale shadow of the real, we can resonate with the way symbols and images put us in touch with realities beyond their material expression.

There are many such testimonials to the role of image in medieval thought and expression. In her book *Image as Insight: Visual Understanding in Western Christianity and Secular Culture*, Margaret Miles quotes a very modern-sounding Thomas Aquinas, who appreciated the intrinsic value of created reality and the ways it functioned in the epistemological process. He says, "The image is the starting point of our knowledge. It is that from which our intellectual activity begins, not as a passing stimulus, but as an enduring foundation."[4] John C. Hirsh comments about medieval texts: "Imagery often plays a crucial role, conveying meaning less by argument than by wonder, a trait poet and mystic both share."[5] And Rosemary Drage Hale explores the topic of sensory perception and memory in medieval mystical experience. When we read medieval mystical texts, she writes, "we miss something of the sensory dynamic of the world or culture of medieval mystics if we persist in interpreting their experience solely as 'visions.'...Perhaps we can begin to do more than translate the words if we take a 'hermeneutical turn'—instead of reading the texts, we could be learning to sense them."[6]

The 1974 volumes celebrating the seventh centenary of Bonaventure's death contain an article by Marigwen Schumacher entitled "Mysticism in Metaphor."[7] She posits that Bonaventure's word choice and selection of images in several of his sermons suggest the extent to which he was in touch with his own religious experience. She writes that there is "an intrinsic, inescapable relationship between the 'what' of Bonaventure's thought and the 'how' of his expression—mysticism tangible through metaphor."[8] Schumacher also picks up on Hale's suggestion about the role of the senses: "To touch—to probe—to, in a way, invade the mythic impulses of Bonaventure's heart and mind, is, I feel and think, an as-yet-unexplored path into his contact with God." Bonaventure's vividness of expression and sensitivity to nuance and cadence pulls the reader into the beauty and thence into the spiritual depth of what he is saying. Bonaventure lived in a world that included "the Gothic smile, the delicate tracery, intricate enamels and wood-carving, amazingly graceful flora and fauna, perfection of craftsmanship even to the tiniest detail, accompanied by soaring and grand cathedrals of exquisite, fragile strength and powerful beauty—all these bespeak a lyric freshness of awareness of God's world. Mosaics and stained glass windows radiated a kind of 'mural poetry' that could not have but influenced those who saw them."[9]

Schumacher goes on to link Bonaventure's poetic and harmonious expression to the joy of Francis, the wandering troubadour of mystic rapture. Francis was clearly endowed with what some have called enthusiasm—Bonaventure often used the term *fervor*—a gift Bonaventure admired and in his own literary-mystical way, possessed. Schumacher describes it as the gift of being God-inspired, touched, attuned, gifted with that rare ability to "see" the direct equation between the divine and the human, and express it in words both powerfully taut and simply clear.[10] In *The Distancing of God*, Bernard Cooke writes of Bonaventure: "From his 'father in God,' Francis of Assisi, Bonaventure had inherited a contemplative awareness of the pervading divine presence. This mystical consciousness caused every detail of experience to be Word of God, to speak of God's loving blessing of human life....The symbol world of

Franciscan spirituality has a freshness that springs from its discovery of the mystery dimension of the ordinary."[11]

Schumacher investigates the poet-preacher-mystic's own personal, intuitive, inspired, nonrational contact with Deity. She cites the article on Bonaventure from the *Dictionnaire de spiritualité*:

> Throughout the periods of religious history, there has perhaps never been found a saint who has made the world hear an invitation to mystical union as broad and as urgent as the Seraphic Doctor. For these reasons, among many others, the spiritual doctrine of St. Bonaventure, totally infused as it is with unction and poetry, constitutes a unique monument in mystical literature.[12]

Bonaventure was a brilliant rhetorician and a learned theologian, but "there is something more that throbs and pulses through his works."[13] British author Sara Maitland reminds us to follow Roland Barthes's invitation to take pleasure *(jouissance)* in the unresolved text, the ending that opens up rather than closes down. She notes that these are obviously the kind of texts in which the great mystics wrote of reaching enormous space in which words fail.[14] Certainly *The Journey of the Soul into God* and many other of Bonaventure's texts fit this description.

Our understanding of Bonaventure's skill as poet in the service of mysticism can be sharpened by a distinction made by Maurycy Suley in an article on the cross in Bonaventure's mystical works and sermons.[15] Suley notes a distinction between spiritual growth that comes as a result of grace and the sacraments, and that which comes through personal assimilation of the works of salvation by listening and meditating on the word of God through prayer and contemplation. Meditation, prayer, contemplation, preaching and hearing the word of salvation provide a different but not separate way from that of the sacraments and doctrine. In the former, one is transformed through the practice of the contemplative gaze upon the images and symbols of redemption. Bonaventure begins and ends the Prologue in *The Tree of Life* with this idea. "No one will have the intimate and lively experience of such a feeling [of being nailed with Christ to the cross] unless, far from forgetting the Lord's passion, or being ungrateful for it, he rather contemplates—with vivid representation, penetrating intelligence, and loving will—the labors, the suffering, and the love of Jesus crucified" (LV Prol. 1). And, "These instances I call fruits, because their full flavor refreshes and their rich substance strengthens the soul who meditates upon them and carefully considers each one; abhorring the example of unfaithful Adam, who preferred the tree of the knowledge of good and evil (Gen 2:17) to the Tree of Life" (LV Prol. 5).

I began our discussion of Bonaventure's spirituality of the cross by attending to the nuances of his style, language, and use of metaphor, because I find that his exposition of the passion of Christ must be read and heard with an inner contemplative ear. Bonaventure's theology and spirituality of the cross reflect much of the tradition he inherited, but their central role in his theological system and the manner of presentation are distinctive. When one spends time absorbing this material, one begins to move beyond analysis and knowledge to a felt sense of what Bonaventure is trying to communicate about the experience and meaning of gazing on the cross.

Images of the Imitation of the Cross *(Imitatio Crucis)*

Bonaventure's treatment of the cross can be found primarily in *The Tree of Life, The Mystical Vine, The Office of the Lord's Passion* and secondarily in *The Soul's Journey into God, On the Perfection of Life for Sisters, The Major Life of St. Francis, The Minor Life of St. Francis,* and several sermons. Bonaventure inherited, brought to new heights, and influenced the future of the tradition of devotion to the suffering humanity of Christ.[16] He borrows from twelfth-century texts of Bernard of Clairvaux and Ekbert of Schönau, who had written a very popular treatise entitled *Wound of Love (Stimulus amoris).* Like his predecessors, Bonaventure writes in an "intimate, affective, apostrophic style, marked by familiar address to Christ."[17] He extends the gospel material with graphic descriptions of the details of the passion, such as Christ being spit upon, hurled to the ground, pushed and pulled by his tormentors, stretched on the cross, left with gaping wounds. He is among the earliest writers to write about Mary's mental anguish at Christ's suffering. Bonaventure influenced many later texts on the passion, including one of the most popular in the Franciscan tradition, entitled *Meditations of the Life of Christ (Meditationes vitae Christi),* a work probably composed in the Franciscan milieu of northern Italy at the end of the thirteenth century or the beginning of the fourteenth.[18]

Much of this material is inspired by Old Testament texts from the Psalms and Isaiah that were applied to Christ (Ps 22:18 "They have numbered all my bones"; Isa 1:6: Christ suffers from the sole of his foot to the top of his head; Isa 53:4: Christ covered with bruises and wounds like a leper; Ps 45:2–3: Christ's suffering and beauty is above that of humans; Isa 63:1–2: describes the red apparel of a man in the winepress). In *The Tree of Life*, Bonaventure begins with a pericope from Paul's letter to the Galatians, "With Christ I am nailed to the cross" (Gal 2:20) and employs the metaphor of a tree to map the events of Christ's life, dividing the meditation into twelve fruits arranged in three groups, covering the origin, passion, and glory of Christ. In *The Mystical Vine*, Bonaventure builds on the words, "I am the true vine" from John's Gospel (15:1). The events of the Passion are compared to the cultivation, pruning, and tying up of the vine. Throughout, "Bonaventure stresses the desirability of conforming to the Passion of Christ, participating in his sufferings so that we may regain the image of his divinity." We are invited to embrace the disfigured body of Christ "in language which is physical, intense, and reciprocal."[19] He writes in *The Mystical Vine*: "Let us embrace our wounded Christ whose hands and feet and side and heart were pierced by the wicked vine-tenders; let us pray that he may deign to tie our hearts, now so wild and impenitent, with the bond of love, and wound them with love's spear (VM 3.6)."[20]

As many scholars have noted, Bonaventure's spirituality is an extensive, more systematic presentation of the spirituality of Francis, one characterized primarily as *imitatio Christi*. Bonaventure writes of Francis in the *Life:* "A gentle feeling of compassion transformed him into the one who wanted to be crucified" (LM 8.1). This spirituality of the cross, inspired by Francis, is most visible in *The Life of St. Francis*, in which Bonaventure traces the steps of Francis; in *The Tree of Life*, which leads the reader through a series of meditations on the origin, death, and resurrection of Christ so that one might imitate more closely the dynamics of the life of Christ; in several sermons; and in *The Soul's Journey into God*, in which Francis's experience of the cross on Mount Alverna provides the starting point. This keynote theme finds its fulfillment in the final moments of the text, thus making the cross an overarching image for the entire work.[21]

Whoever loves this death can see God....Let us, then, die and enter into darkness. Let us silence all our cares, our desires, our imaginings. With Christ crucified let us pass out of this world to the Father so that when the Father is shown to us, we may say with Philip: *It is enough for us.* Let us hear with Paul: *My grace is sufficient for you,* and rejoice with David, saying: *My flesh and my heart have fainted away: You are the God of my heart, and the God that is my portion forever.* (*Itin.,* 7.6)

Here, "the spiritual journey as enacted by Christ, and by Francis in imitation of Christ, is unthinkable without the mystery of cruciform love."[22] The cross is a presupposition of mystical union. The discussion of the life of Christ, for Bonaventure, revolves around the specifically Franciscan understanding of the poor Christ.

For Bonaventure, Jesus' life had "normative significance in the spiritual search for an authentic human existence. Spirituality is, above all, the journey of the human soul 'into God.' And that journey is made by conforming one's personal life to the mystery of the eternal Word enfleshed in the history of Jesus."[23] The culmination of that life is the cross—the ultimate sign of God's love for humanity. Imitation of the cross has taken endless forms across the centuries. Some of those forms are better left behind, such as the extreme forms of asceticism that characterized some medieval practices. But one effect of meditation on the cross that seems fairly constant across the centuries is its ability to nurture compassion in the viewer. Of course, this presumes that the motivation for contemplation of the cross is love, but when that is the case, it can create an identification with, and sensitivity to, the suffering of others. Leonardo Boff reminds us that compassion is not to be confused with masochism, in which a person stops with the feeling of pain. Rather, compassion means the desire to identify with the pain of another, to feel together with, to suffer in communion.[24] With this counsel to keep the compassion of God at the forefront of our reflections on the cross, let us turn to Bonaventure's images.

Fire

Francis had a heart of flesh that could feel, sing, praise, vibrate, weep, be moved. One has to presume that the saints who asked to experience the pain of Christ on the cross did so because they were in love, desiring to walk with, stand in solidarity with, and actually feel the pain of the Beloved. Bonaventure uses a number of images from the tradition to speak of the pilgrim's encounter with the cross—fire,[25] forms of the stigmata, nudity, and tears. In the *Little Flowers of Saint Francis (Fioretti)*, a fourteenth-century collection of anecdotes about Francis, fire is a recurrent image.[26] In one example, we read of Francis's reception of the stigmata on Mount Alverna. The text recounts that a copy of the crucified Christ was produced in Francis through a "mental fire." The symbol is further developed in the story that the whole mountain also caught fire and "seemed to burn among bright flames that illuminated all of the mountains and valleys around as if the sun shone over the land."[27]

In *The Major Life*, Bonaventure says that Francis was "assigned an angelic ministry and was totally aflame with a Seraphic fire" (LM Prol. 1). Francis's vision of the seraph on Alverna was given so that as Christ's lover, Francis "might learn in advance that he was to be totally transformed into the likeness of Christ crucified, not by the martyrdom of his flesh, but by the fire of his love consuming his soul" (*incendium mentis;* LM 13.3). On Alverna, Francis "burned with a stronger flame of heavenly desires....His unquenchable fire of love for the good Jesus had been fanned into such a blaze of flames that many waters could not quench so powerful a love" (Ct 8:6–7; LM 13.1, 2).

Extending (and mixing!) the metaphor somewhat, Bonaventure writes of Francis: "Like a glowing coal, he seemed totally absorbed in the flame of divine love. Whenever he heard of the love of God, he was at once excited, moved and inflamed as if an inner chord of his heart had been plucked by the plectrum of the external voice" (LM 9.1). Inspired by Francis's witness, Bonaventure writes at the end of *The Soul's Journey into God*: "But if you wish to know how these things come about, ask grace not instruction, desire not understanding...God not humans, darkness not clarity, not light but the fire that totally inflames and carries us into God by ecstatic unction and burning affections. This fire is God and his furnace is in Jerusalem (Isa 31:9); and Christ enkindles it in the heat of his burning passion, which only he truly perceives who says: My soul chooses hanging and my bones death (Job 7:15)" (*Itin.* 7.6).

Bonaventure is not the first to use the image of fire to portray an all-encompassing union with Jesus. We find this image in one of the sayings of the desert fathers, those eccentric fourth-century monks who went to the desert to fight the demons and live in humble deference to one another. The story goes: "A brother came to the cell of Abba Arsenius at Scetis. Waiting outside the door he saw the old man entirely like a flame."[28] Throughout the tradition, this fire, enkindled in the passion, is extended to embrace all forms of intense union with God and to the opening of heaven, effected by the paschal event. But *heaven* is not reserved exclusively for life beyond history; indeed, it is intended to be experienced now at those moments when heaven is glimpsed on earth. Poet Julian Budenz plays with the metaphor of fire in "Heaven."

I shall term it seeing
I shall name it light

We saw

We were plunged into white light
For ten thousand years
We saw the prisms of ourselves
And of our friends

And of the friends of our friends

We remembered the morning gold of the elm
In New England autumns
We remembered the burning bushes
Of October afternoons

They were as we remembered

And not dying
And the light was living and caressed us
And the next ten thousand years
We danced and we sang the light

And the next we saw and we saw

The light burned us like locust blossoms
We flamed like love
Like incense burning like spring
In luminous showers
We saw as we saw and we saw white light

We shall pass the term
We shall know the name.[29]

This cluster of images supports and fills out Bonaventure's image
of God as fire—a fire of love enkindled in the heat of Christ's burning
passion, an image intended to invite the reader to enter into the mystery
of union with Christ on the cross. The image provides space in which to
move, to reflect on experiences in which we felt ourselves to be "all
flame." Such experiences suggest gift, self-abandonment, total absorp-
tion, freedom, and spontaneity. Can reflection on such experiences
move us toward insight into what Francis must have experienced and
about what Bonaventure is trying to tell us through his image of falling
asleep with Christ on the cross? And even beyond these insights, can we
imagine ourselves, at some basic, primitive level, facing the cross and
becoming "all flame"?

Tears

For most people, the Franciscan tradition evokes images of joy not
tears. And in some instances tears are indeed a sign of joy. Bonaventure
writes of Francis at the crib of Greccio: "The man of God stands before
the crib, filled with affection, bathed in tears and overflowing with joy"
(LM 10.7). When his father was pursuing him in anger, Francis begged
for deliverance with a flood of tears that produced an experience of excessive joy (LM 2.2). And one day, while weeping for his sins (Isa 38:3-5),
Francis experienced the joy of the Holy Spirit's forgiveness (LM 3.6).

But the symbol of tears is linked above all with redemption.
Bonaventure asks readers to weep for their sins and for others, to weep at
the sufferings of Christ, indeed to join their tears to those of Christ. Again,
Francis is the model. Bonaventure often recalls how Francis wept daily
and so weakened his eyes by tears that he lost his sight (DM, 69, 122, 138;
LM 5.8; 8.1). According to Thomas of Celano, Francis's first "official" biog-
rapher, Francis "wept bitterly because of the Passion of Christ, which he
almost always had before his eyes. Remembering the wounds of Christ, he
filled the roads with laments, without finding consolation." And after his
experience before the crucifix at San Damiano, Francis had a "holy compassion for the Crucified" fixed in his soul (2Cel 10).

The sources also tell us that Clare's prayer was often suffused with tears. The author of *The Legend of Saint Clare* presents an image of Clare as another Mary Magdalene, weeping and kissing the feet of Jesus.[30] And in her sleep, an angel of darkness comes to Clare to deter her from weeping, threatening that it will cause her to go blind or to dissolve her brain (CL 19). Clare wept when a sister was sad or tempted (CL 38), and when Clare wept at prayer, her tears moved other sisters to tears of sorrow as well (Proc 1.7; 3.7; 6.4; 10.3). Clare wept with the suffering Christ and even wept as she taught the novices to do the same (CL 30).

Bonaventure tells us that Francis "strove with constant sighs of sorrow to root out vice and sin" from his heart, and admonishes us to follow him in drenching the couch nightly with weeping (DM, 63; LM 10.4). In a sermon on Luke 19:46—"My house will be a house of prayer," Bonaventure mentions three things necessary for prayer. The first is getting ready; the second is attentiveness; and the third is passionate joy (RF 8). Bonaventure uses the metaphor of "being scrubbed clean" to describe the repentance of the first stage of prayer. One must be scrubbed clean from stubborn pride, from sensual amusement, and from frenzied activity. It is in the second stage of "scrubbing" that he uses the language of tears. He cites 1 Samuel, Judith, and the Psalms. Anna and Judith purified themselves with tears and weeping (1 Sam 1:10; Jdt 12:78), and the psalmist is worn out groaning every night, drenching his pillow and soaking his bed with tears (Ps 6:6).

In his meditation on the passion, *The Mystical Vine*, the reader also encounters an abundance of tears. In this text, Bonaventure presents a graphic picture of the bloody, sweating Christ—our son, brother, and spouse condemned. He writes: "Who would not be filled with sorrow at the sight? Who could keep back sobs and tears? As it is a devout act to rejoice for Jesus, so it is devout to weep for him....Pour out a torrent of tears for him who is dying in such bonds, since he first wept for us. Stand close to him as he hangs, be still and see to what a bitter, shameful death he is condemned" (VM IV.3–4). Bonaventure scolds those whose hearts are made of stone and those whose hearts may even be as hard as diamonds. Only an ossified heart would be unable to weep at the sight of the suffering Lord. Through the vehicle of his text, Bonaventure not only uses words that speak about hearts being softened so that they might weep, but, as we have seen, the text puts us close to experience, so that readers who enter into its texture and flow are likely to have effected in themselves what the text is suggesting. Notice the switch from imperative to declarative sentences here:

> O heart diamond-hard, immerse yourself in the plenteous blood of our kid and lamb; rest in it and become warm; once warm, be soft-ened; once softened, let flow a fountain of tears. I will therefore seek, and then find, a wellspring of tears in the sorrow, the cross, the nails, and finally, the scarlet blood, of Jesus most mild. I will consider and I will understand, as much as he grants me to do so, the ruddiness of body and soul of the Lover different from any other, Jesus most loving. (VM XV.3)

In an earlier chapter he describes the kind of careful, meditative attention to the cross we have been discussing—a kind of loving attention that can bring the cross to life, making it real and compelling. He entreats the reader:

> Look upon the face of your anointed, O Christian soul, and let your tearful eyes behold his torments; lift up your grieving heart to see the manifold afflictions he found while he was seeking you. Open your eyes wide upon the face of your anointed; listen with eager ears to any word he may speak while in such pain. And whatever you hear, store as a most precious treasure in the secret vault of your heart. (VM VI.3)

This tradition of tears that Bonaventure inherits and passes on is one that may be quite foreign to modern sensibilities. But contemporary theology, especially in its feminist forms, is recovering our affective side and its relationship to bodiliness—both linked to the gift of tears. In our culture, the physical expression of tears is more acceptable for women, and perhaps those women who understand this gift most deeply can be our guides. Elizabeth Johnson reminds us of the relational nature of weeping. We weep not only for our own sins but for the sins of the world that cause endless suffering for those we love. She suggests that "women do more than a fair share of the crying in the world." With Jesus, who weeps over Jerusalem, Rachel weeps over her children and South American women weep for the "disappeared."[31] Physical tears symbolize the depth of religious mourning.

Weeping is a deeply human activity. Gregory of Nyssa called tears "the blood in the wounds of the soul" *(Funeral Oration for Placilla)*. As it is natural for a wound to bleed, except among the bloodless, so it is natural for Christians to weep for their sins and for the suffering Christ. Tears bring about not only personal consolation but can also lead to the purification and peace of the world. Conversion that produces tears of affection cannot happen unless we *feel* deeply for ourselves and for our world and act on those feelings. For Francis, Clare, and Bonaventure, this journey is centered on loving contemplation of the crucified. To cut ourselves off from feeling is to cut ourselves off from compassion for the world and from imitating a compassionate God.

Bonaventure's theology and spirituality of the cross also provoke reflection on a renewed sense of the rituals in which we weep for our sins and for the sins of the world. In the past, frequent rote confession in the sacrament of penance led many to a numbness about sin and perhaps the eclipse of compunction. The same may be true of the penitential rite with which we begin each Eucharist. For many worshipers, these words and ritual gestures have become routine and empty, no longer capable of moving us to the profound sense of loss and mourning that is at the heart of conversion. We are embarrassed to weep and gnash our teeth. Bonaventure's powerful texts on the cross can function as an invitation to bring new life to this confession by connecting it with events from the local community and the world. Every week we become aware of new expressions of violence and indifference to humans and the environment. By bringing these stark and sinful realities to worship, we can arouse in the community feelings of deep sorrow and expressions of tears that will give renewed truth and feeling to the words, "I confess to almighty God and to you, my brothers and sisters...."

Nakedness

A third image that Bonaventure associates with the cross is nudity. The theme of spiritual nudity was popular in the twelfth and thirteenth centuries. Jean Châtillon traces the origins of the phrase "naked, to follow the naked Christ" *(nudum Christum nudus sequere)* to the correspondence of St. Jerome.[32] Ambroise Nguyen Van Si writes that in the Middle Ages spiritual nudity functioned as a symbol of distance from the world and evangelical stripping, usually linked with the birth and death of Christ.[33] Bonaventure has recourse to this image when he speaks of St. Francis and Franciscan poverty.[34] In his text *On the Perfection of Life,* Bonaventure exhorts his readers to embrace poverty by calling to mind the poor beginnings and poor ending of the Lord. On the cross, Christ was stripped and despoiled of everything—his clothing, his body, his life, even his divine glory (DPV III.5). Bonaventure calls on Bernard of Clairvaux, who wrote, "See the poor Christ, born without decent shelter, lying in a manger between an ox and an ass, wrapped in poor swaddling clothes, fleeing into Egypt, riding an ass, and hanging naked upon a gibbet."[35] And in his *Defense of the Mendicants,* written to counter the attack of Gérard d'Abbeville, Bonaventure suggested that the way of poverty was the best way to imitate Christ in his extreme state of nudity (AP 7.8-9).

Perhaps the most famous use of the image of nudity can be found in Bonaventure's *Life of St. Francis,* in which he recounts the story of Francis's confrontation with his father before the bishop. "Drunk with remarkable fervor," Francis strips himself naked in front of everyone. He then clothes himself in the rags of a beggar. Bonaventure goes on, "Francis accepted it gratefully and with his own hand marked a cross on it with a piece of chalk, thus designating is as the covering of a crucified man and a half-naked beggar. Thus the servant of the Most High King was left naked so that he might follow his naked crucified Lord, whom he loved" (LM 2.4).

This story of nakedness at the beginning of Francis's conversion account is complemented with one at his death. Bonaventure says of Francis's last hours: "And so, in fervor of spirit, he threw himself totally naked on the naked ground so that in that final hour of death, when the enemy could still attack him violently, he would struggle naked with a naked enemy....In all things he wished to be conformed to Christ crucified, who hung on the cross poor, suffering and naked" (LM 14.4). In the end, however, the theme of nudity is completed with that of clothing, for Bonaventure writes of how Francis was clothed in body and soul with Christ crucified. The nudity of the disciples is hidden by the glorious clothing of the cross (LM 15.1).[36]

Bonaventure also associates nudity with the poverty of renunciation. While Francis's life dramatized the rejection of material reality, Bonaventure extends this stripping to the intellectual life as well. He writes, "Whoever desires to attain the height of poverty should renounce in some way not only worldly wisdom but also learning, that having renounced such a possession, he might enter into the mighty works of the Lord (Ps 70:15-16) and offer himself naked to the arms of the Crucified. No one can be said to have perfectly renounced the world if he still keeps the purse of his own opinion in the hidden recesses of his heart" (LM 7.2).

The image of nudity invites us to reflect on this most common of human experiences. There is the forced nudity of the prisoner, who like Jesus, experiences humiliation or degradation. There is the nakedness of the poor, who do not have the means to clothe themselves properly. In contrast, there is nudity that is chosen. This kind of nudity can take the form of simplicity of dress and life, or psychological, intellectual and spiritual openness. There is also the nudity of illness, of bathing, and that most precious nudity of lovers, childbirth, and children. Throughout all these experiences, one notes some common threads. Nudity produces vulnerability. Clothes serve to protect vulnerable skin from damage. Clothes also hide bumps, scars, warts, and crooked limbs. Naked, I am not able to hide the truth of my physical being. But the choice to be nude with one's beloved can be the surest sign of trust and surrender to another. It is in this moment of simple, loving openness to another human being that many of us glimpse what the saints might have meant when they talked about standing naked before God—even though the Neoplatonic heritage did not allow them to see that this spiritual experience can also be deeply embedded in the physical.

Nudity also creates an odd kind of democracy. The clothes we wear usually point to class and status, although they can also signal the freedom to express one's particular personality. But all of us come into the world naked and in a true sense leave the world naked. At these moments all human beings share a common humanity in its stark simplicity and nothingness. When one is mindful of these common experiences of life and death, it becomes more difficult to lord it over one another, to be arrogant, or to treat each other with disdain. The nakedness of the cross can be a symbol of the linkage of these various experiences. In our willingness to be vulnerable with each other, we can learn to stand in solidarity with our suffering sisters and brothers. The cross stands as assurance and hope to those who languish in prisons, who are tortured, who suffer the ravages of war and famine. Bonaventure's counsel to live simply and humbly is connected to the imagery of nakedness—literal and dramatic in the case of Francis, metaphoric and reflective in Bonaventure.

The Tree of Life

We have seen how Bonaventure likes to link opposites as a way of dramatizing the condescending love of God. The opposites he proposes are ultimately those of the divine and the human, brought together in startling clarity in the incarnate Christ. One of Bonaventure's favorite names for Christ is Mediator. In addition to the restorative function of the incarnation, Bonaventure also sees it as establishing friendship between God and humans. In the *Breviloquium*, he offers the following image: "Nor could humans have recovered the friendship of God except through a fitting Mediator, who could touch God with one hand and human beings with the other, who would be the likeness and the friend of both: God in divinity, and human in humanity" (*Brev.* IV.4). This short passage suggests the image of a child's cut-out paper figures linked to one another; the telephone ad—"Reach out and touch someone"—or, in a more artistic vein, Picasso's wonderful painting entitled "Le Rond," in which figures join hands and swirl in a circular dance. This horizontal image of the divine-human link is complemented by one much more favored by Bonaventure, that of the tree. The wooden tree of the cross becomes the tree of life.

Bonaventure begins his work entitled *The Tree of Life* with Paul's statement in Galatians 2:20: "With Christ I am nailed to the cross." In this text, Bonaventure explicitly refers to the role of the imagination in the spiritual life. He says, "Because imagination assists understanding, I have arranged in the form of an imaginary tree the few passages selected from many, and have disposed them in such a way that, in the first or lower branches, the Saviour's origin and life are described; in the middle branches, His passion; and in the top branches, His glorification" (LV Prol. 2). The quotations on each branch are in alphabetical order for easy remembering, and there is a spiritual fruit growing from each branch.

This tree is reminiscent of the tree in Genesis 2:9. Its roots are watered by an eternally gushing fountain that becomes a great and living river that irrigates the whole garden of the church. There are twelve branches. The leaves serve as medicine, "for indeed the word of the cross is the power of God for salvation to all who believe (Rom 1.16)" (LV Prol. 3). The flowers are fragrant, drawing our desires. "This is the fruit born of the virginal womb, and ripened on the tree of the cross to delectable maturity by the midday heat of the Eternal Sun, that is, by Christ's love" (LV Prol. 3). Like the hands of Christ extended horizontally to link us to God, the tree of life images the vertical link between earth and heaven. The flavorful fruits of this tree "refresh and strengthen the soul who meditates upon them and carefully considers each one; abhorring the example of unfaithful Adam, who preferred the tree of the knowledge of good and evil (Gen. 2.17) to the Tree of Life" (LV Prol. 5).

The point of this image is to invite us to reflect on God's love shown on the cross, but above all, it reveals the intimate connections that God has established with us in Christ. The image is a vertical one, stemming in part from Bonaventure's deep sense of the hierarchical nature of the universe. But while today we shy away from ladders and hierarchies to describe the spiritual life and our relationship with God, I think we do share with Bonaventure an appreciation of the deeper experience of the profound solidarity and loving abandon that God shares with us. Transposed into a new twenty-first century key, the image of the tree of life can feed our hunger for a truly incarnational understanding of the faith and of God's presence in and to the world.

The Vine

A related horticultural symbol is the vine, to which Bonaventure devotes an entire treatise, *The Mystical Vine: Treatise on the Passion of the Lord.* This text contains the most graphic depiction of the details of the crucifixion. In this text, Bonaventure states frequently that his aim is to move the reader to empathy, to tears, to a heart that sorrows with the sorrows of the beloved savior (VM IV.3; XI.2; XV.1). The vine is pruned, bound, hung on a trellis that resembles a cross; the leaves of the vine are Christ's last words; the flowers are virtues; the rose is the flower colored by Jesus' blood. This is certainly a text that merits careful meditation—especially perhaps during the penitential season. Here I can suggest but a few of its main themes.

In this text, Bonaventure compares the pruning of the vine to the stripping endured by Jesus in his passion. In the incarnation, Jesus was humbled and made less than a man. "His glory was cut away with the knife of shame, his power with the knife of abjection, his pleasure with the knife of pain, his wealth with the knife of poverty" (VM II.2–3). He was born poor, lived poor, and died on the cross the poorest of all (VM II.3). And then even his "friends and relatives were cut from him with the knife of fear, so that there was none to comfort him among all those who were dear to him" (VM II.4). But this cutting is consoling because of the "abundance of fruit it yielded" (VM II.4). Thus does Bonaventure give his readers a way to understand, in the light of the cross, the stripping that life inevitably brings through troubles, violence, illness, and aging. Bonaventure interprets Jesus' words, "It is consummated" (John 19:30) as a model to help us "persevere in the face of all our troubles, until following our Guide, Jesus most kind, we reach the end of all our tribulations and can trustingly say with him: 'It is consummated'; that is: 'By your help, not by my own strength, I have fought the good fight, I have finished the course, I have kept faith' (2 Tim 4:7)" (VM XII.2).

A second image is that of the binding of the vines. Bonaventure notes seven kinds of binding suffered by Christ: the virgin's womb; the manger; the ropes with which he was tied at his arrest; the ropes with which he was dragged to the tribunal; the ropes with which he was affixed to the scourging post; the binding of the crown of thorns; and that of the iron of the nails that held him on the cross. The one who is freedom itself is bound for the sake of our own freedom. Bonaventure entreats, "Let us be bound with the bonds of the passion of the good and most loving Jesus, so that we may also share with him the bonds of love" (VM IV.5).

Marked with the Cross

Bonaventure used another image to speak of human conformity to the cross—that of being signed or clothed with the sign of the cross—on the forehead; by wearing the Franciscan habit; and in Francis, by the stigmata.[37] In the *Major Life*, Bonaventure notes that Francis's ministry was to

...mark with a Tau the foreheads of those who moan and grieve, signing them with the cross of penance and clothing them with his habit, which is in the form of a cross. But even more is this confirmed with the irrefutable testimony of truth by the seal of the likeness of the living God, namely of Christ crucified, which was imprinted on his body...by the wondrous power of the Spirit of the living God. (LM, Prol. 1)

At the end of the *Life*, Bonaventure recounts the seven incidences in which Francis bore the arms of heaven emblazoned with the sign of the cross (LM 13.10). These signs culminate in the stigmata:

Now, finally toward the end of your life you were shown at the same time the sublime vision of the Seraph and the humble figure of the Crucified, inwardly inflaming you and outwardly marking you as the second Angel, ascending from the rising of the sun and bearing upon you the sign of the living God....The first six were like steps leading to the seventh in which you have found your final rest. (LM 13.10)

The stigmata is the sign that Francis had reached the summit of gospel perfection, that is, a sign that he served as an example to others.

In the Prologue to *The Tree of Life*, Bonaventure speaks again of this cruciform state. He tells us that the true worshiper of God and disciple of Christ who wants to conform to the crucified Savior should strive to "carry about continuously, both in his soul and in his flesh, the cross of Christ until he can truly feel in himself" what Paul says to the Galatians (2:20): "With Christ I am nailed to the cross." (LV Prol. 1). We might ask what it means to "carry the cross of Christ continuously in soul and flesh." In the second section of *The Tree of Life*, Bonaventure suggests an answer. After dealing with Christ's origins in part I, Bonaventure moves to the passion in part II (part III deals with Christ's glorification). The four sections in part II recount Christ's passion and death in some detail. Bonaventure wants to convey a number of points.

The first is to assure the reader that Christ was fully human, suffering all the pains that we know as human beings. Bonaventure then leads the reader through a detailed account of Christ's passion and death. The account focuses on how Christ related to others, especially those who were his enemies and those who let him down—Judas the traitor, the guards, Peter, the high priest, the Jews, Pilate, Herod, the soldiers, and those who mocked Jesus. We watch to see how Jesus responds to the challenges of these hostile relationships. His behavior is characterized in these ways: meekness, silence, gentleness, mildness, submissive speech, charity, forgiveness, sweetness, love, grace, and words of blessing.

These chapters are quite concrete in terms of presenting the most difficult of human relational situations and the ideal response that Jesus always gives. One can imagine Bonaventure himself, as administrator of the Franciscan Order, faced with all kinds of opposition and contention. In this text, he might have been reminding himself and the friars how to respond to people who betrayed or mocked or walked away from them. These are situations in which imitating Christ is challenging and difficult indeed, but possible to those who bear the marks of the cross in their being.

Bonaventure also wants the reader to note the effect of the cross on Mary and Mary Magdalene. He sees this primarily in terms of compassion. With Mary we are to feel desolation and to experience the Lord's word of consolation to her because her soul had been more "deeply pierced by a sword of compassion than if she had suffered in her own body" (LV II.28). Mary Magdalene also provides an example. Even though the disciples fled, she does not go away. She too is "ablaze with the fire of divine love," burning with such a powerful desire and wounded with such an impatient love that nothing had any taste for her except to be able to weep and lament with the psalmist, "Where is your God?" (Ps 42:4; LV II.32).

Bonaventure pleads and prays:

O human heart,
you are harder than any hardness of rocks
if at the recollection of such great expiation
you are not struck with terror,
nor moved with compassion
nor shattered with compunction
nor softened with devoted love. (LV II.29)

...grant to me that I may ponder [these events] faithfully
in my mind and experience toward you

my God crucified and put to death for me,
that feeling of compassion
which your innocent mother and the penitent Magdalene
experienced at the very hour of your passion. (LV II.32)

Bonaventure wants the reader to develop an affection, a feeling for being nailed to the cross with Christ through contemplating "the labor, suffering, and love of Jesus crucified with vividness of memory, sharpness of intellect and charity of will" (LV Prol. 1).

One can also reflect on the fruits of this experience of being marked by the cross. Zachary Hayes suggests:

> When the human person responds to the offer of God's grace in an appropriate way, the basic effects of this response may be seen in a firm sense of fidelity to God, a strength of character in oneself, and an increasing generosity and love of one's fellow human beings. The fullness of grace is found when the human person is lifted above him or herself to love God above (and in) all creatures, and to love not only those who belong to one's household, but even one's enemies. This depth of love is the fullest meaning of the journey of human existence in the likeness of Christ.[38]

Conclusion

This brief excursion into some of the images that Bonaventure associated with the cross whets our appetites to spend more time with his texts. Bonaventure invites one to linger over the images; to allow them to wash over us; to penetrate the affective levels of the psyche that are most effectively touched by symbol and image; to understand their particular meaning for our time; and to gain insight into how to translate that meaning into action. I began with Marigwen Schumacher's suggestion that Bonaventure's style, his choice of language and images, is reflective of his being in touch with his own experience of the Crucified. She wrote, "To touch—to probe—to, in a way, invade the mythic impulses of Bonaventure's heart and mind, is, I feel and think, an as-yet-unexplored path into his contact with God." She posits that there is "an intrinsic, inescapable relationship between the "what" of Bonaventure's thought and the "how" of his expression—mysticism tangible through metaphor.[39] Our appreciation of these images completes the hermeneutic circle from our experience of the cross to Bonaventure's written description of his experience of the cross, to our reading of his text, and back to our own experience of the Crucified. I close with a section from one of Bonaventure's sermons on St. Francis in which he lays before his audience a most compelling and burning question: "Do you desire to imprint Christ crucified on your heart?"

> How is it that we, wretched as we are, have such cold hearts that we are not prepared to endure anything for our Lord's sake? Our hearts neither burn nor glow with love. Ardent love is a quality of the heart and the stronger this love burns in a person's heart, the more heroic and virtuous are his deeds. Do you desire to imprint Christ crucified on your heart? Do you long to be transformed into him to the point where your heart is aflame with love? Just as iron when heated to the point where it becomes molten can take the imprint of any mark or sign, so a heart burning fervently with love of Christ crucified can receive the imprint of the Crucified Lord himself or his cross. Such a loving heart is carried over to the Crucified Lord or transformed into him. That is what happened to St. Francis....The cross or sign of the cross imprinted on his body symbolized his love of Christ crucified and by the flame of that love he was totally transformed into Christ.[40]

NOTES

1. *The Bakhtin Reader: Selected Writings of Bakhtin, Medvedev, Voloshinov*, ed. Pam Morris (London: Edward Arnold, 1994), cover, 74–80, 119.

2. It is important to note ways in which medieval treatments of the Passion fueled anti-Semitic sentiment in their portrayal of Jews as beasts or an unharnessed mob, and labeled them as responsible for the death of Jesus. During the thirteenth century, the status of European Jews worsened (in 1242 approximately ten thousand volumes of Jewish works were burned in Paris in the Place de Grève), leading to efforts to remove Jews from western Europe altogether (Jews were expelled from England in 1290 and from France in 1306). In *Texts of the Passion: Latin Devotional Literature and Medieval Society* (Philadelphia: University of Pennsylvania Press, 1996), Thomas H. Bestul discusses the role of the new orders of Franciscans and Dominicans in anti-Jewish persecution.

Although Bestul comments that there is no evidence of Bonaventure's direct involvment in polemical activities against Jews, he cites Bonaventure and John Pecham (d. 1292) as authors who wrote within the larger context of the anti-Judaizing activities of the friars and details several anti-Jewish passages (several of which are adaptations of passages from the work of Ekbert of Schönau) in Bonaventure's work (93). "It is the case that many of the major thirteenth-century narratives of the Passion in which the role of the Jews is given special attention were written by friars" (92). Since Bonaventure spent many years in Paris, an "arena in which some of the most dramatic of the persecuting activities against the Jews took place," it is unlikely that he would have been unaware of, unaffected by, or even possibly implicated in, the hostility toward Jews (43-48 and 90-98).

3. Regis Armstrong, "Starting Points: Images of Women in the Letters of Clare of Assisi to Agnes of Prague," *Spirit and Life: A Journal of Contemporary Franciscanism* 1 (1991): 44, 48.

4. Thomas Aquinas, *Opusc.* 16, *De Trinitate* 6.2 ad 5. Quoted in Margaret Miles, *Image as Insight* (Boston: Beacon Press, 1985), 143.

5. John C. Hirsh, "Religious Attitudes and Mystical Language in Medieval Literary Texts: An Essay in Methodology," in *Vox Mystica: Essays on Medieval Mysticism in Honor of Professor Valerie M. Lagorio* (Cambridge: D. S. Brewer, 1995), 17.

6. Rosemary Drage Hale, "'Taste and See, For God is Sweet': Sensory Perception and Memory in Medieval Mystical Experience," in *Vox Mystica: Essays on Medieval Mysticism in Honor of Professor Valerie M. Lagorio* (Cambridge: D. S. Brewer, 1995), 14.

7. Marigwen Schumacher, "Mysticism in Metaphor," in *S. Bonaventura 1274-1974* (Grottaferrata, Rome: Collegio San Bonaventura, 1973), II: 361-86.

8. Ibid., 362.

9. Ibid., 364.

10. Ibid., 365.

11. Bernard Cooke, *The Distancing of God: The Ambiguity of Symbol in History and Theology* (Minneapolis: Fortress Press, 1990), 163.

12. Schumacher, 366. *Dictionnaire de Spiritualité* (Paris: Beauchesne, 1936ff.) I, col. 1842.

13. Ibid., 384.

14. Sara Maitland, *A Big-Enough God: A Feminist's Search for a Joyful Theology* (New York: Henry Holt and Company, 1995), 111.

15. Maurycy Suley, "La Croce Nella Vita Del Cristiano Negli Opuscoli e Sermoni Di S. Bonaventura," *Miscellanea Francescana* 96/1-2 (1966): 113-17.

16. See Thomas H. Bestul's *Texts of the Passion* for an excellent analysis of this important medieval tradition; and Ewert Cousins, "The Humanity and the Passion of Christ," in *Christian Spirituality III: High Middle Ages and Reformation*, ed. Jill Raitt. World Spirituality Series 17 (New York: Crossroad, 1987), 375–91.

17. Bestul, 44.

18. Ibid., 48. English translation, *Meditations on the Life of Christ*, trans. Isa Ragusa and Rosalie B. Green (Princeton, N.J.: Princeton University Press, 1961).

19. Ibid., 46.

20. (VIII, 165).

21. See Frances M. Biscoglio, "Cross, Tree, Bridegroom, and Circle: Marking in the Mystical Journey of Bonaventure and Jacopone da Todi," *Studia Mystica* 11 (Summer 1988): 32. For the relationship between the mystical death on the cross of the *Itinerarium* and Francis's *Canticle of Brother Sun*, see Ilia Delio, "The *Canticle of Brother Sun*: A Song of Christ Mysticism," *Franciscan Studies* 52 (1992): 1–22.

22. Zachary Hayes, "Bonaventure: Mystery of the Triune God," in *The History of Franciscan Theology*, ed. Kenan Osborne (St. Bonaventure, N.Y.: Franciscan Institute, 1994), 119.

23. Ibid., 85.

24. Leonardo Boff, *Saint Francis* (New York: Crossroad, 1985), 27–28.

25. Bonaventure also uses the symbol of fire to point to purification and damnation. In a sermon on Lamentations 1:13—"He has sent fire from on high down into my bones"—Bonaventure explores the image of fire (RF 24), describing it as grace (the zeal of God, hatred for sin), guilt (passion, greed, and anger enkindled by the devil), and repentance (purifying substance to be endured because it will strengthen us). The fire of guilt can only be quenched with the water of tears (Ps 6:6 and 42:1). While the fire of our present problems can be beneficial if we endure them with patience, the fire of eternal damnation can be escaped by no one and is to be dreaded. The antidote to eternal fire is humility.

26. See John V. Fleming, *An Introduction to the Franciscan Literature of the Middle Ages* (Chicago: Franciscan Herald Press, 1977), 63ff.

27. *Fioretti*, Consideration III. Cited in Boff, *Saint Francis*, 28.

28. *The Sayings of the Desert Fathers*, trans. Benedicta Ward (Kalamazoo, Mich.: Cistercian Publications, 1975), 13.

29. Julian Budenz, "Heaven," *Cross Currents* 41/2 (Summer 1991): 250.

30. Renewed interest in Mary Magdalen brings these symbols to our attention in a fresh way. See *Mary Magdalen and Many Others* by Carla Ricci (Fortress, 1994); *Mary Magdalen: Myth and Metaphor* by Susan Haskins (Harper-Collins, 1993). Some earlier accounts are also now available. See *The Life of Saint*

Mary Magdalen and of her Sister Saint Martha: A Medieval Biography by Rabanus Maurus (c. 784–856) and *Les perles, ou, les larmes de la Sainte Magdeleine* by César de Nostredame (Exeter, U.K.: University of Exeter, 1986).

31. Elizabeth Johnson, *She Who Is: The Mystery of God in Feminist Theological Discourse* (New York: Crossroad, 1992), 259.

32. Jean Châtillon, "Nudum Christum nudus sequere: Note sur les origines et la signification du thème de la nudité spirituelle dans les écrits de saint Bonaventure," *Bonaventura 1274–1974* (Grottaferrata, 1974), 4:719–72.

33. Ambroise Nguyen Van Si, *La théologie de l'imitation du Christ d'après Saint Bonaventure*, Bibliotheca pontificii athenaei antoniani, 33 (Rome: Edizione Antonianum, 1991), 114–15.

34. Francis does not use this image at all. It occurs twice in Clare's writings, once in her *Testament* (TestC 45) and once in *The First Letter to Blessed Agnes of Prague* (1LAg 27).

35. Bernard of Clairvaux, *Sermones*, 3, *In Tempore Resurrectionis Domini*, 1.

36. Nguyen Van Si, *La théologie*, 116.

37. For a discussion of the role of the stigmata in claims about Francis's mysticism, see Bernard McGinn, "Was Francis of Assisi a Mystic?" in *Doors of Understanding: Conversations on Global Spirituality in Honor of Ewert Cousins*, ed. Steven L. Chase (Qunicy, Ill.: Franciscan Press, 1997), 145–74.

38. Hayes, "Bonaventure," 100.

39. Schumacher, "Mysticism in Metaphor," 362.

40. Bonaventure, "Sermon on St. Francis," Oct. 4, 1262 (IX, 586–90), emphasis added.

AFTERWORD

"Behold, the One you seek has been lifted up"

Elizabeth A. Dreyer

The Cross Today

This excursion into the theology and spirituality of the cross in the Christian tradition has brought to light forgotten or neglected texts and images used by our ancestors in the faith. We have explored the uses to which this language was put and gained insight into the ways in which the meaning of the cross was deeply embedded in specific historical, sociocultural and ecclesial settings. This collective witness of the church down the ages points to the virtual inexhaustibility of the cross's meanings. These essays have also reminded us that these texts are linked to existential situations in which Christians sought to live as faithful disciples of Jesus. In each age, Christians struggle to understand how the cross discloses the shape and form of Christian existence.

A frequent commentator on the cross, British Anglican Alister McGrath, reminds us that the point of delving into the meaning of the cross is this: Christ's destiny is *our* destiny. It is our experience that fuels the search for knowledge of the tradition, and it is to our experience that we return. The past challenges us to gaze at the cross and to ask in all honesty and simplicity: What do *we* think happened there?[1] And what difference does what happened there make for us and for our world?

Nathan Mitchell reflected on how the liturgical language and imagery of the cross have evolved over the centuries and raised questions about how the cross functions in contemporary ritual. If we were to examine our worship with an eye to "catching ourselves in the act of negotiating our relation to mystery," what would we discover? Do we see ourselves as

236

being about the business of "negotiating rapture"? When do we ponder the poetry of the cross or listen to music inspired by the event of Calvary? What is our awareness of the cross when we celebrate the sacraments of baptism and Eucharist? Does the passionate, erotic intensity of early medieval prayer to the cross strike a chord? What kind of intensity do we associate with the cross today—an intensity that leads the community to "suffer in sympathy with the One who has created all things"—the "One who clothes the heavens with clouds, but who is wrapped in a robe of scorn, beaten and wounded?" Is Christ's "blood in any way contiguous to ours?" In the midst of our global diversity, do we express and ritualize the meaning of the cross in ways that respect our differences? In each culture the cross will heal, defend, save, protect, free, forgive, and give refuge and life in distinctive ways.

As we search for the meaning of the cross in our spiritualities and theologies, its enigma remains as scandal and foolishness. If today's church considers it old-fashioned to put the cross at the center of Christian faith and theology, Jürgen Moltmann counters that only the cross can bring the freedom that changes the world because it is no longer afraid of death. "Today the church and theology must turn to the crucified Christ in order to show the world the freedom he offers."[2]

Karl Rahner affirms Moltmann's basic thesis. In a series of meditations for Good Friday, he reflects on the cross as a source of the Christian call to be countercultural. This stance may include refusing to take advantage of others, speaking the truth, and confronting injustice and hatred. John Cavadini interprets Augustine's spirituality of the cross as above all a spirituality of creative critique in which one breaks open the circles of meaning that had seemed closed. For example, when Christians act with compassion toward the neighbor, they reclaim that neighbor from the "empire's" intent to see human identity as simply another vehicle for its glory. The cross leads to critique and protest.[3] And Rahner reminds us that it is especially when such behaviors seem hopeless to effect change that the cross comes into play. Paul wrote to the Corinthians, "We are afflicted in every way possible, but we are not crushed; full of doubts, we never despair. We are persecuted but never abandoned; we are struck down but never destroyed" (2 Cor 4:8-9). It is in hopelessness, particularly, that the folly and powerlessness of the cross begins.

For Rahner, the mysterious identification between Jesus and every human being allows us to say, "Wherever you come across someone who is dying, you find me, the one dying on the cross."[4] We perceive the dying person either as entering into emptiness and nothingness, or into the "sheltering incomprehensibility which we call God." For believers, the cross and resurrection are the guarantee of this sheltering incomprehensibility. "The climax of history that makes known its meaning and the victorious finality of its goal *within* history itself is the cross, the death and the resurrection of Jesus in one event. Here God's "Yes" to the world and the world's to God become historical, unambiguous, and irrevocable....This cross is the salvation of the world."[5]

However, it has become a methodological truism that our understanding of the past is conditioned by present experience and questions. An "objective," "pure" past is simply not available to us. Nor do we view the tradition as an unbroken historical trajectory. We are aware of the vulnerability and ambiguity of all traditions. The goal of these chapters has been an open yet critical assessment. The intent was not to lead the reader out of this tradition, nor to reinforce a universalizing, dominating ideology, but to appreciate our history and to explore how it can enrich the present.[6]

In this century, aspects of traditional theologies and spiritualities of the cross have been found wanting. There is a perception that the cross has been misunderstood in ways that mislead Christians into masochism, guilt, depression, and paralysis when faced with the crying needs of the world. It has been suggested that the cross was used to advocate neglect of ego-development and to counsel suppression of one's needs and gifts under the guise of imitating the suffering Jesus. Moral theologies have used the cross as an instrument of moral persuasion, threatening punishment and nurturing deadening fear by preaching that if we do not behave, someone will die.[7]

Others, rejecting what was perceived as a false asceticism, flee from even the suggestion of renunciation—demanding a Christianity of comfort and security, devoid of the cross altogether. Spiritualities that eschew suffering, denial and pain abound in our own time, raising the question about how traditional understandings of the cross can be transformed in ways that speak meaningfully to a postmodern world. What *is* the existential significance of the cross today?

Contemporary Discussions on the Symbol of the Cross

In order to link our discussion of the cross in the tradition with the present more concretely, let us examine briefly four contemporary discussions on the cross. Those who ponder and struggle with the cross in our own time can be seen to mirror, *mutatis mutandis*, Jerome Murphy-O'Connor's portrayal of Paul as one who felt very deeply about the crucifixion of Jesus. Like Paul, we are challenged to allow the cross to redefine our relationship to the world. The first group addresses the relationship between the suffering of Jesus on the cross and the Trinity. Does the fact of the crucifixion of Jesus alter the way we think about God, from One who is impassible to One who is filled with compassion? A second area explores the cross from the perspective of psychology. How do we think of the cross in terms of the dynamics of the human psyche and of our relationships with one another? Third, the cross has become an important focus in the theologies and spiritualities of liberation. How does the cross function as a symbol of identification with, and liberation of, those whose lives are characterized overwhelmingly by suffering and oppression? Finally, feminist theologians call attention to the difficulties traditional presentations of the cross present for women as they try to re-form this doctrine in ways that take seriously the full humanity of women.

A Suffering God?

A major question in contemporary theology addresses the connections between the cross and our image and understanding of God. Classical approaches have imaged God as impassible, that is, incapable of suffering or change. In this view, God is shielded from being affected by, and therefore dependent on, anything outside of God. For a suffering God would be a finite God—in other words, no God at all. In order to preserve the changeless nature of deity, the suffering endured by Jesus on the cross has been attributed to Jesus' humanity alone, since suffering could not be predicated of God as such.

This classical understanding of the relationship between the cross and the triune God is being challenged. Kenneth Leech writes, "Christ endured crucifixion as one who was in the form of God. So Christians have dared to say that God was crucified. It was God who

239

hung there. If this is so, then in our relationship to the cross, we are entering into something very close to the mystery of God's being."[8] Europeans addressing a theology of the suffering God out of the experience of World War II and the Holocaust include Hans Urs von Balthasar,[9] Johannes Metz[10] and Jürgen Moltmann.[11]

Moltmann engages in a theology of the cross in response to a "protest atheism" that perceives the classical Christian God as an absurdity in light of a history of violent inhumanity. According to Moltmann, the only ground for faith and hope in such a world is a theology of the cross—a theology that recognizes in the crucified Christ suffering in God's very being.[12]

Moltmann suggests that since we need a revolutionary concept of God, we need to take up the theology of the cross today in a way that goes beyond the limits of the traditional doctrine of salvation. Who is the God in the cross of the Christ who is abandoned by God?[13] He concludes that in the Son's passion, the First Person assumes the passion of the world, suffering the pain of abandonment. In the death of the Son, death reaches God's very self, and the Father suffers his Son's death for love of abandoned human beings. Thus, human suffering transpires *within* God. God *is* affected by suffering. God is crucified.[14] Our image of God remains incomplete, he claims, if we limit it to the ways in which God reveals Godself through positive, life-giving experiences. Our image of God must also somehow incorporate the negativity of the cross. Thus, if the cross is to offer access to God, it will do so by pointing to the paradox that power is found in weakness, speech in silence, life in death.

Process theologian David Ray Griffin also finds the classical notion of God unsatisfying. As an alternative, he explores what he calls a naturalistic understanding of the triune God, in which the way God acted in Jesus is seen as the norm for the way God has acted in creating and sanctifying the world. If we take Jesus not only as a special instance of God's saving activity, but also as a special revelation of the way God acts in general, we arrive at a notion of God as exercising "nonretaliatory, suffering love."[15] In every place that Jesus' nature is present, some aspect of God is revealed. Therefore, God's presence on the cross reveals something of God.[16]

We see, then, that it has become a *desideratum* of many theologians to find ways to speak about a God who remains passionately engaged in the sorrows of the universe. Elizabeth Johnson suggests that in light of the extreme and widespread suffering of creation, we need to find ways to predicate suffering of the holy mystery of God who cherishes our beloved world.[17] Theologians seek to name a God who responds to the agonies of the world with sadness and joy, anger and challenge. Jesus on the cross is an obvious starting point to speak about God's real engagement in the pain of the world. If the union of human and divine natures in Christ is as profound as Christian theology has always contested, then does not the cross "belong not to the human Jesus alone but also to the person of the divine logos?"[18]

Instead of understanding suffering as a passive reception of the action of some "other," theologians envision suffering as something that is chosen inasmuch as it becomes a consequence of loving others. Thus, the cross is seen not as something that just *happened* to Jesus, but as an effect of Jesus' choice to love the world. From this perspective, "the symbol of divine suffering appears not as an imperfection but as the highest excellence."[19] Human participation in the cross is then understood as the experience of suffering that is integral to loving others. One cannot truly love another who is suffering unless in some way there is participation in that suffering. Genuine love for humanity involves becoming vulnerable, opening oneself to the sorrows as well as the joys of the other. Therefore, God's presence in the cross of Christ calls for a more nuanced understanding of God's transcendence. God is wonderful, not only because God is the loving Creator of the universe, but because God is *at the same time* the lowly, suffering One on the cross.

Related to the issue of impassibility is the need to reassess classical understandings of God's power. The cross has always stood for the kind of power that is present in weakness. God's power, then, is not a dominating, controlling power, but rather a power that is visible in the incarnation, death and resurrection of Jesus—God's free and loving choice to empty God's self of divinity *(kenosis)* for our sake.

Ronald Goetz has suggested that this interest in integrating suffering into our idea of God is so widespread that it is tantamount to the rise of a new orthodoxy. He attributes this development to four factors. To the decline of Christendom, he attributes the difficulty modern persons have in believing in God's "mighty power and deeds." Second, the rise of democratic aspirations inevitably creates links between the concept of divine sovereignty and that of political sovereignty—with the outcome that both are rejected. Third, it is difficult to imagine an all-powerful God who refuses to act to alleviate the suffering and evil with which the world is filled. Finally, the scholarly reappraisal of the Bible presents a God who is personal, passionate, jealous, concerned and capable of suffering.[20] But ultimately, for Goetz, a suffering God only exacerbates the problem of evil. "God, the fellow sufferer, is inexcusable if all that he can do is suffer."[21]

Gerhard O. Forde takes an even stronger counter-position against those exploring the viability of a suffering God. In Forde's monograph on Luther's Heidelberg Disputation of 1518, a *locus classicus* for Luther's theology of the cross, Forde laments the lack and/or inadequacy of recent treatments of the cross in English.[22] He suggests that the malaise of the theology of glory is the ultimate source of contemporary angst, not the theology of the cross.[23] He voices concern about what he sees as the "sentimentalization" of the cross in an age that is overly concerned about victimization. Thus, he takes a very critical stance toward theologians in search of a suffering God. "'The suffering of God,' or the 'vulnerability of God,' and such platitudes become the stock-in-trade of preachers and theologians who want to stroke the psyche of today's religionists....'Misery loves company' becomes the unspoken motif of such theology."[24] Forde turns to Luther for a corrective that retrieves the ultimate language of sin, law, accusation, devil and damnation in order to balance the penchant for the penultimate language of affirmation, comfort, support and self-esteem. In Luther's words, a true theologian of the cross is one who sees all of reality through the cross, who "says what a thing is."[25]

In the ongoing debate about how to relate the cross to the triune God, theologians can be aided by an awareness of the various approaches to the cross articulated in the preceding essays. While it is true that throughout the tradition a dualistic, Neoplatonic outlook prevented theologians from theorizing about a God susceptible to change, much less suffering, we have seen the ways in which existential engagement with the cross functioned in the lives of past Christians. A broader and deeper appropriation of this tradition sheds light on how the cross functioned in a variety of historical, sociocultural settings and can assist theologians in their quest to make the cross an integral part of the way we image God, and of the ways creation relates to that God.

"BEHOLD, THE ONE YOU SEEK HAS BEEN LIFTED UP"

Psychological Approaches

In his letter to the Romans, Paul wrote, "We know that our old self was crucified with him so that the body of sin might be destroyed, and we might no longer be enslaved to sin....But if we have died with Christ, we believe that we will also live with him" (Rom 6:6, 8). Ellen Charry aptly frames what appears to be a chasm between traditional piety's understanding of the self and that of a post-Freudian, heavily psychologically oriented world. Contrasting the fourteenth century (a time frame that can be extended both backward and forward to include wider segments of the tradition) with the present, she notes that given our desire

> to enhance self-esteem, cultivate assertiveness, and seek personal ful-
> fillment, fourteenth-century piety and devotionalism appear frankly
> bizarre. While in a way both centuries might be said to be seeking
> perfection of the self—one by abolishing it, the other by cultivating it—
> late medieval devotion and late modern values, are, nevertheless, like
> ships passing in the night. They face in different directions, one
> anchoring happiness in knowing and loving God, the other seeking
> to investigate the world by using the self as the fulcrum.[26]

Relationships between the loss and the discovery/recovery of self and between self-knowledge and knowledge of God have been a hallmark of the Christian spiritual tradition. The issue is crystallized in the paradox of the cross, in which the meaning of death as the final loss of self becomes irrevocably reversed.[27] English Benedictine Sebastian Moore addresses this issue as part of a larger project in which he has sought to understand the primary mysteries of the Christian faith—especially Christology—from the perspective of contemporary psychology. In *The Crucified Is No Stranger*, Moore uses Jungian categories to envision the true or authentic self in terms of the person of Jesus, and to explore the crucifixion as a hermeneutic key by which to understand the destructive human tendency to kill what is good and free within.

In chapter 8, Elizabeth Dreyer called attention to the ways in which Moore reflects on the human phenomenon of refusal of the fullness of life to which God is impelling us and which our whole being dreads. This refusal, Moore suggests, is motivated by fear.[28] Moore imagines Jesus as the embodied symbol of this dreaded yet very much desired self, this "destiny

243

of being human," this "unbearable freedom." The crucifixion of Jesus thus becomes the central drama of the human refusal of the true self.[29] This refusal is not an atmosphere but an act—in fact, a murderous act.[30] And yet in the very destruction of the innocent One, death proves to be without power. Within the ambit of the human psyche, Moore suggests that we experience ourselves as crucifiers of Jesus and of our best selves. When believers are confronted with Jesus crucified, the evil in their lives becomes *explicit* as the destruction of their true selves, made concrete in the person of Jesus on the cross. One also experiences this evil as resolved in the forgiveness of God, of which the cross is the symbol. In the cross, we are *accepted* at our very worst, as destroyers of goodness.

Thus, the believer becomes both the crucifier and the crucified.[31] One's worst self sets out to destroy one's best self, the identity of which lies deep in the biblical tradition in the story of Genesis, where we are told that we are created in the image and likeness of God. One's best self is *not* one's full potential in the sense of "I'm #1" or "I'm OK, you're OK." No, our true self is symbolized by none other than the sinless, Crucified One. This realization provides an existential, inward sense of *that which is crucified.*[32] Moore speaks of this in terms of the alienation of the conscious ego and the total self, in which humans have their place in God's world. One may thus understand salvation as the overcoming of this "protean alienation."[33]

Moore is aware of the danger of misreading this psychological interpretation of the meaning of the cross. It is all too easy to think of the self in egoistic terms, or to emphasize the link between Jesus and humanity at the expense of the differences. Theologian and educator Parker Palmer also calls attention to this danger in a reflection on his experience of depression. Depression, he says, was the vehicle that led him away from a false self, characterized by over-intellectualization, concern with abstractions over experience of God, an inflated ego, and a distorted ethic filled with "oughts" rather than genuine insight into his existence. For him—and he underlines the truth that this may not be the case for others who suffer from depression—depression brought him to a place where he came to understand that the self is not special or superior, but rather a "common mix of good and evil, darkness and light—a place where we can finally embrace the humanity we share with others."[34]

244

Against critics who view the psychological import of the truths of the faith as necessarily self-centered, Palmer confirms that he did *not* experience embracing his wholeness as narcissistic, as obsession with self at the expense of others. He writes, "When I ignored my own truth on behalf of a distorted ego and ethic, I led a false life that caused others pain—for which I can only ask forgiveness. When I started attending to my own truth, more of that truth became available in my work and my relationships. I now know that anything we can do on behalf of true self is done ultimately in the service of others."[35] Moore's analysis supports this account and links it to the cross: "In the man on the cross I find an identity and a world to live it in, that my education and my gradual acceptance of it declared to be impossible."[36]

Mystics can be described as those who seek an ultimate identity because they are not satisfied with the world's answers to their self-questioning. Mystics see in the Christ-figure crucified the powerful symbol of the self that they seek to become. The only way to this identity is through the sinfulness that has put them there. "*This* dimension of the confessed crucifier, is the vigour, the honest humanity, the political realism, of his commitment to an ultimate human identity and mission."[37] This theological/psychological account of the cross is light years away from Luther's rendering of the theology of the cross, and yet in its reliance on the need to reach out constantly for "the real" and for "truth," one cannot help but think of Luther's statement that a theologian of the cross is one who sees all of reality through the cross, who "says what a thing is."

For Moore, identification with the Crucified means death to the ego and a new flourishing of the person's "real being." In his explanation of why Paul placed such importance on the crucifixion of Jesus, Jerome Murphy-O'Connor suggests that, for Paul, it was the key to salvation. In his suffering, Jesus revealed to the community what they could become. Jesus' "generosity shattered the stifling bonds of their egocentricity" (page 33, above). Jesus died for all, so that "those who live might live no longer for themselves" (2 Cor 5:15). This process is Spirit-directed and creative, *not* narrow and self-preoccupying, as mortification or self-discipline can sometimes be understood. Rather, Moore goes on, Paul "is talking about the mystery of the crucified as it daily enlarges our lives in freeing us of our ego-illusions. Far from being an emotional hari-kari, mortification is an emotional liberation, turning the energy that we expend in unconsciously strangling our life into the freeing of it."[38] Moore concludes that since God in Christ revealed the root of sin in us as self-crucifixion, we can experience forgiveness as a liberation from ourselves, a "liberation that we enjoy anew each time we find the cross in our lives, identify with the crucified, and so let the ego die." Thus forgiveness equals liberation; liberation powers the ongoing askesis. The Christian life is simply the prolongation of God's forgiveness of human beings in Christ.[39]

The Cross in Liberation Theologies

Liberation theologies are another major impetus behind a reevaluation of the theology of the cross. In light of the history of colonization, in which the symbols of cross and sword were joined to enslave and mistreat entire peoples, the meaning of the cross has become fraught with ambiguity.[40] How are we to talk about the cross in relation to the suffering masses across the globe? Hugo Assmann writes,

> The theology of liberation, as an effective process of critical reflection on historical practice, will have to go back to the theology of the cross. It will also have to strip it of the alienating mystifications that have accrued to it....It will have to give back to the man Jesus his full integrity as a human being, and give his death the historical and political meaning that in fact it possessed.[41]

Jesus' commitment to the poor throughout his entire public life disturbed the social, political and religious status quo and led to his death on the cross. This link between Jesus' life of concern for outcasts and the cross is an important hermeneutical key for a theology of the cross today.

Liberation theologians view the cross from the perspective of present suffering, resistance to oppression and liberation. Their starting point for theology is the experience of a crucified world, inviting Christians to keep their eyes trained on the ways in which the cross is embodied in history. For them, the suffering of Jesus on the cross and human suffering mutually interpret one another. Like Paul, there are Christians who carry in their bodies the dying of Jesus, a dying that manifests the life of Jesus and his love for others (2 Cor 4:10-11; Rom 6:5-6; Gal 2:20 and 6:14). But the ultimate goal is liberation from death, a liberation symbolized in the cross and resurrection of Jesus. Liberation perspectives see the cross not as an isolated symbol, but as one that is tightly linked with Jesus' entire life and with the lives of all Christians who followed after him. The cross is a symbol of God's standing against all suffering, not advocating it. The only human suffering that has value is the suffering that comes when one loves enough to resist the suffering of others.

For example, in *Jesus the Liberator*, Salvadoran theologian Jon Sobrino identifies the world's poor and suffering peoples with the cross. For Latin American Christians, the symbol of the cross leads them to fight for liberation, not to be resigned to their plight. The poor make Christ present through "the bare fact of being massively on the cross."[42] If we do not forget those who are being crucified today, Sobrino reminds us, it will be more difficult to forget the crucified Jesus.[43] This contemporary situation calls to mind the role of martyrdom in Origen's theology. In Peter Gorday's analysis, Origen interprets martyrdom as the culmination of a life of virtue. In the second century, as in the twenty-first, martyrs follow Jesus to the cross, undermining the demons of idolatry and falsehood. It is in the cross of Jesus that the community discovers the full significance of love that leads to suffering and death.

Ultimately, the cross reveals the love of God in a powerful and unique way. The cross reveals that nothing is an obstacle to God's desire to say a definitive, saving, welcoming irrevocable yes to the world.[44] The cross is the ultimate message that God has drawn near to be "with us" and "for us." What God's suffering on the cross says, finally, is that the God who fights against human suffering wants to show solidarity with human beings who suffer, and that God's fight against suffering is also waged in a human way.[45]

In *Passion of Christ, Passion of the World*, Leonardo Boff works out a theology of the cross that places the cross firmly within its social-cultural-political matrix. He argues that Jesus did not see his death in the formal, abstract, juridical, sacrificial and substitutionary terms of later theologies of redemption. Rather, the cross is to be understood as God's solidarity with the world in its suffering. God takes up suffering into God's being not to eternalize it (a criticism of his reading of Moltmann and others) but to suppress it. For Boff, the cross in itself is a symbol of hate, the vehicle used by human forces to kill Jesus, and a quality totally absent from God's being. Only the cross of love, symbol of Jesus' fidelity—a consequence of the cross of hate—can be projected within God.[46] The manner of God's suffering, then, is as the fruit of love and of God's infinite capacity for solidarity. Genuine love takes up the pain of the "other" because it loves the other and wishes to share in the other's pain.[47]

In liberation theologies, the knowledge of God that comes through the cross is a committed knowledge. To know the Crucified means to choose to be involved in confronting and working to eliminate the suffering of the body of Christ in history—that is, what liberation theologians call the "crucified people."[48] In Ignacio Ellacuría's terminology, since the crucified Lord is present in the crucified people, "coming to terms with" God on the cross has to be accompanied by carrying the cross and taking responsibility for the crucified.[49] The cross was the result of Jesus' choice to stand with and for the marginalized. Thus, the cross reveals a God who stands in solidarity with the endless agonies of the world and calls us to do the same. The cross calls us to an *imitatio crucis* that confronts human suffering in responsibility and solidarity.

The Cross and Feminist Theologies

Feminist theologians approach traditional theologies of the cross with reserve.[50] Women and other marginalized groups have become aware of the ways in which the doctrine of the cross has been misused to condone and even glorify suffering in ways that perpetuate, rather than confront, the agonies of the weak and oppressed. As a result, many women experience the cross as an instrument of violence—spiritual, psychological and physical.[51] Indeed, this misuse of the symbol of the cross becomes ironic in the extreme in light of recent attempts to understand the cross as the polar opposite of violence—a sign of the final defeat of all violent and controlling behaviors.[52]

Women seek to expose ways in which the cross has been used to justify or glorify suffering that has been harmful to them. We are now aware that without some sense of self and of authentic freedom, silent suffering merely prolongs behaviors that are destructive to self and ultimately harmful to the community. "Power in weakness" is not genuine power if it is exercised because of coercion, fear, or the desire to please those in the dominant group who set the rules. If the symbol of the cross is to point to an authentic participation in the life of God, then vigilance must be exercised to maintain a distinction between the genuine power of divine weakness and the interiorized weakness of subordination and inequality.

It is the actual, historical suffering of women and women's response to that suffering that become the starting point for feminist approaches to the theology of the cross.[53] In addition to a critique of classical theologies of the cross, women and other oppressed groups add their own voices, documenting the experience and meaning of the cross in their lives. In particular, they ask how the suffering of women might shape language about God. "What theological concepts support this kind of speech? To what understanding of God does the symbol of the suffering God give rise?"[54] Elizabeth Johnson allows that when we look upon all the violated women of the world, we rightly say, *Ecce homo*, for indeed they are images of the Crucified.[55]

Feminist theologian and ethicist Sally Purvis interprets the cross as "an intellectual, spiritual, and communal resource for radical change."[56] She finds support for this position in the way Paul points to the cross as the subversion of the meaning of power—a theme we have encountered often in these essays. Christ crucified becomes the new standard for wisdom and for power. The cross symbolizes the power of life, not of death and control. The cross reveals a power that brings forth life even from the desolation of defeat and death. What appears as folly and weakness becomes the source and sign of a power that is not coercive, dominating, or manipulative. For Paul, the cross reveals that the most violent efforts to manipulate and control the power of God for life are overcome by another kind of power that the world perceives as weakness.[57] Purvis underlines the unexpected and unpredictable nature of this power. Because the cross reverses the status quo, Purvis suggests that the cross must be reclaimed for feminist theology as a resource that must be restored and enacted against violent and manipulative behaviors.[58]

This brand of power becomes a model for a theology of the cross that focuses on relationship. The cross teaches us to be with and for each other in receptivity, freedom and forgiveness. The kind of power revealed in the cross is to be nurtured and made visible in the Christian community. "The power of the cross functions as a kind of organizing principle for the Christian community."[59] It is the power to build up not to tear down (1 Cor 1:18-25). It is the power to confront unjust suffering and to make the suffering life inevitably brings meaningful. At another level, we call this kind of power hospitality; that is, we choose to allow the reality of others to affect our ideas, our affections, our commitments—to acknowledge that we are most able to become who we are intended to become when we share with, and open ourselves to, others.

Speaking about the role of the cross in ethics, Barbara Hilkert Andolsen and Beverly Wildung Harrison criticize Christian ethicists who place inordinate stress on self-sacrifice. In this brand of ethics, Jesus' life, and in particular his death on the cross, is presented as a model of one who pours himself out completely in service to others. Thus, Jesus' followers should also live a life of complete self-giving. This interpretation of the cross is seen to serve women poorly to the extent that women, who have been conditioned by Christian culture to live lives of total self-giving, are encouraged toward self-immolation *for the sake of sacrifice*. Harrison asserts that Jesus did not desire death on the cross as a manifestation of total self-surrender; rather, he accepted death as "the consequence of his unswerving commitment to mutual love. Jesus remained faithful to radical love even when his fidelity resulted in a life-endangering confrontation with the forces of loveless power—forces which threaten the dignity of persons. It is not suffering itself which Christians should seek. Rather we should emulate Jesus' absolute dedication to love which highlights human dignity."[60] Jesus' sacrifice on the cross was no abstract exercise in moral virtue. "His death was the price he paid for refusing to abandon the radical activity of love—of expressing solidarity and reciprocity with the excluded ones in his community." The aim of love is not to perpetuate crucifixions, but to bring an end to them in a world where they go on and on.[61]

But questions about the cross cannot be reduced to an examination of the ways traditional theologies of the cross are experienced as suffocating and coercive. The focus must extend to the ways in which Christian women today encounter and understand the cross as the revelation of, and access to, the loving power of God. One must also bring forward specific texts of the Christian tradition and examine them afresh. The essays in this volume do just that. In all ages, the tradition is both well used and abused. But in every age, we are invited to return to the original texts, situate them in their context, allow them to speak to us, and question them in light of the particular experiences of the moment—filled as they are with both joy and sorrow.

Conclusion

Leonardo Boff cites Paul Ricoeur's statement that symbols and myths "make you think."[62] It is our hope that this exploration of language, images and meanings of the cross in the Christian tradition has had the effect of "making us think." In the cross we discover something about God's love—as awful and terrifying as this may be. Jesus' commitment to be with and for people led to his tragic end on the cross. We are also reminded of the truth that amid the darkness of evil and suffering, the cross stands as a beacon of light. There is no magic here. Jesus is not rescued from death. Rather, new life comes out of death. Nor does the cross make suffering glorious in itself. Suffering is not to be sought as a badge of fervor in some literal imitation of Jesus. But suffering does come, inevitably, and the cross endows it with meaning and dignity.

Suffering does not have to lead to despair, since the cross tells us that God is alongside us in our pain. "The powerful image of a God who knows what human suffering and pain are like, who *understands* at first hand what it is like to be weak, frail and mortal, is authorized by the cross of Jesus Christ."[63] Through faith, the cross awakens the realization that historical failure is not the last evidence of what the future holds. The cross stands as a symbol of the hope that is born of resurrection. Death, we believe, will never have the final word. Prayer and ritual of the cross function to create a new world. Celebration of the cross and resurrection is "a passionate human outcry against extinction; it rebels against the ending of the waltz, the fading of the rose, the dying of the light....It is resistance—even rage and rebellion" against the seeming finality of the darkness.[64]

Throughout the tradition, the cross has stood as a symbol teaching Christians how to live—not in fear, but in love, courage and hope. It is by means of Jesus' humanity and, in particular, his death on the cross, that we have access to the truth of what it means to be human, what it means to be good. It is on the cross that the humanity of God is most perfectly revealed as God's compassion in Jesus. With Augustine, we may see the cross as a lampstand, with Christ the lamp shining into the world. The texts we have pondered in these pages help us to rediscover that the cross, like everything else about Jesus, is about being fully and completely human. Through simple, silent contemplation of the cross, one comes to ever deeper awareness of who God is and of who we are.

These events in the life of the incarnate Jesus compel the Christian
community to link faith to "real" living. Language and ideas, symbols
and images of the cross remain empty rhetoric unless they are anchored
in action in and for the world. An authentic encounter with the cross can
never be divorced from love-in-action that leads to a more just world.
Kenneth Leech writes, "The Jesus who died, the Jesus who was deliberately killed, was the same Jesus who taught, who went about doing good
(Acts 10.37ff.), who healed the sick, cleansed the lepers, and cast out the
forces of evil."[65] The cross of Christ is not a call to resignation in the face
of unutterable pain or to a life of masochistic pursuit of suffering, often
called "the way of the cross."

Rather, the cross calls us to recognize solidarity with the Christ
who has confronted pain and death once for all. It calls us to "minister
to the wounded Christ as he is found broken and bruised on all the highways of the world."[66] Jesus' mission and strategy are clearly stated at the
beginning of Luke's gospel:

> The Spirit of the Lord is upon me, because he has anointed me to
> bring good news to the poor. He has sent me to proclaim release to
> the captives and recovery of sight to the blind, to let the oppressed
> go free, to proclaim the year of the Lord's favor. (Lk 4:18–19)

The call to continue Jesus' mission to bring good news to the
poor finds its foundation and thrust in the cross. We return to the
words of an Easter homily by Karl Rahner, cited by Nathan Mitchell in
chapter 2:

> Christ is already in the midst of all the poor things of this earth,
> which we cannot leave because it is our mother....He is in all tears
> and in all death as hidden rejoicing and as the life which triumphs
> by appearing to die. He is in the beggar to whom we give, as the
> secret wealth which accrues to the donor. He is in the pitiful defeats
> of his servants, as the victory which is God's alone. He is in our
> powerlessness as the power which can allow itself to seem weak,
> because it is unconquerable. He is even in the midst of sin as the
> mercy of eternal love patient and willing to the end.[67]

That the power and wisdom of God are disclosed in the utter powerlessness and obscenity of the cross stands in dialectic with a theology that

proclaims harmony between the historical world and God. For Bonaventure, the cross reveals a God who in infinite love condescends to walk with us in all our frailty. For Origen, the cross is a power that leads Christians to live the moral life of compassion and action for justice. For the poor and marginalized, the cross stands as proof of God's tender love and compassion, bringing hope. For the educated and the affluent, the cross warns against arrogance and empire-building.[68] The learned who proudly claim to be wise, says Augustine, are like travelers who can see the destination they want to reach but have no way of reaching it. In Bonaventure's language, they lack poverty and humility. John Cavadini in chapter 6 referred to our proclivities to pridefulness as a "failure of imagination."

In each historical period, Christians turn to the cross for understanding, meaning, encouragement and challenge amid the particular joys and sufferings distinct to each era, geography and situation. Yet in and through these concrete and specific circumstances, we conclude that the meaning of the cross is love. Paul sets the tone by teaching that divine goodness and the cross can be related only by love. And in his exegesis of Ephesians 3:17–18, Augustine takes the cross as the symbol of the Christian life, that is, a life "rooted and founded in love." The breadth, width, length and height of the cross symbolize good works done in charity, with perseverance, works done out of love for God, and in grace, where the life of love is ultimately rooted.[69] In the end, the message of our exploration into the imagery of the cross in the tradition is this: The cross continues to have the power to reinvest the imagination with new images, whose most profound meaning is that in Christ's life, death and resurrection Christians are invited and enabled to live not in fear, guilt, domination, arrogance, or compulsions, but in love.

> Be strong, then, my weak and wretched soul, and rise aloft: on the wings of faith and hope, fly to this garden of love; concentrate the scattered vision of your mind, and follow the zeal of the bee in gathering for yourself the honey of devotion. Rise to the paradise of love—rise, I say, to the heights of the heart: behold, the One you seek has been lifted up (Ct 7:1).[70]

NOTES

1. Alister McGrath, *The Enigma of the Cross* (London: Hodder & Stoughton, 1987), 107, 114. See also *Luther's Theology of the Cross: Martin Luther's Theological Breakthrough* (Oxford: Blackwell, 1985); *The Mystery of the Cross* (Grand Rapids, Mich.: Zondervan, 1988); *Making Sense of the Cross* (Leicester, England: Inter-Varisty Press, 1992); *What Was God Doing on the Cross?* (Grand Rapids, Mich.: Zondervan, 1992).

2. Jürgen Moltmann, *The Crucified God: The Cross of Christ as the Foundation and Criticism of Christian Theology* (San Francisco: Harper & Row, 1974), 1.

3. See John Cavadini, chap. 7, above.

4. Karl Rahner, *Opportunities for Faith: Elements of a Modern Spirituality* (New York: The Seabury Press, 1970), 27.

5. Ibid., 29–30.

6. J. Wentzel Van Huyssteen, "Tradition and the Task of Theology," *Theology Today* 55/2 (July 1998), 218.

7. For a provocative treatment of the ethical, spiritual and pastoral dimensions of the tradition's teaching on the cross, see Ellen T. Charry, *By the Renewing of Your Minds: The Pastoral Function of Christian Doctrine* (Oxford and New York: Oxford University Press, 1997).

8. Kenneth Leech, *We Preach Christ Crucified* (Cambridge, Mass.: Cowley Publications, 1994), 12.

9. Hans Urs von Balthasar wants to insert the incarnation within the Trinity. By becoming a human being and taking on the human condition, God as Trinity assumes suffering and death. He transforms the idea of changelessness in God from a static state to one of constant change and process ("Mysterium Paschale," in *Mysterium Salutis*, ed. Johannes Feiner and Magnus Löhrer [Petropolis, Brazil: Vozes, 1974]).

10. Johannes Metz has developed the idea of the "memory of suffering and of the death of Jesus Christ" *(memoria passionis et mortis Jesu Christi)*, that dangerous, subversive remembering of those who have been persecuted throughout history. Such a dangerous memory functions as a catalyst for ever more radical and committed forms of discipleship dedicated to combatting all forms of oppression (see *Faith in History and Society: Toward a Practical Fundamental Theology*, trans. David Smith [London: Burns & Oates, 1980]).

11. Moltmann, *The Crucified God*.

12. Ibid., 227.

13. Ibid., 4.

14. Ibid.

15. David Ray Griffin, "A Naturalistic Trinity," in *Trinity in Process: A Relational Theology of God*, eds. Joseph A. Bracken and Marjorie Hewitt Suchocki (New York: Continuum, 1997), 25.

16. See Jon Sobrino, *Jesus the Liberator: A Historical-Theological Reading of Jesus of Nazareth*, trans. Paul Burns and Francis McDonagh (Maryknoll, N.Y.: Orbis Books, 1993), 243.

17. Elizabeth A. Johnson, *She Who Is: The Mystery of God in Feminist Theological Discourse* (New York: Crossroad, 1992), 246. See also Jan Lambrecht and Raymond Collins, eds., *God and Human Suffering* (Louvain: Peeters Press, 1990).

18. Ibid., 251.

19. Ibid., 266.

20. Ronald Goetz, "The Rise of a New Orthodoxy," *Christian Century* 103/13 (April 16, 1986), 385–89.

21. Ibid., 389.

22. Gerhard O. Forde, *On Being a Theologian of the Cross* (Grand Rapids, Mich.: Wm. B. Eerdmans, 1997). In Forde's opinion, Walthar von Loewenich's *Luther's Theology of the Cross* (Minneapolis: Augsburg, 1976; a translation of the German published in 1929) and Alister McGrath's *Luther's Theology of the Cross* (Oxford: Basil Blackwell, 1985) focus on Luther's theological development rather than on his theology of the cross per se.

23. Ibid., xiv.

24. Ibid., viii.

25. Ibid., x. See Luther's *Theses for Heidelberg Disputation*, 20–21.

26. Ellen T. Charry, *By the Renewing of Your Minds*, 176. For a popular feminist treatment of this and related issues see Carol Lee Flinders, *At the Root of This Longing: Reconciling a Spiritual Hunger and a Feminist Thirst* (New York: HarperSanFrancisco, 1998), 59–98.

27. For other treatments of the relationship between spirituality and a psychoanalytic perspective, see W. W. Meissner, *Life and Faith: Psychological Perspectives on Religious Experience* (Washington, D.C.: Georgetown University Press, 1987); *Ignatius of Loyola: The Psychology of a Saint* (New Haven, Conn.: Yale University Press, 1992); and *Thy Kingdom Come: Psychoanalytic Perspectives on the Messiah and the Millennium* (Kansas City: Sheed & Ward, 1995), which examines the cross in the context of eschatological movements. See also J. H. Smith and S. A. Handelman, eds., *Psychoanalysis and Religion* (Baltimore: Johns Hopkins University Press, 1990), and Peter J. Gorday, "The Thought of David Bakan: Overview and Implications for Christology," *Pastoral Psychology* 47/1 (1998): 19–32.

28. Sebastian Moore, *The Crucified Is No Stranger* (London: Darton, Longman and Todd, 1977), x. For a feminist critique of Moore's position, see

Cynthia S. W. Crysdale, "Feminist Theology: Ideology, Authenticity and the Cross," *Église et Théologie* 28 (1977): 245-63.

29. Moore, *The Crucified Is No Stranger*, x.

30. Ibid., 2.

31. Ibid., 7.

32. Ibid., 11.

33. Ibid.

34. Parker Palmer, "All the Way Down: Depression and the Spiritual Journey," *Weavings* 13/5 (Sept./Oct. 1998), 39-40.

35. Ibid., 40-41.

36. Moore, *The Crucified Is No Stranger*, 15.

37. Ibid.

38. Ibid., 92.

39. Ibid., 94.

40. See Virgil Elizondo and Leonardo Boff, "1492-1992: The Voice of the Victims," *Concilium* 1990/6, vii. For a theology of the cross that focuses on the North American context, see Douglas John Hall, *Lighten Our Darkness: Toward an Indigenous Theology of the Cross* (Philadelphia: Westminster Press, 1976); *Thinking the Faith* (Minneapolis: Fortress Press, 1989); *Professing the Faith* (Minneapolis: Fortress Press, 1993); *Confessing the Faith* (Minneapolis: Fortress Press, 1996).

41. Hugo Assmann, *Theology for a Nomad* (Maryknoll, N.Y.: Orbis Books, 1976), 86. Cited in Yacob Tesfai, ed., *The Scandal of a Crucified World: Perspectives on the Cross and Suffering* (Maryknoll, N.Y.: Orbis Books, 1994), 6.

42. Sobrino, *Jesus the Liberator*, 264.

43. Ibid., 235.

44. Ibid., 231.

45. Ibid., 245.

46. Leonardo Boff, *Passion of Christ, Passion of the World* (Maryknoll, N.Y.: Orbis Books, 1987 [1977]), 110.

47. Ibid., 114.

48. Sobrino, *Jesus the Liberator*, 254ff.

49. Cited in Sobrino, *Jesus the Liberator*, 252. See also Jon Sobrino, "The Crucified Peoples: Yahweh's Suffering Servant Today—In Memory of Ignacio Ellacuría," *Concilium* 6 (1990): 120-29; and *The Principle of Mercy: Taking the Crucified People From the Cross* (Maryknoll, N.Y.: Orbis Books, 1994).

50. See, for example, Joanne Carlson Brown and Carole R. Bohn, eds., *Christianity, Patriarchy and Abuse: A Feminist Critique* (New York: Pilgrim Press, 1990); Dorothy Soelle, *The Strength of the Weak: Toward a Christian Feminist Identity*, trans. Robert and Rita Kimber (Philadelphia: Westminster, 1984); Rosemary

Radford Ruether, *To Change the World: Christology and Cultural Criticism* (New York: Crossroad, 1983); Elizabeth Janeway, *The Power of the Weak* (New York: Knopf, 1980). In *Touching Our Strength: The Erotic as Power and the Love of God*, Carter Heyward challenges the model of power as control and opts for a power that is linked to *eros*. She asks whether the cross can function as a symbol not of atonement but of an eroticism that draws us to others in liberating and empowering ways (San Francisco: Harper & Row, 1989).

51. For a personal account of the ways in which teaching on the cross functioned negatively in a woman's life, see Roberta C. Bondi, *Memories of God: Theological Reflections on a Life* (Nashville, Tenn.: Abingdon Press, 1995).

52. See the discussion of the work of René Girard in the Introduction, above.

53. See Cynthia Crysdale, *Embracing Travail: Retrieving the Cross Today* (New York: Continuum, 1999).

54. Johnson, *She Who Is*, 265.

55. Ibid., 263-64. Johnson goes on to cite Asian theologian Virginia Fabella, who writes that all over the world desperately poor women "are today the Christ disfigured in his passion" ("A Common Methodology for Diverse Christologies?," in *With Passion and Compassion: Third World Women Doing Theology*, eds., Virginia Fabella and Mercy Amba Oduyoye (Maryknoll, N.Y.: Orbis Books, 1988), 110.

56. Sally Purvis, *The Power of the Cross; Foundations for a Christian Feminist Ethics of Community* (Nashville, Tenn.: Abingdon Press, 1993), 14.

57. Ibid., 50-51.

58. Ibid., 81. See also Elisabeth Moltmann-Wendel, "Is There a Feminist Theology of the Cross?," in *The Scandal of a Crucified World: Perspectives on the Cross and Suffering*, ed. Yacob Tesfai (Maryknoll, N.Y.: Orbis Books, 1994), 87-98.

59. Ibid., 53.

60. Barbara Hilkert Andolsen, "Agape in Feminist Ethics," in *Feminist Theological Ethics: A Reader*, ed. Lois K. Daly (Louisville, Ky.: Westminster John Knox, 1994), 155.

61. Beverly Wildung Harrison, "The Power of Anger in the Work of Love," in *Weaving the Visions: New Patterns in Feminist Spirituality*, ed. Judith Plaskow and Carol P. Christ (San Francisco: Harper & Row, 1989), 222-23.

62. Boff, *Passion of Christ, Passion of the World*, 128.

63. Ibid., 156-58, 118.

64. See Nathan Mitchell, chap. 3, above.

65. Leech, *We Preach Christ Crucified*, 54.

66. Ibid., 31.

67. Karl Rahner, "Easter: A Faith That Loves the Earth," in *The Great Church Year*, ed. A. Raffelt, trans. Harvey D. Egan (New York: Crossroad, 1994), 196.

68. See Hall, *Lighten Our Darkness*.

69. Augustine, *Sermons* 53.15–16; 165.2–5, 9.

70. Bonaventure, *The Mystical Vine*, XXIV.1.

Index

Index

a person, 76–78, 81; as protective sign, 13, 58; sign of the cross, 58, 148–54, 164, 165, 228–31; as source of sacramental power, 56, 76; and tradition, 5–19; as tree of life, 226–27; as tree of "silly fruit," 14–15, 161–64, 165; veneration of, 60, 74, 72; as vine, 227–28; "way of the cross," 87; *see also* specific topics and persons, e.g.: Liturgy; Origen
Crossan, John Dominic, 55
Crouzel, Henri, 108–9, 128, 135, 136–38
Crown of thorns, feast of, 63
Crucified Is No Stranger, The (Moore), 204–5, 243–44
Crucifixion, 7; forbidding of, 22; of Paul, 29–33; *see also* Cross
Culture, 87
Customaries, 73

Daly, Robert, 109
Daniélou, Jean, 128
De inventione crucis dominicae, 62
De Lubac, Henri, 13, 131–35
Defense of the Mendicants (Bonaventure), 224
Devil, 178
Devotio moderna, 80
Didache, 56, 57
Disputed Questions on Evangelical Perfection (Bonaventure), 201
Distancing of God, The (Cooke), 213
"Dream of the Rood, The," 5, 61–62, 76–77
Dreyer, Elizabeth, 15–16, 243
Dualism, 110, 127, 242; *see also* Manichaeism
Dunstan, archbishop of Canterbury, 73

Ekbert of Schönau, 215
El Guadalupano, 84
El Nino Fidencio, 84–85
Ellacuria, Ignacio, 248
Erikson, Erik, 118
Ethelwold, bishop of Winchester, 73
Eucharist, 40–41, 56, 59–60, 76, 80, 88, 174, 185, 223
Eucharistic Prayer, 58, 59–60
Eusebius of Caesarea, 114, 136
Exaltation of the Holy Cross (f), 62
Exhortation to Martyrdom (Origen), 102, 113–14

Faustus the Manichaean, 172
Faye, Eugène de, 127–28
Feasts of the cross, 61–64
Feminist theology, 248–50
Fénelon, 138
Fidencistas, 85
Finding of the Holy Cross (f), 62
Fire, 217–20
Forde, Gerhard O., 242
Forgiveness, 155–56
Fortunatus the Manichaean, 170–72
Fortunatus, Venantius, 75, 77, 79
Francis, St., 217–18, 220–21, 223, 224; Bonaventure and, 94, 100, 201, 203, 213–14, 218, 220–21, 224, 228–29; Clare of Assisi inspired by, 195–96; cross as centerpiece of theology and spirituality, 15, 223, 224; humility, 201, 203
Frend, W. H. C., 114

Gitard, René, 7
Gjerlow, Lilli, 65
Gnosticism, 95, 98, 126, 127, 128, 133
God: suffering of, 239–42; *see also* Jesus Christ; Trinity
Goetz, Ronald, 241–42
Good Friday liturgy. *See* Liturgy
Good thief, confessor, feast of, 63
Gorday, Peter, 1, 247
Gregory of Nyssa, 223
Griffin, David Ray, 240
Guardini, Romano, 133

Hale, Rosemary Drage, 212–13
Hall, Douglas John, 6
Harl, Marguerite, 138
Harrison, Beverly Wildung, 250
Hartmann, Prosper, 115
Haveluck, Bob, 86
Hayes, Zachary, 192, 193, 194–95, 197, 231
Helena, St., 62
Heraclius, 62
Hippolytus, 57
Hirsh, John C., 212
Holy Eucharist. *See* Eucharist
Homilies on Ezekiel (Origen), 103
Homilies on Jeremiah (Origen), 104
Homilies on Leviticus (Origen), 103–4
Homilies on Numbers (Origen), 104
Humility, 15, 199, 200–4

INDEX